The Search for Stability in Russia and the Former Soviet Bloc

Studies in Disarmament and Conflicts:

THE DYNAMICS OF THE ARMS RACE

INTERNATIONAL TERRORISM AND WORLD SECURITY

ARMS CONTROL AND TECHNOLOGICAL INNOVATION

CONTEMPORARY TERROR: Studies in Sub-state Violence

THE HAZARDS OF THE INTERNATIONAL ENERGY CRISIS

THE ARMS RACE IN THE 1980s

SOUTH-EASTERN EUROPE AFTER TITO: A powder-keg for the 1980s?

REASSESSING ARMS CONTROL

THE ARMS RACE IN THE ERA OF STAR WARS

PERSPECTIVES ON THE ARMS RACE

THE ARMS RACE IN AN ERA OF NEGOTIATIONS

SPACE AND NUCLEAR WEAPONRY IN THE 1990s

CONTROLLING THE INTERNATIONAL TRANSFER OF WEAPONRY AND RELATED TECHNOLOGY

RISING TENSION IN EASTERN EUROPE AND THE FORMER SOVIET UNION

The Search for Stability in Russia and the Former Soviet Bloc

Edited by

DAVID CARLTON

and

PAUL INGRAM

LONDON AND NEW YORK

First published 1997 by Ashgate Publishing

Reissued 2018 by Routledge
2 Park Square, Milton Park, Abingdon, Oxon, OX14 4RN
52 Vanderbilt Avenue, New York, NY 10017

Routledge is an imprint of the Taylor & Francis Group, an informa business

Copyright © David Carlton and Paul Ingram 1997

All rights reserved. No part of this book may be reprinted or reproduced or utilised in any form or by any electronic, mechanical, or other means, now known or hereafter invented, including photocopying and recording, or in any information storage or retrieval system, without permission in writing from the publishers.

Notice:
Product or corporate names may be trademarks or registered trademarks, and are used only for identification and explanation without intent to infringe.

Publisher's Note
The publisher has gone to great lengths to ensure the quality of this reprint but points out that some imperfections in the original copies may be apparent.

Disclaimer
The publisher has made every effort to trace copyright holders and welcomes correspondence from those they have been unable to contact.

A Library of Congress record exists under LC control number: 97002266

Typeset by Manton Typesetters, 5-7 Eastfield Road, Louth, Lincolnshire, UK.

ISBN 13: 978-1-138-35345-9 (hbk)
ISBN 13: 978-1-138-35379-4 (pbk)
ISBN 13: 978-0-429-42763-3 (ebk)

Contents

List of Abbreviations		vii
Notes on Contributors		ix
Preface by Carlo Schaerf		xi

1 Post-Cold War Challenges to Stability in Eastern Europe and the Former Soviet Union   1
Georgi Arbatov

2 Russian Domestic Politics, Foreign Affairs and Geopolitical Considerations   15
Alexei Arbatov

3 Transition to Democracy: Explanatory Models   23
Sondra Z. Koff and Stephen P. Koff

4 Dancing on the Edge of the Chasm: The Struggle for Survival in the Former Soviet Union   45
Derek Braddon

5 Energy in the Former Soviet Republics   61
Victor Gilinsky

6 The Present State and Future of Science in Russia   77
Sergei Kapitza

7 The Kremlin's Chechen Policy   91
Ruslan I. Khasbulatov

8 The Chechen Crisis: Predictable and Unpredictable Consequences   105
Alexei Vasilyev

9	Theories of Post-communist Nationalism *Andrus Park*	119
10	The Legacies of Soviet Communism *David Carlton*	141
11	NATO Enlargement and Russian Policy in the 1990s *Alexander Nikitin*	149
12	A Cooperative Security Approach to Addressing Instabilities in Eastern Europe: The Role of NATO *Lamberto Zannier*	157
13	Instabilities in the Former Soviet Union and Eastern Europe and the Role that OSCE Can Play *Herman De Fraye*	167
14	The Role of Memory and Identity in the Process of Change, with Special Reference to the Former Soviet Union and Eastern Europe: Psychological Perspectives *Rita R. Rogers*	191
Index		205

List of Abbreviations

Btu	British thermal unit
CFE	Conventional Forces in Europe (Treaty)
CIS	Commonwealth of Independent States
CMEA	Council for Mutual Economic Assistance
Comecon	Council for Mutual Economic Assistance
CSCE	Conference for Security and Cooperation in Europe, now called the Organization for Security and Cooperation in Europe
EU	European Union
FSU	former Soviet Union
GATT	General Agreement on Tariffs and Trade
GDP	gross domestic product
GDR	German Democratic Republic
GNP	gross national product
GWh	gigawatt-hour
IFOR	Multinational Peace Implementation Force (Bosnia)
IMF	International Monetary Fund
INF	Intermediate Nuclear Forces
JCG	Joint Consultative Group (of CFE)
kWh	kilowatt-hour
MIC	military–industrial complex
Minatom	Ministry of Atomic Energy and Industry (Russia)
NACC	North Atlantic Cooperation Council
NATO	North Atlantic Treaty Organization
OCCP	All-national Congress of the Chechen People
OECD	Organization for Economic Cooperation and Development
OSCE	Organization for Security and Cooperation in Europe
PFP	Partnership for Peace
R&D	research and development
START	Strategic Arms Reduction Talks
Tcf	trillion cubic feet
UN	United Nations

WEU	Western European Union
WMD	weapons of mass destruction
WTO	Warsaw Treaty Organization

Notes on Contributors

Alexei Arbatov (*Russian*) is a Member of the Russian Duma and Deputy Chairman of its Defence Committee. He is also associated with the Institute of World Economy and International Relations, Moscow.

Georgi Arbatov (*Russian*) is Director Emeritus of the Institute for the USA and Canada, Moscow, as well as a member of the Russian Academy of Sciences. He is author of *The System: An Insider's Life in Soviet Politics*.

Derek Braddon (*British*) is Research Director at the Research Unit in Economics, University of the West of England, Bristol.

David Carlton (*British*) (*co-editor*) is Lecturer in International Studies at the University of Warwick. He is author of *Anthony Eden: A Biography* and of *Britain and the Suez Crisis*. He is co-editor of 14 previous volumes in this series.

Herman De Fraye (*Belgian*) is Director of Protocol and External Relations for the Belgian Senate, Brussels.

Victor Gilinsky (*US*) is a former Commissioner of the US Nuclear Regulatory Commission.

Paul Ingram (*British*) (*co-editor*) is a Researcher at the Oxford Research Group and an Oxford City Councillor. He is conducting postgraduate research in the Department of Politics and International Studies, University of Warwick.

Sergei Kapitza (*Russian*) is a member of the Russian Academy of Sciences. He is also a member of the Council of the Pugwash Conferences on Science and World Affairs.

Ruslan Khasbulatov (*Russian*) is a former Chairman of the Supreme Soviet, Moscow. He is now associated with the Plekhanov Institute, Moscow.

Sondra Z. Koff (*US*) is Professor of Political Science at the State University of New York at Binghampton.

Stephen P. Koff (*US*) is Professor of International Relations at Syracuse University, New York.

Alexander Nikitin (*Russian*) is Director of the Centre for Political and International Studies, Moscow. He previously served with the Soviet Permanent Mission to the United Nations in New York.

Andrus Park (*Estonian*), now deceased, was a member of the Division of Humanities and Social Studies in the Estonian Academy of Science, Tallinn.

Rita R. Rogers (*US*) is Professor of Clinical Psychiatry at the University of California Medical School, Los Angeles.

Alexei Vasilyev (*Russian*) is Director of the Institute for African Studies, Moscow.

Lamberto Zannier (*Italian*) is Deputy Head of the Italian Delegation to the Organization for Security and Cooperation in Europe. He was formerly Head of Department, Arms Control and Co-operative Security Section, Political Affairs Division at NATO, Brussels.

Preface

The International School on Disarmament and Research on Conflicts (ISODARCO) held Winter Courses in 1994, 1995 and 1996 to consider developments involving the former Soviet Union and Eastern Europe. Many of the papers presented in 1994 and 1995 have already been published in *Rising Tensions in Eastern Europe and the Former Soviet Union*. Most of the chapters in this volume were presented to the Ninth Winter Course held at Andalo (Trento), Italy, between 28 January and 4 February 1996. The holding of this Course was made possible by the financial contributions of various organizations and the generous collaboration of several individuals without which this meeting would have not been possible and to whom we extend our deepest gratitude:

- The John D. and Catherine T. MacArthur Foundation;
- Dr David Carlton and Dr Eng. Giancarlo Tenaglia, Directors of the Course;
- The Rectorate and Physics Department of the University of Rome 'Tor Vergata';
- The Autonomous Trentino-Alto Adige Region;
- Dr Isabella Colace of the ISODARCO office in Rome.

For hospitality we are indebted to the Hotel Gruppo Brenta.

All opinions expressed in the chapters of this book are of a purely personal nature and do not necessarily represent the official view of either the organizers of the School or of any organizations with which these writers may be affiliated.

Carlo Schaerf
President and Director of ISODARCO

1 Post-Cold War Challenges to Stability in Eastern Europe and the Former Soviet Union

Georgi Arbatov

Introduction

The course of events points to Eastern Europe and the former Soviet Union (FSU) as, the focal point of danger for the destabilization for international relations in general – at least at present. As time goes by it is becoming ever more obvious that the end of the Cold War caught not only the governments but also the specialists and the general public in countries on both sides of the recently-deceased 'Iron Curtain' by surprise. That is why, up to now, not one of these governments has had a coherent, long-term policy about this area. Whether such a state of affairs was unavoidable is a separate topic, but in my opinion this could have been avoided, thereby saving us from many troubles and uncertainties.

Eastern Europe

The East European countries differ in terms of their past, their historical traditions and peculiarities, their present situation and the problems they face today. Nevertheless, there are factors which allow us to regard them as an entity, united by some similarities and common problems. There are perhaps two special cases. One is the former German Democratic Republic (GDR), which is going through the process of reunification, with massive, though not always maximally effective help from the former West Germany. And the second is the former Yugoslavia, which was much more distant from the 'Socialist Commonwealth', but now presents a most extreme case of destabilization.

What, then, are the principal factors which allow us to speak about the East European countries as an entity? The first is that they experienced decades dominated by the centralized, administratively planned economy. This was more or less a copy of the Soviet system, although with differences in some important areas such as the partial acceptance of private property (in Poland almost the whole agricultural system was privately run). Now, as all of them are turning (or trying to turn) towards the market economy, most are suffering from more or less severe difficulties. Second, after several decades of existence as Soviet satellites (albeit enjoying some occasional limited independence) they have become truly independent states, free both in their foreign policy and in their internal affairs. Third, in the past, all East European countries had to copy, in substance, the totalitarian or authoritarian political system of the Soviet Union. Then, after the major changes in the Soviet Union during the *perestroika* experience, they (often belatedly) joined the process, making really revolutionary changes and the building of a completely new political system inevitable. However, in this endeavour, only a few of them could benefit from the experience of past democratic traditions. At the outset they had neither real parliaments nor political parties, nor a civic society, nor democratic legal systems. In addition, all the old institutions of the state were discredited, as were a large proportion of civil servants. There were almost no available reserves of trained, experienced bureaucrats who had not been tarnished by their service to the old social order. Fourth, after many years of very strict ideological control and intensive indoctrination, the populations of these countries suddenly found themselves in an ideological vacuum, robbed of any ideals and open to any influences from the extreme left to the extreme right – hard-line communism, fascism, monarchism, anarchism, all sorts of mysticism, pure greed and the deification of money and wealth. Of course, the West is ideologically pluralistic as well but, in the course of a long history, drawing on democratic traditions and a rich experience of struggle for the support of public opinion, the liberals and the labour movements won some influence and the establishments themselves learned to 'sell' attractive ideas to the majority. They were also able to deal with extremist forces by isolating and ridiculing them – although sometimes this was not completely successful, as the presence of fascist movements in some advanced European countries proves. Many East European countries and former republics of the Soviet Union have not yet mastered this art at all. Fifth, most of the East European countries have inherited national problems – sometimes very serious ones – from the past. Under the old regimes they were suppressed. Now, with their newly won freedom, centrifugal forces have gained momentum. This has already split some countries (for example, Czechoslovakia); it has created problems and conflicts in some others (for example in Romania and Bulgaria); and in the former Yugoslavia, as well as in parts of the FSU, it has led to bloody wars.

This situation in East European countries has created significant problems and threats of destabilization. A few examples may be cited. Let us start with the economy. The situation again was different in different countries. The West, having proclaimed its determination to help them to build market economies, appeared to favour the model of reforms, proposed by the International Monetary Fund (IMF), which earned the nickname 'shock therapy' (the initial addressees had been the Third World countries with the principal goal of squeezing debts out of them). This was not only recommended but imposed on the East European countries in that acceptance of this particular model was made a condition for receiving financial assistance. Nevertheless, I do not want to shift all the blame for this on to the West for, in each of the East European countries, there were some home-grown enthusiasts for 'shock therapy'. Moreover, it should not be assumed that these people were motivated by any malicious designs; more probably there were serious gaps in their knowledge of practical economics – in the West as well as in their own countries – and even greater gaps in their knowledge of contemporary economic theory. They had been raised on the works of Karl Marx and what they saw around them in the years of Communist rule was not even an outdated version of Marxism, but totalitarian economic practices very often implemented by economically semi-literate or illiterate leaders. Consequently, the remedies which the reformist economists tended to propose was to do exactly the opposite. The teachers they picked out from the West were mostly arch-conservative economic thinkers, mostly fanatical monetarists, often considered in their own countries not as messiahs, but as extremists. While an understandable emotional reaction, it was hardly a reasonable answer to the problems.

In this way, the 'unholy' union of the IMF together with advisers and some 'radical' economists in Eastern Europe and the FSU came into being. Of course, not all economists in the former socialist countries were so unprofessional and easily deceived. And not all of the post-socialist governments were so naive and economically illiterate. Hence the results differed between various countries.

Hungary suffered a little from this treatment, but less than many others because not only did it have some good economists and leaders with common sense, it also had a fairly sound policy before the onset of the major changes started and had already practically begun market reform in the 1970s. Consequently the experiments blessed by the IMF did not harm the country too much.

Although the 'shock therapy' reform was proclaimed to be a great success there, Poland was not so lucky; the resulting impoverishment of the majority of the population and large-scale unemployment led to the changing of prime ministers in quick succession. Subsequently, in parliamentary elections the 'communists' (they changed the name of the party, of course) have eventually won, while the advocates of the 'shock therapy' have lost.

The Czechs elected a most militant fighter for 'shock' reform in prime minister Vaclav Klaus. In his speeches he was always tremendously radical and would fight like a lion against the very notion of the 'regulated' or 'socially-oriented' market. His line was: 'You either have a market or not. All adjectives are out of place.' But as soon as he became prime minister he turned out to be a very pragmatic and prudent man, always ready to compromise about the principles and to sacrifice theoretical purity for the well-being of the economy. Therefore his country – in addition to being better developed than its neighbours – avoided most of stupidities of 'shock therapy' and is now in relatively good shape.

In summary, then, some of the East European countries are in a relatively decent situation, while others suffer from serious difficulties but, so far, they have avoided both catastrophic failures and stunning successes. The economic situation has not destabilized any of these countries (except perhaps Romania), but nor has it enhanced their stability. However, some danger signs have become visible. For example, there is dissatisfaction on the part of the populations with economic policy and its social consequences. Most of the people were obviously glad to get rid of communist domination, but it was difficult for them to understand why living standards should be lower than under the communists. If they were then told that there were no alternatives to the model of economic reform which the government had chosen, they started to look for the alternative in their recent past. That is the main reason why the former communists have already won elections in Lithuania, Poland, Hungary, Bulgaria and Slovakia and have become one of the big political forces even in the former GDR. And the first post-communist (and fiercely anti-communist) governments have nobody to blame for their defeats but themselves.

This is an important and thought-provoking phenomenon. After celebrating freedom from communism, the majority in one country after another in absolutely free elections voted for communists. This is very probably what will also happen in Russia, particularly because many of those who called themselves democrats very soon showed themselves to be power-hungry influencemongers, some proved to be vulnerable to corruption and some even became proponents of authoritarianism or totalitarianism.

The difference is that this shift to the Left in East European countries can be seen as a rather healthy development. The ex-communists, who came to power in these countries are, in reality, liberal social democrats. And this is what is really needed after communist dictatorship rather than proponents of a hard-boiled capitalism, who neglect the social needs of the population and are social-Darwinist in their real beliefs. In these countries, therefore, developments leading towards a market economy and political democracy will most probably continue. But, to my personal regret, the former communists in Russia are dominated and influenced not by people of this kind, but by hardliners, who are not very educated and whose main preoccupation is with power rather than the well-being of the country. This may be true even of some of those in Russia who call themselves 'social democrats'. But the lesson has to be learnt. In short, it is politically dangerous to ruin a country's economy and you are lucky if you then have a political force which will save you from violent upheavals, like the social democrats in Eastern Europe, even if they were, or at least called themselves, latter-day communists. In the event that the economy continues to deteriorate and this seriously affects the lives of the population, more extreme forces will sooner or later inevitably win and this may lead to a real destabilization. But the shift to the Left we are currently witnessing in the East European countries is not like this. On the contrary, this shift is of a stabilizing character.

In what situations can destabilization occur? First, it can result if there is a rise of nationalism, accompanied by internal or even external conflicts; second, if there is a return to power of hardline rather than 'social-democratized' communists, seeking a kind of totalitarian rule with a corresponding foreign policy; third, if there is a shift to right-wing radicalism.

In Eastern Europe, however, provided Russia is not involved, destabilization, although it can create some problems and threats, will hardly be on a scale that can affect the whole world or even the European continent. In short, I do not foresee new 'Yugoslavias' happening there. But mention of the former Yugoslavia suggests one other point we should not overlook: such events in East European countries can adversely affect the relations between Russia and the West. Likewise, acceptance of countries of this region into the North Atlantic Treaty Organization (NATO) would be unfortunate. For, in Russia, it will be understood as an anti-Russian act – though after events in Chechnya, East European countries cannot be condemned unreservedly for aspiring to NATO membership.

Russia and Other Parts of the FSU

Little by little, Russia is becoming an ever more destabilized and destabilizing part of the FSU – although, even before Chechnya, the situation in Georgia, Nagorno-Karabakh, Tadjikistan and Moldova seemed, in some ways, perhaps even more ominous. But Russia was, and will remain, the most important and potentially dangerous member of the newly independent states.

First, there is the sheer size of the country. Second, there is, of course, its military might – it has the second-largest army in the world and a terrifying arsenal of modern weapons, (including a second-to-none nuclear capability). Added to this is its large economic potential and a wealth of natural and intellectual resources. As soon as the country climbs out of its deep economic and political crises, all of this will become very impressive and will make Russia a great power or, if it opts for a very active world role and is willing to pay the price, even a superpower.

The sources of destabilization in Russia do not differ greatly from those in the East European countries. At the same time the driving forces of destabilization are much more mature in Russia and are therefore more dangerous. Most difficult are the internal problems – economic, political, ideological and national. A second tier of problems facing Russia concerns the so-called near-abroad. The former republics of the Soviet Union are bound to Russia by numerous ties of an economic, political, cultural and demographic nature (25 million Russians living there, not to mention millions of mixed marriages). And at the same time many of these republics feel alienated by some events of ancient and modern history, particularly by the memory of imperial oppressions. A third tier of problems arises from relations with its former allies in the Warsaw Pact and in the Council for Mutual Economic Assistance. Finally, there are severe problems arising from the relations with the rest of the world, especially with the West.

Let us start with the first tier of problems, and concentrate, in particular, on the economy. A popular current story in Russia nowadays is about mountain-climbers. Two friends were climbing high in the mountains when one of them slipped and fell into a deep crevasse. His friend started to shout: 'Ivan, are you alive?' Seconds later he heard from below: 'Yes!' 'Didn't you break your neck?' 'No.' 'And your legs and hands?' 'They seem all right.' 'Then climb back immediately! I'll try to help you.' 'Impossible! I'm still in freefall!' This story is, of course, really about Russia's present economic (and not only economic) situation. Russia is still falling. But some feel euphoric that, so far, they are still alive and still in a tolerable, if not in a good, condition. As to the freefall, many (including myself) have not yet given up hope of a soft landing and a consequent recovery.

As far as the long-term prospects are concerned, such optimism is probably justified. For this, as was already mentioned, is a country endowed with tremendously rich natural and intellectual resources, with educated, gifted people and a trained labour force, and with great industrial and agricultural potential. Such countries do not perish so easily. This we know, indeed, from Russia's own history.

The present state of affairs is mainly a result of gross mismanagement, with some ups and downs – though with an overall inefficiency – during more than 70 years under communist rule. During the last two years of Mikhail Gorbachev's rule, and for more than three years after him, Russia experienced practically no 'ups', and was really close to a freefall. While this is, of course, bad enough, if at the root of troubles is mismanagement, it does mean that there is light at the end of the tunnel – one only has to eliminate the mismanagement and learn to manage the country properly. To do this, one first needs a democracy – at least an elementary one – which makes it possible for the public to know the truth about the state of affairs. And one needs a political system, which will permit the people to influence effectively the policy-making process.

The road to recovery is marked by three extremely dangerous pitfalls which may affect Russia. One would be the curtailment of democracy and the restoration of an authoritarian (or even totalitarian) rule. So far, Russia has avoided a full move in this direction, although it has taken some dangerous steps towards it.

The second potential pitfall would be a full breakdown in the economy, which was ailing for a long time but which suffered a devastating blow with the so-called 'reform' associated with the name of Yegor Gaider. In reality this policy unleashed an unprecedented inflation, a sharp decline in production, growing unemployment, the deintellectualization and moral degradation of society, rising crime and corruption and the undermining and, to a large measure, the destruction of arts and culture, science, education and healthcare. This was absolutely misunderstood in the West, which seemed to see this 'reform' as genuine, and which encouraged and almost imposed it on the Russians not only by force of persuasion but also by threats to deny or promises to give, financial assistance. Maybe this occurred because the West really thought that a session of 'shock therapy' could save the Russian economy. The other explanation, which regrettably is more and more popular in Russia, is that the whole enterprise was a Western conspiracy, designed to undermine the 'arch-enemy' once and for all, to deindustrialize it and to transform it into another Third World country. It was noticed in Russia that, among conditions for credits put forward by the IMF, such items as the level of unemployment and the dynamics of production are not included, although they are of primary importance as indicators of the country's economic situation and economic health. All this stimulated feelings of national humiliation, which is always a fertile ground for the rise of nationalism.

And here we come to the third pitfall: a possible upsurge of nationalism and 'neo-imperialism' in Russia. This is also a great, maybe a mortal, danger. Its causes obviously cannot be reduced to economic failures. Among other factors would be the sudden dissolution of the Soviet Union. The recent falling apart of an empire creates a constant source of nostalgic feelings and encourages not only imperial ambitions but, often, very sensible desires to bring the country back together. Such desires for a kind of reunion are natural and everything depends on what means are chosen to achieve these ends. It should not be forgotten that, in the Russian case, the problem is by no means limited to sentiment, for many Russians feel that, together with the Union, they lost something very tangible. They perceive this loss not only in terms of the size of their country, which so easily can be mistaken for greatness, but also, without the Union (or an empire), in terms of less security. As a result, because some of the former republics were not too friendly, they sought to retain nuclear weapons or tried to join NATO. In addition, other republics have become a battleground for internal conflicts, in which they have tried to involve Russia (or Russia volunteered to be so).

All this has had very adverse consequences. Many Russians who lived in these republics suddenly felt discriminated against, deprived of their rights or, even worse, were in a very physical danger, caused by an armed conflict raging around them. Some of them had already fled and become refugees – which in the present economic conditions has doomed them to misery. And their numbers may multiply. In general, the fate of the 25 million Russians who, after the demise of the Soviet Union, suddenly found themselves 'abroad' creates very dangerous problems. In the event that they feel really threatened and they make a mass exodus to Russia, it could lead to a virtual explosion of most militant chauvinism which will simply sweep away all Russia's so-far modest democratic achievements and radically transform its foreign policy. In this connection the West could, perhaps, effectively influence a number of former Soviet republics, so that they do not permit any discrimination and injustice against Russian minorities living on their territory.

As to 'neo-imperialism', the problem largely depends on the future of the Commonwealth of Independent States (CIS). I do not believe that the breakdown of the Soviet Union was either inevitable or desirable for Russia, for the other republics, or for the West. But at the same time it clearly could not survive as an empire or as a unitary state; it had to be transformed into a really democratic federation. Nevertheless this is now 'spilt milk'; more important is the future. A desire to restore the Union will live and will remain a strong source of Russian policy, and much will depend on the direction which these moods and activities take. Russian nationalists, particularly the more extreme ones, talk about restoration of the empire, or plan for it, by any and every means, including violence. If it comes to a new dictatorship, these plans could result in a terrible war which would dwarf all horrors of former Yugoslavia.

In fact, militant nationalism is becoming more and more popular among Russia's ruling elite. It might be that their economic failures, together with their inability to rule by democratic means, is pushing them again and again towards the authoritarianism and even totalitarianism that was exercised for decades in the country. This in turn makes them turn to rabid nationalism which can not only assure massive support at home, but also excuse the most cruel and bloody actions within their own country. I was bewildered and shocked by the attitude of the West towards such a bloody development in Russia. First there was its support for the action committed by President Boris Yeltsin and his team against the parliament in 1993. Then there was its attitude towards the genocide against one of Russia's own smaller peoples, the Chechens in December 1994 – something which can have devastating results for Russia as a whole, turning it into a dictatorship and eliminating all the modest achievements in the direction of democracy and human rights. The West, it seems, does not understand that, before its very eyes and with its assistance, Russia is slipping back into the condition of a police state, and a highly militarized one, which is demonstrating its total disregard for the human rights of its citizens. This promises to become a highly criminalized and corrupted state, swiftly degenerating into intellectual and moral degradation.

Let us now turn to the dangers of neo-imperialism and nationalism as the greatest threat to stability. The Soviet Union could not disappear into thin air. It survives in the minds of millions of its former citizens. The idea of making it function in some way (if not as a federation, then as a loose confederation or as a package of treaties about economic, security, ecological and humanitarian cooperation) is alive and will motivate people to act. This makes it all the more important to search for a suitable way to restore some form of cooperation – although after events in Chechnya this has of course become an even more difficult task. Among other things, it demands from the Russian people honesty. They have to understand that the republics (like Russia) were oppressed by the totalitarian centre, but that they see the oppression and injustices as having come from Russia, with which they identified the totalitarian empire. And the Russians will only fool themselves if they do not understand that there were some good reasons for this belief. This past has left a legacy of suspicion and mistrust, and only Russia itself can destroy this legacy, by persuading other republics that all of this has been left behind and that contemporary Russia has no imperial ambitions. It cannot be done by words alone (who believes them nowadays?). Only practical policies can do this job.

The ground can be cleared by these means for natural trends and forces of integration to assert themselves in the CIS countries. Indeed, good and fair relations with other states of the CIS should be the first priority for Russian foreign policy.

Some forms of integration of the CIS (or most of it) is in the interests not only of Russia and other members, but also of the West. In the years of the

Cold War the West was interested in promoting the disintegration of the former Soviet Union. But now the Cold War has ended the situation has changed. Today stability in the whole region has become a matter of the highest concern. Stable, peaceful and responsible policies may be expected, however, only from a Russia which is not only internally but also externally secure.

The Quest for Stabilization

The dangers exist and they are real. This means that there is urgent need for positive action. Such action should be concentrated in the following directions. First, the root of destabilization is catastrophic economic failure. It has led to an overall decline in Russia, to a rapid and substantial deterioration in the living standards of the majority of the population and a dramatically increasing gap between them and the small number of the 'new rich', thereby adding to social tensions. The task of overcoming economic crises is of course in principle, and also from the practical point of view, Russia's own concern and responsibility. No doubt some of the economic misdeeds are irreversible. One cannot, for example, undo 'shock therapy'. People were robbed of their savings, inflation was let loose and a crisis broke out in practically all producing branches of the economy. But the free fall can be stopped by pursuing a viable industrial policy, pushing through a sensible agrarian reform and creating a dependable safety net, which will save people not only from hunger and misery, but also from being recruited by left or right-wing extremists and becoming victims of another demagogue and dictator. Crime and corruption can and should be fought more effectively. All of this must be done by the Russians themselves. However in the face of such difficulties, foreign assistance is also welcome and a Russian economic revival is, moreover, also in the interests of the Western donors. So, what in realistic terms can the West do? I have several times been asked by Westerners how they could help. My answer has always been: first, do not give any more bad advice and, second, be absolutely honest and do not create any illusions among the Russian people about the help that is on offer.

The major task, then, is to create conditions, which would make East European countries and Russia, together with other countries of CIS, attractive to foreign investments, which of course cannot be a full substitute for the independent efforts of these countries. A fresh look is also needed at the activities and the role of international financial institutions, such as the IMF or the World Bank. Bretton Woods and its decisions are now at least two eras behind us; and their reform should not be reduced to the elimination of the dollar's gold standard.

Second, it is of crucial importance for Russia to finally see the institutionalization of the positive political changes achieved since the beginning of *perestroika*. In the West the argument is sometimes heard that stability in Russia is more important for the West than democracy. This is not only a crass example of hypocrisy but also one of the biggest political fallacies because, in this particular region and at this particular period of history, without democracy there also cannot be any stability. In this matter it is to be hoped that Russia can depend to some degree on Western understanding and assistance. The West should not of course interfere in Russian domestic affairs – although this is sometimes done anyway without invitation and almost always in a direction – that is not in favour of democracy and stability. But, since the end of the Cold War, the opinions of the West, its sympathies and antipathies have become a serious moral and political force in Russia and quite a few countries of the neighbouring region. True, as testified by the first signs of a revival of anti-American, anti-Western sentiments, we have already passed the peak of this Western influence, fuelled by the deep disappointment at the results of the 'shock therapy' and Western support of bloodshed in Russia. But this influence still remains a political factor, which could, and should, be used for the development of democracy, not to its detriment. The West, including the United States, can also be of important practical help. The Russians need their experience in building up democratic institutions, and in creating civic society and a really democratic legal system. Clearly, not everything from this experience will be appropriate for Russia, but much of it can facilitate and speed up the difficult and complicated process of democratic changes. And only democratic development can ensure stability.

Third, in the present situation, with a public opinion that has learned a lot and gained rich political experience, any revival of the Cold War and hostile relations with the West would work in the long run against stability – both inside Russia and in the character of its foreign policy. It is difficult to imagine that majority of the Russian or American peoples will ever again believe in the 'enemy' and accept as the only, or at least the principal, villain the opposite side. But this is only a small part of the story – the fact is that both sides have become too soon and too easily euphoric about the state of international relations after the end of the Cold War. For this important change in international relations is not yet wholly irreversible. Consider a 'worst case' scenario: events in Russia alone (for instance, a full economic collapse, followed by chaos and dictatorship, or a victory of extreme nationalists and neo-imperialists, with the same results) could have a deplorable effect. The truth is that, after the end of the Cold War, although it was a unique opportunity, we failed to put international relations fully into order. First, the whole infrastructure of the Cold War has remained practically intact in the form of the tremendous arsenals of all kinds of weapons, including nuclear and other weapons of mass destruction, militarized policy, militarized mentality and mammoth defence industries (which have become a heavy economic and social burden and a source of militaristic influence on policy). Second, we have also inherited from the Cold War a heavy legacy of conflicts, as well as hostile attitudes left by the local wars of these times. The years since the end of Cold War have shown how difficult it is to get rid of this legacy. Soviet troops left Afghanistan a long time ago, but the war there goes on and on. The killing fields of Cambodia continue to see killings. Then there is the tremendous amount of weapons, spread practically without any control all over the world. And, in addition, there are plenty of people who are real guns for hire. It must surely be a matter of general concern that these subjects are not yet on the agenda of negotiations and international discussions. And who thinks today seriously about the 'new world order'? I myself am not very fond of this term. It somehow awakens in my memory the German vocabulary of the Second World War, in particular, the *Neue Ordnung*. But let us ignore the words and consider only the substance. It is clear that the international system after the end of the Cold War cannot remain the same, that radical changes are inevitable. Yet there is, one has the feeling, a striking general lack of understanding that a whole era in history of international relations has come to an end. And this makes it necessary to start a fundamental review for the whole situation.

The end of the Cold War created opportunities to move in a better direction but it did not remove all obstacles and resolve all problems. We have to work out a new agenda for giving mankind a chance to make a real breakthrough in its evolution. But how to do it? Here we have to turn to very practical issues. As in every work of construction, everything has to begin with preparing the construction site. First, it has to be cleared of the debris of the Cold War. In particular, we must remove the tremendous amounts of armaments, which otherwise have to be constantly guarded, kept in safe condition and prevented from getting into the wrong hands. But it is a striking and sad fact that, since the end of the Cold War, arms control negotiations have come almost to a standstill. One gets an impression that governments are much more concerned about the salvation of their defence industries and corresponding laboratories than about destruction of mostly redundant weapons or the conversion of redundant defence industry and science. Arms control treaties were for the most part worked out during the Cold War, when distrust and other reasons made slowness explicable. Apart from that, we could not foresee, at that time, that a slow timetable in a situation of instability could become a source of additional dangers. That is why it might be reasonable to try to renegotiate some parts of the already signed treaties in order to speed up the destruction of nuclear weapons anticipated by them.

Maybe the most important among the other problems are poverty and ethnic conflicts, usually very closely connected with the danger of revival of neo-imperialist ambitions. Maybe Russians feel the weight of these problems better than many others. As well as understanding the crucial importance of economic problems, Russians see the need for new approaches to the tremendous difficulties of the poorest countries, as well as to the intricate and politically complicated issues faced by the countries trying to build a market economy.

The end of the Cold War gives us a chance to deal with such problems in a different way. Many of the problems to which we have to pay great attention nowadays become international – a clear example being environmental issues. But this is true also of many economic problems. Here, then, is an area where Russian–American cooperation is a condition for success. Meanwhile it is important not to permit the relations between two countries to sour even further. Russia is not at the end but in the midst of or even on the eve of deep changes. This itself is an important reason not to leave Russia in isolation, but rather to involve it as much as possible in world affairs – and to do it not an act of charity but with clear understanding of its present and future role.

2 Russian Domestic Politics, Foreign Affairs and Geopolitical Considerations

Alexei Arbatov

The Principal Domestic Opinions on Foreign Policy

Traditional Western analysts describe Russian foreign policy thinkers and players as belonging to three basic groups: reformers, reactionaries and centrists. These descriptions were inaccurate in 1993 and, as demonstrated by the election campaign of 1995, are even less adequate for the foreseeable future. There are at least four major groups trying to affect Russian foreign policy. Of these, two are idealistic and the other two pragmatic, with numerous subdivisions and tints within them.

The first idealistic group, most vividly represented by Yegor Gaidar, Andrei Kozyrev, and Viktor Chernomyrdin, is distinguished by conspicuously pro-Western policies (by deeds if no longer by words), with a heavy tilt towards economic determinism. The principal idea of Kozyrev and his allies was to pursue urgently the integration of Russia into the West economically, politically and even militarily. They did not recognize the enormous obstacles, stemming from Russia's uniqueness, its current transitional state and heritage and the implications of its specific geopolitical situation for its national interests. Nor did they allow for the possibility, despite the end of the ideological schisms, of significant divergences between Russia and the West on regional and global issues, including arms control and conflict resolution. At the same time this group was quite indifferent to, and uninterested in, Russia's relations with the 'near-abroad', least of all with the Transcaucasus and Asian republics. But after cooperating with Ukraine and Belarus in disbanding the Soviet Union, and after signing initial basic agreements with them and Kazakhstan in Minsk and

Alma-Ata, excellent relations and integration with those states was largely taken for granted.

The second idealistic group consists primarily of active communists and neo-imperialists (such as Gennadi Ziuganov, Alexander Lebed and Konstantin Zatulin), whose primary goal is the restoration of the Soviet Union. They believe in the genuine desire of the former Soviet nations to reunite (against the will of their elites) and to revive the centralized economic, military and political potential of the superpower. In terms of foreign policy towards the 'far-abroad' they are mostly isolationist and suspicious of the West. These people could not reconcile themselves to the demise of the Soviet Union, although they do not advocate reunification by military force. They generally take a tougher stand on relations with Ukraine and the other republics, and advocate a policy of pressurizing them with respect to territorial, ethnic, economic and military issues of discord. This faction understands the many weaknesses of the Russian position in the world, but is keen to demand that the West recognize Russia's 'special interests, rights and responsibilities' in the 'near-abroad'. At the same time they have suggested diversification of attention to alternative economic and political partners (China, India and Iran) and have called for expansion in exports of arms and nuclear technology and materials as a promising way of earning hard currency.

The third group is liberal-pragmatic (including Grigori Yavlinsky, Vladimir Lukin, Sergei Karaganov and myself). Although no doubt quite Westernized in their upbringing and outlook, their principal difference from the first group is that they do emphasize the necessity of adopting a distinctive Russian foreign policy and distinctive security priorities based upon the specifics of Russia's geopolitical position and transitional domestic situation. This implies that the highest priority should be given to Russian relations with other former Soviet republics. Most of them have advocated maximum concessions and flexibility in relations with other former Soviet republics – the only exception concerning the preservation of centralized control over nuclear weapons and the need for the urgent elimination of those outside Russia. Their aim is to overcome the inherent fears in these other former Soviet republics of revived Russian imperialism and attempts at domination. As for relations with the United States and its allies, these politicians and intellectuals have never doubted their preference for the Western model of economic and political development, and they have consistently advocated stronger and more stable relations with NATO and Japan. At the same time, however, they have argued that improvements in the relationship with the West does not automatically imply acceptance of all the proposals of the current Western governments. They were quite critical, for example, of many aspects of US policy in the early 1990s, sharing many of the views of the US liberal foreign policy community. Nor were they in favour of the lax concessions made by Russia in 1992–93 and argued in favour of more equal and fair deals with the West. This group is generally sceptical about too heavy a reliance on the promises of Western economic aid and consider sound national security policy as having a value in its own right regardless of the foreign credits a different policy might earn. They operate on the principle that rejection of utopian expectations and naive illusions will prevent disappointments and mutual recrimination later.

Finally, the fourth group, which could be characterized as reactionary-pragmatic, consists of radical nationalists (like Vladimir Zhirinovsky and Nikolai Lysenko) and, on their extremes, overt fascists. This group is wholly devoted to the goal of the revival of the Russian superpower role on the premise of Great-Russian nationalism, a fundamentalist version of orthodox Christianity, anti-semitism and across-the-board anti-Western political activities. They are prepared to reinstate the Soviet Union by military force if necessary, and advocate economic blockades and open intervention on the side of separatists in the Baltic States, the Crimea, Moldova and Georgia. In addition, they are prepared to resume alliance with all radical anti-Western regimes, such as Iraq, Libya, North Korea and Cuba, encourage nuclear proliferation where it reduces the West's control, and call for the abolition of the United Nations and the division of the world into spheres of influence under the Great Powers. They call for a renunciation of UN sanctions against Iraq and in the Balkan context, and they call for the sending of arms and volunteers to help those they favour. Naturally, these hardliners have been in favour of crash military build-ups and oppose the second Strategic Arms Limitation Talks Treaty, the Conventional Forces in Europe Treaty, and unilateral cuts and withdrawal of Russian troops. This group appeals, then, to the most primitive instincts of the impoverished masses and young capitalists alike, unscrupulously varying their tactics, slogans and allies.

Foreign Policy: the First Phase

In 1992 Russian foreign policy was dominated by the first of these groups. But for all its good intentions, Boris Yeltsin's administration, and its Foreign Ministry in particular, had several serious and interrelated deficiencies. They failed to formulate or specify in general terms the new Russian national interests and priorities abroad. There was no new formula that was distinct from either a scaled-down neo-imperialist version of hard-nosed traditional Soviet ambitions, or from a new version of the utopian slogans of Mikhail Gorbachev's 'new political thinking' (such as 'universal defence of human rights in the world', 'strategic democratic initiatives', striving 'to have no enemies and being friendly with all nations of the world' and so on). Hence, for two years, Russia did not put forward any realistic initiative on conflict resolution, arms control or adaptation of multilateral organizations to cope with post-Cold War problems. On most issues Russia merely followed the Western lead.

A further problem stemmed from the first one. Russian foreign policy-makers failed to recognize in time that their first priority after the disintegration of the Soviet Union should have been relations with Ukraine, Kazakhstan, Georgia and the other republics of the former Soviet Union, however messy and unglamorous they were. These relations were the key not only to the protection of Russia's economic, political and security interests, but also to Moscow's relations with the United States, Western Europe and neighbouring states in Asia; and moreover, they were vital to the very prospects of Russian democratic reforms at home. This vacuum was quickly filled by other governmental agencies, military field commanders, parliamentary factions and political parties, acting independently of each other, openly challenging the Minister of Foreign Affairs and the President.

One other deficiency was that, in dealing with the West, the government produced a widespread impression, mostly justified, of a never-ending sequence of easily given unilateral concessions with respect to UN sanctions on Yugoslavia, Iraq and Libya and arms sales to Iran; and with respect to the Western position on the rights of Russian minorities in the Baltic States, the South Kurils and other areas. Even such ill-conceived concepts as Russia's bid for membership of NATO and possible participation in the United States' Strategic Defense Initiative programme found their way into official policy. These policies then became a vulnerable target for the right-wing opposition, which attacked the Foreign Ministry for selling out Russian interests to the West. In addition, the apparent absence of substantive political and security gains achieved at negotiations produced a common perception of foreign policy merely as an adjunct of other tactics to obtain credits and economic aid from the West. Perhaps Gaidar and his team looked at it precisely in this way, thereby consciously influencing official Moscow's policy, but when substantial Western economic aid was not forthcoming, except from Germany, this policy came to look altogether impotent and humiliating.

Finally, this policy did not rely upon any substantial domestic constituency. The Foreign Ministry operation was characterized by disorder and numerous mishaps. Contrary to expectations, precisely in the crucial founding phase of the new course of the newly created state, there was a complete lack of interest in any comprehensive analysis of major policy issues, in sharp contrast, for example, to the time when Eduard Shevardnadze was Foreign Minister. Experts from the Academy of Sciences and the new, independent think-tanks and foundations were ignored. The decision-making pattern was highly irregular and divorced from external input, and for a long time no serious efforts were made to bring on board parliament, the mass media or the academic community to forge a solid domestic political basis for foreign policy. Even within the Foreign Ministry passive opposition to its leadership became quite strong, arising from disagreements over the principles behind the policy and the dissatisfaction with the loss of traditional prestige and the role of this institution. What was even worse, Kozyrev, the Foreign Minister (together with other close associates of the President, such as Gaider, Gennadi Burbulis and Mikhail Poltoranin) on several occasions openly involved foreign governments in domestic political clashes within Russia. This left them open to accusations of conspiracy against their own people and encouraging Western intervention in domestic affairs. Even on a presidential level, in times of acute domestic crisis, US support was sought for the actions against the opposing branch of the government – that is, in March 1993, in September and October 1993, as well as when resignations in the Russian government were contemplated in January 1994, and on some earlier occasions.

It is hard to say what the main reason for such acts was. It could have been the lack of political culture, or the naive idea that there could be full intimacy in relations with the United States, or blind hatred of political opponents at home. Needless to say, nothing could have discredited Russian foreign policy more and compromised its authority in the eyes of public opinion, thereby preparing the ground for a chauvinistic backlash later on. For their part, while the Western powers were ready to stop considering Russia as a foe, they politely declined enthusiastic appeals for instant alliance. They exercised restraint, though bargaining on all issues of any substantive nature from economic assistance to strategic arms reduction. At the same time, in Russia this pro-Western policy was increasingly perceived as a humiliating course of unilateral concessions, exchanged for very little benefit to Russia (all the more so as foreign credits and aid had not been used efficiently), and hence detrimental to Russian prestige and economic, political and security interests. The West also perceived it as a policy of concessions and very quickly learned to take it for granted.

Foreign Policy: the Second Phase

In 1994 foreign policy came under the growing impact of an eclectic combination of the first and the fourth schools of thought. While there was continued interest in courting the 'far-abroad', there now grew an increasing interest in the 'near-abroad' – hence the Chechen issue came to prominence. This happened for a number of reasons. First, there was a growing mood in favour of Russian self-assertiveness, of finding a clear-cut Russian national mission within world politics and in defending it with all available instruments, including military power. Second, there was an increasing aversion to the idea of a New World Order with 'universal values', international legal encroachments upon the actions of Russia, and other 'idealistic' propositions as guidelines of policy. Third, greater credence was given to anti-Western sentiments, which started to appear more prominently in the public consciousness and within political debate. Fourth, Russian relations with the 'near-abroad' came to the foreground of theoretical debate and practical policy-making, dwarfing other international concerns, the only exception relating to obtaining foreign credits and economic assistance. Fifth, and most important, all the above features culminated in an expanding support for what was called the Russian 'Monroe Doctrine'. For the first time it was expressed officially in Yeltsin's appeal to the United Nations in early 1993 to delegate to Russia the mission of ensuring stability by organizing peacekeeping operations in the former Soviet Union's geopolitical space. This line was elaborated by Kozyrev at a number of ministerial meetings of the Organization for Security and Cooperation in Europe (OSCE), of the Group of Seven, the CIS and the Baltics.

There were a number of reasons for this profound shift. The fundamental explanation was a deterioration in Russia's economic and social state, and a growing dissatisfaction with the results of the reforms within the population. This made political leadership more vulnerable to the mounting pressure from nationalist and aggressive opinion, but also from within the bureaucracy, the military and security establishments, industrial groups and young private capitalists. Moreover, the aggravating political conflict between the executive and legislative branches of government made the support of the military and security institutions much more important, and the rival factions of the new ruling elite were trying to attract that support by neo-imperialist appeals. The deficiencies of the foreign policy of 1992–93, considered above, backfired as well. In this sense, having failed to formulate palpable and imaginative new Russian national priorities, the leadership started to succumb to the more base feelings of the general public and its most superficial, primitive features, most widely appealing to insulted national pride and resorting to a policy of the 'non-idealistic' Zhirinovsky-type.

The logical outcome of this shift was the large-scale military adventures, most clearly shown in Chechnya, which started in December 1994. This conflict led to a bloody quagmire and by early 1996 had acquired all the classic features of the hopeless involvements in Afghanistan and Tajikistan. Nonetheless it had the effect of a cold shower on new Russian expansionist tendencies, as well as a destructive effect on the economy, on the morale of the army and on activities in the 'far-abroad'.

A New Phase: the Challenge for the Future

In the near future Russia's foreign policy will most probably evolve as a compromise between the second and the third positions, with the first and the fourth becoming largely marginalized. But domestic and foreign challenges for the Russian policy-makers are enormous indeed.

The first, and most urgent, problem will be ending the war and the crisis in Chechnya, without either escalating it to the whole of the Northern Caucasus or provoking the disintegration of the rest of Russia as a result of defeat, withdrawal and recognition of secession. Another issue will concern the reorganization of Russia's relations with the 'near-abroad' to encourage natural integration (especially in economic matters) without engaging in imperial encroachments. Finally, it will be necessary to reform Moscow's relations with the West, providing for more equal and fair interactions without reviving mistrust, even if, as a result, such relations are on a narrower basis. In these relations there needs to be a growing role for arms control agreements, the implementation of existing treaties and the achievement of new ones. The problems of the expansion of NATO to the east and Russian cooperation with the West on peacekeeping in the Balkans and other areas will also be of the utmost importance.

3 Transition to Democracy: Explanatory Models
Sondra Z. Koff and Stephen P. Koff

Introduction

Two quotations from recent publications say a great deal about the transition to democracy in Russia. The first is from a former US Ambassador to the Soviet Union who, in a book about his experience in that country, notes that he discussed the speed of change in that nation with Mikhail Gorbachev. The Ambassador mused that Gorbachev should have moved more quickly in dealing with the Soviet republics. The Soviet leader responded that

> ... I can see you are a professor now, because your question is academic. In some abstract sense, it is probably right that I moved too slowly, but I did not have the luxury of living in the abstract. I lived in a harsh world of political reality... .[1]

The second quotation comes from a journalist discussing the probable outcome of the Russian parliamentary election of December 1995. He wrote:

> Scores of millions of Russians will vote ... in parliamentary elections, and a large majority of them will, in one way or another, register displeasure, even disgust, at what he [Boris Yeltsin] has done since the collapse of Communist rule, in August of 1991. Although a segment of urban population clearly values the many new civic and economic freedoms, what used to be called the masses have become utterly disaffected by industrial and agricultural decline, imperial collapse, unchecked organized crime, the rise of economic oligarchies, and Yeltsin's brutal assault on Chechnya, a disaster that cost tens of thousands of lives last winter and is far from over.[2]

This transition, which was achieved with a minimum of violence and a great deal of speed, has prompted questions from many people. Much has been written about the subject. Some works have dealt with abstractions and theoretical models, while others have focused on explanations of specific behaviour patterns. This chapter will focus on selected models of transition.

It is noteworthy that a group of people have come to be known as transition theorists or 'transitologists'. Obviously, they endeavour to provide universal explanations of the transition from autocracy to democracy. Many try to compare developments in Latin America and Southern Europe to generate general ideas about the transition process in Eastern Europe. There is even controversy about the possibilities of recognizing universal theories. One approach invokes 'legacies of the past'. Here, transformation results from the cultural, social and institutional structures which, in part, developed from the ideas of V. I. Lenin and the Russian Revolution of 1917. It indicates that it is the persistence of the past experience which sets the parameters of the liberalization process. An opposite position is entitled the 'imperatives of liberalization'. It emphasizes that totally new institutions can be created and the strictures of the past be overcome. Clearly, the legacy of the past, especially the Leninist influence, makes comparison of Eastern Europe with other regions most difficult. On the other hand, where totally new institutions are developed, similar conditions, especially economic ones, can be identified across regions and provide the bases for comparison.

Many models of transition can be described as abstract ideas about the processes and foundations necessary for democracy. However, some, especially those focusing on the economic base which seems to be required for democracy, involve specific advice for change. Essential to the transitologists' arguments is agreement on a precise meaning of democracy. This has caused all sorts of problems, the resolution of which is important because each definition of democracy has its own implications. The age-old issue of whether democracy is basically a process or a set of values or norms receives a great deal of attention.

Some scholars, such as Giovanni Sartori, believe that democracy is a process. In a discussion of Robert Michels' 'Iron Law of Oligarchy' Sartori wrote:

> In short democracy on a large scale is not the sum of many little democracies. Political democracy is, *in primis*, a method or procedure by which, through a competitive struggle for sanctioned authority, some people are chosen to lead the political community. Democracy, then, is the product, or the sequence of effects (secondary and composite) that result from the adoption of that method.[3]

The process school emphasizes the role of leaders, political bargaining, the balance between government power-holders and responsible opposition, effective political parties, interest groups and similar things. If the process works and is managed well by the leaders, democracy will develop: rules of the game will emerge and all the actors will play by them and create the institutions they consider necessary for democracy.

On the other hand, those writers with normative concerns generally begin with the notion of the need for certain preconditions for democracy. Often cited are the facts that Germany and Italy never had a true liberal revolution, they developed late and they emphasized economic modernization at the cost of political modernization. Furthermore, these two nations experienced modernization concurrently with the development of national unity. While some aspects of nationalism were progressive, a significant portion of it was reactionary. All these factors contributed to the rise of fascism in both countries.

Clearly those who deal with prerequisites for democratic government invoke social and economic, as well as political transformation. Among the requirements are a different kind of socialization through broadened educational opportunities and exposure to fair mass media presentations. The economic transformation would include industrialization (for Russia this is debatable) which, in turn, would bring about an increase in wealth and an expanded middle class. Although noted often, it should be stated openly that there is an assumption that a greater consensus would develop in the polity and hence extremism would decline. Seymour Lipset's well known *Political Man: The Social Bases of Politics* emphasizes the link between economic development and democracy.[4] He shares this view with many writers.

Gabriel Almond and Sidney Verba argue in their work, entitled *The Civic Culture: Political Attitudes and Democracy in Five Nations,* which has become something of a modern classic, that values, knowledge and attitudes are all central to the foundations of democracy.[5] At least a major core of the population must be knowledgeable about the political system, understand those outputs which impact on them and feel they can, in some way, influence decision-makers. As would be expected, there are considerable methodological differences between the structure- and process-oriented approaches. These will be dealt with below. Since dichotomizing between the process and normative approaches leads to too great a rigidity in explanation. Some middle ground is sought. Rather than simplifying matters, attempts to combine some elements of the two basic approaches tend to create much more complexity as the roles for institutions, leaders and followers, processes and preconditions must also be combined.

Each of these various positions has developed into schools advocating diverse approaches to the study of regime change. Each of these schools – the structuralist, the process-oriented and the mixed – will be discussed in turn. Throughout the presentation it will be noted that the differences between each camp relate to theory, methodology and research design.

Exploring Transition: Three Approaches

The Structuralist School

Analysts of regime change until the late 1970s sought configurational explanations. Thus, they stressed variables of context, such as the aforementioned level of economic development, character of the national political culture, roles of civil society, amount of national integration, and class structure, among others, all of which are presented as preconditions or determinants of democracy. They correlated the features of the *ancien régime* and the new republic. This methodology associates inductively outcomes – that is, democracy or any other type of political system – with the initial conditions, such as the existence of an agrarian class structure. According to this school, outcome is primarily fashioned by conditions, and human activities play no meaningful role. Thus, people who stress the objective conditions of regime transformation are labelled structuralists.

Kitschelt notes that a typical assumption of the structure-oriented school is that political actors do not enjoy a wide variety of choices.[6] Moreover, these may be limited by the distribution of resources as well as the actors' aim to maximize income and/or power. Choices are calculated in light of given institutional parameters and preferences. In terms of their literature, members of the structuralist school use nations as the unit of analysis and they demonstrate a preference for systematic micro-quantitative studies or conceptually defined qualitative comparative endeavours.

A seminal structuralist work is one penned by Seymour M. Lipset, who handles social phenomena on a total societal level.[7] He attempts to dissect the conditions of democracy into several interrelated variables, setting forth a set of conditions that have existed in nations featuring democratic regimes. These are presented as structural characteristics of a society which supports a democratic political system. His primary concern is with social conditions. Demonstrating that the more wealthy a nation, the greater the chances that it will support a democracy, Lipset argues that democracy is related to the state of economic development which includes indices such as wealth, industrialization, urbanization and education. All of these indices were higher in the cases of more democratic countries and thus carried with them the political correlate of democracy. Also, in his discussion he relates legitimacy and effectiveness to the subject at hand as well as to relationships among the contending political forces. Conditions which he identifies with the emergence of democracy are: an open class system, economic wealth, an egalitarian value system, a capitalist economy, literacy and high participation in voluntary organizations. He makes it quite clear that the complex characteristics of a total system have multivariate consequences because each condition enjoys a degree of autonomy within the system. Statistical data support his arguments. He writes:

> The implication of statistical data presented in this paper concerning democracy, and the relations between democracy, economic development and political legitimacy, is that there are aspects of total social systems which exist, can be stated in theoretical terms, can be compared with similar aspects of other systems, and at the same time, are derivable from empirical data which can be checked (or questioned) by other researchers.[8]

As D.A. Rustow notes, this focus on socioeconomic factors represented a breath of fresh air[9] and an improvement on the traditional sterile legal approach. Moreover, the linkage between economic prosperity and democracy has been questioned not only with regard to Africa and Latin America, but more recently in Eastern Europe as well. In these areas, democratic structures have been born in an environment of profound economic decline. Consequently, leaders have had to confront political and economic challenges simultaneously.[10] Also of note is the fact that Lipset's data bears only on function. His variables are presented in terms of correlations which are very different from causation. At best, a hint is furnished as to some sort of causal connection – but with no indication as to its direction. Rustow remarks:

> Lipset's data leave it entirely open, for example, ... whether democracies provide superior schools and economic growth; whether there is some sort of reciprocal connection so that a given increase in affluence or literacy and in democracy will produce a corresponding increment in the other ... .[11]

These and many other questions remain unanswered. It is important to separate correlate from cause. A probe into cause is warranted. To cite Rustow again, '... only by such inquiry can the social scientist accomplish the proper task of exploring the margins of human choice and of clarifying the consequences of the choices in that margin'.[12]

The structuralist school is far from homogeneous. Other scholars have underscored specific historical domestic conditions or the historical sequencing of events as other requisites for democracy. Such studies were sceptical of Lipset's findings. For example, Barrington Moore claimed, in a seminal work, that a dispersal of political and economic power prior to industrialization was advantageous to democracy. He argued that, in order for democracy to emerge, the landed aristocracy, representing the most recalcitrant interest in society, must be in decline. As Moore concluded, '... the route that ended up in capitalist democracy ... was itself a part of history that almost certainly will not be repeated'.[13] Works with a comparative historical orientation arrived at results which contradicted those derived from cross-national quantitative studies, such as Lipset's. Different methods which lead to diverse theoretical positions account for different outcomes. There seemed to be an impasse concerning research on the impact of economic development on democracy.

A thread in the structuralist fabric is that of the economic institutionalists. One research team, Dietrich Rueschemeyer, E.H. Stephens and J.D. Stephens, seized upon this deadlock as a departure point for their own efforts related to the connection between capitalism and democracy.[14] They agreed that cross-sectional correlations do not allow for appropriate inferences about causal sequence. Their methodology differed from what has been discussed so far in that they relied on comparative historical political economy. In an effort to deal with causation their strategy was one of analytic induction based on comparative historical research. Their case studies were linked to a theoretical framework which incorporated past research and analysed successive individual histories as well. By proceeding in such a manner they believed that they could deal with historical sequence and the specific historical context of each factor analysed. Moreover, each case could transform hypotheses used in previous inquiries as well as the broader conceptual framework. As they explain, what emerged was a galaxy of cases explained by a single set of theoretical propositions and a progressively modified theory which was consistent with the cases. Their results thus incorporated cross-national statistical work and were also based on extensive comparative historical analysis. They examined three sets of variables: class power, state structures and transnational power structures. Their efforts confirmed Lipset's results. Capitalism is related to democracy. It favours democratization because it modifies the class structure by strengthening the middle and working classes and weakening the landed class, which was so important to Moore. Although class structure does not explain differences in democratic development across nations, it is of major importance. Rueschemeyer, Stephens and Stephens have thus provided a causal theory portraying the conditions which enhance or impede democratization. However, they reject the notion of a homogeneous pattern of causation throughout history. They conclude that, even though the same variables fashioned democratization in all their cases, '... the combinations of causes and thus the paths to democracy (and dictatorship) were different in different historical contexts and in different regions'.[15]

Previously, reference was made to 'legacies of the past'. Any regime change is affiliated with some type of confrontation with national history. In a path-breaking study Robert Putnam delves into Italian history in an effort to determine its impact on the effectiveness of democratic political institutions.[16] He demonstrated that political traditions, history, social context and values are of significance. Although his study focused on Italy, his conclusions are applicable to Russia. Although it might seem a cliché to assert that the inheritance from the past must be considered in any evaluation of the present, the obvious turns out to be true. Basically, this historical legacy relates to a sense of security – not only political, economic and military security, but also environmental and societal security. More specifically, in the case of the latter, the role of traditional patterns of language, culture, religion, national identity and custom is significant. According to Geoffrey Pridham, the relationship between regime change and national history is '… invariably uncomfortable and perhaps painful, since it requires not merely a rejection of the preceding regime but also a slice of national experience which may have longer roots'.[17] As far as Russia is concerned, the principal problem is that there is no agreement as to the nature of its past.[18]

Central to the debate over Russia's present course and the relevance of standard liberal democracy is a strong, but fractured, state lacking roots in Russian society, a superficial and quasi-military relationship between regime and society, a supranationalism and the underdevelopment of autonomous institutions, including the state which has remained as an administrative force. In addition, mention must be made of militancy and an externally oriented public policy, charismatic salvationism or the 'Russian idea' which encapsulates the divine mission of the nation vis-à-vis the rest of the world, collectivism, and idealism, among other things. Then there is the *Vekhi* tradition, a manifestation of Russian particularism with its emphasis on spiritual and ethical values, opposed to revolutionary authoritarian communism. Also to be singled out is an ambivalent attitude to the West and democracy and the extent and nature of the country's relationship with Europe. These historically created social, political and value structures set the parameters for, and condition, the choices available to decision-makers. Not only do they establish the range of alternatives from which decision-makers may choose, but they predispose them to select a specific one.[19]

A review of the literature reveals a disagreement concerning the impact of the *ancien régime* on regime change. For example, Samuel Huntington recognizes the influence of the preceding regime on the overall transformation process.[20] Conversely, Adam Przeworski writes, '… where one is going matters as much as where one is coming from'.[21] For him, the past's influence on the processes of transition and consolidation of a new regime are neither as direct nor as weighty. Often these discrepancies result from the employment of different theoretical and methodological stances. G.L. Munck advances a political–institutional approach to overcome this impasse.[22] His strategy recognizes the importance of choices during the transitional phase and their effect on emerging democratic institutions as well as the appropriateness of placing actors in the broader context of the transformation. In the Russian case it is noteworthy that there is a bountiful legacy of differing traditions concerning these historical elements which jostle each other. Richard Sakwa writes:

> While historical factors clearly have a role to play in the current transition, there is always a choice of traditions, and the view of the future is coloured by the subjective evaluation of the past. The past weighs particularly heavily on Russian politics. And Russia has still to come to terms with its Tsarist and Soviet traditions, and elements to sustain the democratic experiment can be found although they come in a peculiarly Russian form.[23]

Such a situation only makes analysis and forecasting that much more difficult and controversial.

The structuralist school has weathered severe attacks from clinicians as well as academicians. As soon as the possibility of democratization appeared on the historical horizon, it became much less popular for practical and political reasons. The approach did not appeal to political actors who believed that, through their actions, they had something to contribute to the success of democratization. In the scholarly arena it was recognized that the forces which maintain a stable democracy may not be the same ones that account for its emergence. As Rustow observes, '... explanations of democracy must distinguish between function and genesis'.[24] Kitschelt argues that the structuralist model is probabilistic in terms of prediction. He asks:

> Even if all structural constraints were right, would there have been a rise of the German Nazi party to power in 1933 had it not been for the depression and the unique form of elite politics ushered in by the provisions of the Weimar Constitution?[25]

In a related vein, it is often easier to explain after the event why a particular regime was bound to fall than to predict when it would fall. It has been pointed out that the structural model provides adequate interpretation after the fact but that it is useless beforehand. The timing of any collapse is significant in that collapse can have tremendous consequences in breadth and depth. Unfortunately, this model does not account for timing and timing matters. Przeworski writes:

> The fact that recent transitions to democracy occurred as a wave also means that they happened under the same ideological and political conditions in the world. Moreover, contagion plays a role. Co-temporality induces homogeneity. The new democracies learn from the established ones and from one another.[26]

An in-depth analysis of the characteristics and contradictions of the *ancien régime* and its impact on group life is necessary for an explanation of the timing of transitions.

The quest for a set of unique and identical democratic preconditions has been termed as 'futile'.[27] Many of the requisites have failed to hold up very well in practice and have been disputed on a country-by-country basis. No general law of democratization has been developed nor is it expected. Consequently, it has been suggested that the search for preconditions be '... replaced by a more modest effort to develop a contingently sensitive understanding of the variety of circumstances under which [democratic regimes] may emerge'.[28] Moreover, given the nature of politics in the real world, there has been a call to view the preconditions of democracy as outcomes of disparate types of democratic systems. In other words, they should be considered as dependent, rather than independent, variables.

The Process-oriented School

A different approach is that adopted by the so-called 'process school'. It is less structuralist and its members, being of the opinion that the aforementioned preconditions of democracy are really outcomes, focus on human actions used to move from one type of political regime to another. Democratization is viewed as a complicated historical process with analytically distinct stages which distinguish the most important moments of the process: transition, consolidation, persistence and deconsolidation. Because it is recognized that there are many ways to travel this road, processes and procedures are emphasized. Each phase involves different sets of actors with disparate supporters, preferences, tactics and resources. For example, the transitional phase requires processes and dynamics distinct from those of the consolidation stage. The collective decisions and strategic interactions of each phase are deemed to be important. More specifically, these scholars study leadership, choices, alliances, processes, procedures and sequential patterns that emerge as the road to democratization is travelled.[29]

Democratization may be thought of as a tumultuous and fast game in which all the players manipulate their own vision as well as that of their opponents. At a National Research Council workshop T.L. Karl claimed:

> Democracy is a second-best option; it happens on the installment plan, which means there is no grand design. Instead you make your way as you go. The key to that process of building democracy is the notion of stalemate. In other words, no one group is strong enough to impose its vision and will on the society as a whole. There is stalemate, which means you must compromise about the ultimate outcome, and that compromise is the basis of democratization.[30]

Throughout this game the players' perceptions of preferences and constraints are constantly redefined. Consequently, the regime changes which result from this contest might be completely different from those desired or anticipated by any of the players at the outset. In other words, the resultant policies of government are not completely predetermined.[31]

Not only does the approach of the process-oriented scholars differ from that of the structuralists, but the literature may be differentiated as well. That generated by the process-oriented camp contains a heavy dose of descriptive case studies of regime transformation and lacks systematic cross-national comparison involving a broad array of nations.[32] Karen Remmer notes that these case studies '... privilege domestic over international forces, national peculiarities over broader comparative patterns of similarity and difference and accidental or contingent events over structural or institutional constraints ...'.[33]

A major exponent of the process-oriented school, Giuseppe Di Palma, as is evident from the title of his book, *To Craft Democracies: An Essay on Democratic Transitions*, views democratization primarily as a matter of political crafting which involves the creation of alliances between the leaders of the new order and their opponents, with the scope of leading to an acceptance of democracy.[34] The prime movers craft democracy by selecting the rules of the political game, the institutions, the manner of decision-making, the mediating procedures, the pacts and coalitions that engineer transformation and legitimize political discourse as well as the timing of change. These activities determine differing probabilities of victory for individual actors. With the emphasis on crafting, there is no need for any preconditions. Human action is the prime determinant. It does all. The vital components are political leadership and judgement and the role of specific individuals in the overall process. Thus, democracy can be expected to grow in a wide variety of soils.

According to Przeworski, rather than determining a particular allocation of resources among social groups, democratization creates apparent uncertainties regarding outcomes.[35] Others concur with this notion. For example, O'Donnell, Schmitter and Whitehead refer to 'extraordinary uncertainty ... with its numerous surprises and difficult dilemmas'.[36] This highlights the importance of the path. As Przeworski asserts: '... the final destination depends on the path ...'.[37] More specifically, he notes that the tenure of new democracies depends on their economic performance. It is generally acknowledged that market-oriented reforms are needed, but there is much debate over the method of reform. Przeworski proposes a social democratic path combining state coordination of economic transformation with democratic decision-making processes.[38] In addition to economic choices, there is a series of other agonizing ethical and political choices to be confronted, which determine the path of democratization. The four principal players in the game of regime change are the softliners and the hardliners and, in the ranks of the opposition, the moderates and the radicals.[39]

Assuming that the method used to establish new regimes is critical to their stability, the modes of transition, which in large part will determine whether or not democracy will emerge, are highlighted by process-oriented scholars.[40] Modes of transition can be classified on the basis of the process through which opposition forces replace incumbents. Three different types have been identified: transition from above (transformation, transaction, reform); transitions from below (replacement, breakdown, rupture); and transitions in which government and opposition assume a roughly equal role in system change (transplacement, extrication).[41] There are variations on this typology, and different terms are used to analyse the nature of regime change.[42]

It is the first type of transition that has been the most frequent. Regime changes of this type are based on major foundational pacts which achieve a consensus on four types of issues: military–state relations; the rules of the game as they relate to kinds of political systems and their operation; socio-economic matters, especially those concerning the rules of property; and religious and ethnic cleavages. Combined, these four types of agreement – all interdependent and impacting on each other in disparate ways – have led historically to stable democracies.[43]

Some process-oriented students of transition have focused on one single issue of transition, such as conflict resolution. Helga Welsh claims that the concept of bargaining and compromise, independent of the mode of transition, is critical to gaining insight into the transition process. It is her contention that concentration on diverse negotiation patterns enhances understanding of the transition process. It is thus possible to differentiate various stages in the transition process on the basis of diverse modes of conflict resolution. The successful transition process would have three phases, each one identified by a major means of conflict resolution: command and imposition; bargaining and compromise; and competition and cooperation. Welsh argues that the negotiating pattern provides the framework for the transition process and in turn '... the transition to democracy is also a transition in the modes of conflict ...'.[44] Her argument is a plausible one, in that Karl, at a National Research Council gathering, noted '... that to the extent that modes of transition happen first, by compromise, and second, with as much mass participation as possible within legitimately organized intermediary organizations, durable transitions are more likely'.[45]

An impure process-oriented model is the predictive and advisory one put forward by the American economist Jeffrey Sachs and which, notably, has been implemented. We label it an impure process-oriented model because it views democracy as an end product but contains no room for compromise. Based on a neo-liberal theory, it is sometimes known as the 'shock therapy' model and has been at the basis of Western advice and influence. It has been very controversial. Some say that it will only bring Russia to disaster, while others argue that, if it is given time and proper effort, it will help the economy recover and aid in the building of democracy. On the other hand, Peter Gowan argues that 'shock therapy' has produced naked markets opened to the West by convertibility and privatization, but denied the forms of public subsidy, protection and regulation encountered in every Western country.[46]

Sachs argued that his model represented a problem-solving approach to public policy analyses. Gowan writes:

> Sachs formulated his model to solve one big problem: how should the entire ex-Communist region of Eastern Europe and the USSR be reorganized in order to achieve, in Sachs's words, 'a recovery of human freedom and a democratically based rise in living standards'?[47]

Basic to his ideas was the breaking up of the Comecon region which would lead to competition among the East European nations. Rejecting not only the totally owned and directed economy of communism, he also opposed all mixed economic models that retained a significant role for the state in directing the economy. Among the systems he rejected was social democracy which would continue to give the state a considerable role in the economy. Proponents of social democracy, among other things, see it as a transition position which leaves time for adjustment. Sachs's model leaves no such time for adjustment. He pushes for an immediate commitment to a Western type of free market economy, indicating that 'the main precepts of capitalism [are] open trade, currency convertibility and the private sector as the engine of growth'.[48] In fact, he lists these three among his six 'core reforms' which must be achieved. The other three are corporate ownership as the dominant organizational form for large enterprises, openness to foreign investment and membership in key international economic institutions, including the IMF, the World Bank and the General Agreement on Tariffs and Trade (GATT). The emphasis on international trade and membership in international economic institutions ensures that Russia will take its place in the mainstream global economy. Critics see the interrelatedness of the global economy as working to the advantage of Western capitalist countries, while adding a costly burden to the changed East European economies.

The whole model involves a process whereby the liberalization of most parts of the economy and the privatization of industry and commerce and reliance on international and national trade to bring about growth will cause desired political change and institutional consolidation. The point to be recognized, though, is that democracy, as noted above, is an end product of the process. It is the shock treatment which, while probably expensive in terms of human costs, will lead to a transformation of legal and civil institutions and therefore to a changed civil society and democracy. Within the process there is no emphasis on a popular role in decision-making nor the development of consensus. As a result, it is somewhat curious that supporters of 'shock therapy' have been surprised by the showing of the former communists in the election of December 1995. This model, which brought about economic and social decline for many, saw the people lose confidence in its promises since they were not brought in as partners.

Given the orientation of the process-oriented approach, it is understandable why its supporters view the structuralists, who circumscribe democratic theory with a list of structural preconditions and requisites, as being too pessimistic. It is believed that, in their approach, the system-building stage is confused with system maintenance. Moreover, they are charged with imposing the characteristics of stable democratic regimes as prerequisites on emerging democracies. They are seen as being counterproductive because limits are placed on human activity. Furthermore, the open-endedness of the transition processes is defied and, above all, democratic action is not encouraged.[49] Karl, at a workshop sponsored by the National Research Council, hypothesized that the democracies which have the least chance for survival are those in which no precise strategy of transition is evident at any given time.[50] In light of this, concentration on political strategies and choices is most valuable.

The Mixed School

The point was made earlier that writers on transition have acknowledged that there is considerable complexity in model-building in this field. Hence, there are mixed or hybrid models. In this school of thought single causation is rejected and factors which may fall in different schools of thought are utilized. It is recognized that process is important, but that it should be evaluated in light of preconditions. Thus, there is a need to draw upon and integrate the lessons of the structuralists and process-oriented approaches.

Among the foremost writers who advocate a mixed model is Huntington. He is best known for his ideas about 'waves of democratization'.[51] These involve three long waves which have their roots in the first half of the nineteenth century. In addition, there are two intermediate 'reverse waves'. The first democratic wave which began in the 1820s and lasted for roughly 100 years saw the birth of 29 democratic systems. However, in the early years of the Second World War the first 'reverse wave' developed and the number of democracies in the world was reduced to 12. Stalinist communism and fascism almost obliterated democracy. The second long wave of democratization began immediately after the end of the Second World War and lasted until the early years of the 1960s by which time 36 democracies existed worldwide. However, there was a minor 'reverse wave' in the 1960s which continued until the mid-1970s during which period the number of democracies was reduced by six. It is the distinctiveness of current transitions to democracy which Huntington refers to collectively as the 'third wave' of democratization. This one which is relevant to this paper occurred between 1974 and 1990. In this period the number of democratic states increased from 30 to 60. It is on the basis of these new democratic states and those which followed them that theoretical postulation about transitions have been developed. In the 'third wave' domestic forces are more important than international ones.

Huntington, in discussing transition to democracy, identifies social, cultural and economic factors as necessary preconditions for democracy, but also indicates an important role for central actors. He dichotomizes 'initiating transitions' which involve preconditions and are related to structure and 'advancing transitions' which are related to process. This approach is a very flexible one and enables him to refer to different factors in different areas.

He also postulates five causes of the 'third wave'. First, in authoritarian regimes economic effectiveness can neither be dissociated from the legitimacy of rulers nor the legitimacy of rulers from legitimacy of rules of governance. Second, while emphasizing the importance of economic development, he does not perceive it as a necessary or a sufficient condition, although he does assign importance to the distribution of wealth. Third, he stresses the independent effect of religious doctrine and religious transformation. Fourth, over and above these structural changes, he notes that new cross-national politics influenced by the United States, the Soviet Union, the European Union and the Vatican enhanced the environment for democratic change in the 1980s. Finally, the democratic wave began to snowball. Demonstration effects elsewhere reinforced opposition efforts to achieve democracy in nations where structural conditions were somewhat conducive to regime change. In this explanation of the causes of the 'third wave' the combination of structural and procedural orientations is manifest. However, in that Huntington demonstrates that the mode of transition is related to the nature of incumbent political regimes, he goes beyond the usual structure–process divide.[52]

International Factors

Although the importance of the international context in an explanation of internal politics and political development has long been recognized in the literature of comparative politics,[53] theories of regime transition have neglected international factors or, at best, relegated them to secondary importance. Democracy has primarily been analysed as a product of domestic forces. In some cases it has been implied, however, that foreign influence would most likely play a more significant part in the consolidation phase of change. This underrating of the international dimension is generally surprising, especially in the case of Eastern Europe where it would seem to be most difficult, if not impossible, to escape its effects. Indeed, Pridham argues that this factor has been more decisive and more profound in this region than in others and has, in fact, been labelled a crucial condition to the fate of democratization.[54]

There are numerous actors in this international dimension which has assumed many disparate forms. These include unintentional effects – for example, market forces, and deliberate efforts to exercise influence through a wide variety of activities, such as the erection of trade barriers. Also of influence are international organizations and national governments as well as the galaxy of non-governmental players of various types and dimensions, such as political parties, interest groups, social institutions and entrepreneurs, among others. The nature and amount of influence exercised by an external actor depends on the domestic context of the country in transition, its strategic importance and the type of regime change involved in terms of its speed, style and scope. In any case, these pressures emanating from the international arena are multifaceted. They include political, diplomatic, economic, commercial, moral, cultural, covert, subversive, coercive, persuasive, direct and indirect activities, all of which are translated into the domestic political agenda with mixed results.[55]

Economic transformation via market-driven reforms is ranked high, if not top, among the priorities of regime change. Technical assistance and Western financial aid are necessities. Thus, Russia is dependent on Western economic aid and access to Western-dominated economic institutions. Because of their impact on the efficiency and competitiveness of industrial ventures, the availability of global capital and capital flows into a region are prime determinants of economic success. Limited domestic economic resources have increased the impact of international forces on regime change. In fact, Remmer refers to the '... internationalization of processes of domestic political choice ...'.[56] International organizations have been generous – and indeed, more active than private lenders or investors – with loans, credits and aid to Eastern Europe in general and to Russia in particular.[57]

But many critics argue that, while many promises of aid have been made, actual delivery of assistance has been meagre.

Of the international organizations involved, the European Union (EU) may be singled out for attention. The relationship which the EU has cultivated with Russia is related to the notions of democratization through incorporation and democratization through convergence.[58] Its primary objectives have been to support Russia's movement towards a market economy, a pluralist democratic society and international integration. The Phare and Tacis programmes are developing economic and political links between the EU and Russia, and the Democracy Programme supports the activities and efforts of non-governmental bodies. The EU fulfils its objectives by providing financial grants in aid, but awards are linked to establishment of a pluralistic polity with no institutionally favoured party, free trade unions, movement towards a free market economy and respect for human rights, among other conditions. Such requirements play an important role in strengthening democratic trends in Russia.

Although most attention has focused on the economic transformation, it must be recognized that Russia, as well as other East European nations, must build the institutions and skills necessary for effective constitutional democracy and civil society. It is this facet of nation-building that has occupied a secondary place. In short, a culture of democracy and an environment friendly to democratization must be cultivated; leaders and citizens are to be trained in the ABC of democracy, and the EU and other external resources are to be used for this task.

In view of the extensive burden assumed by international actors in regime change and the acknowledgement of the relationship between the international and the national contexts in the literature of comparative politics, it is surprising that these actors have not played a prime part in the above-mentioned theoretical models. Their role cannot be ignored. In fact, it is impossible to escape the impact of the international system. Schmitter and Karl have noted that Russia, as well as the nations of Eastern Europe, are caught in a paradox.[59] Although their transitions were rapid, bloodless and definitive, their consolidation phase will probably be lengthy, conflictual and inconclusive. Difficulty will be experienced in choosing and becoming used to an appropriate brand of democracy. Their forecast is that the most probable outcome will be 'unconsolidated democracy' because of the conditions imposed by reliance upon the EU and the West. Influence from these sources has definitely determined the course and content of democratizing impulses.

Remmer presents a long list of international factors related to democratization. Among other things, these include:

... global value change, global modernization, shifts in the orientation of the Catholic church, foreign policy changes on the part of the European Community and other world powers, and demonstration effects ... economic sanctions, military defeats, international sporting events, multilateral pressures ... and improved communications technology.[60]

She notes that questions must be answered concerning the relevance and importance of these factors, as well as the effects of interaction among and between domestic and international variables. These are not simple questions to answer, given the fluidity of international pressures, a nation's linkage to the international system, and its internal politics and their receptivity to external influence.

Summary and Conclusion

Quite clearly, students of regime change, despite having a shared agenda, have generated a large body of heterogeneous literature riddled with debate. A major point of disagreement, as mentioned previously, is the issue of comparability of regime transitions in Eastern Europe in general, and in Russia in particular, with other regions of the world. In one camp are those, such as Schmitter and Karl, who accept the appropriateness of cross-regional comparisons.[61] Post-communist regimes are viewed as a variation on the general theme of democratization. Although it is recognized that regime changes in the East and the South have differing points of departure in terms of their socioeconomic and institutional structures, the nature of the collapse of the previous regime (of larger magnitude in the East), the role of external forces (more prominent in the East) and the sequence of processes (more vague in the East), inclusion of East European nations in the case base is welcomed because of the various historical and cultural contexts which enrich the sample.

On the other hand, a group of scholars, personified by Kenneth Jowitt and Valerie Bunce, claim that, because of these and other diversities, but especially because of a unique historical legacy, it is inappropriate to group the Russian case with others.[62] This group are of the opinion that some efforts at comparison are highly suspect because of the differences between East and South. This particularly applies to the transfer of concepts and arguments from one region to another because of the diverse contexts is open to question. Furthermore, as a result, the validity of predicting development in the East on the basis of the southern experience is challengeable.

It would seem that a more comparative approach is appropriate. For years Soviet studies have represented an area study and, in a sense, an independent discipline. The assumption of a true comparative orientation would foster intra- and interdisciplinary collaboration which is critical to an examination of many of the issues related to post-communist transitions, such as military–state relationships, interactions between 'hardliners' and 'softliners', and preconditions, to cite a few. Further progress towards the generation of a generalized theory of post-communist transitions would be achieved if common patterns across diverse cases were detected. But undertaking efforts at comparison does not necessarily indicate an expectation of similar outcomes. Uncovering differences is just as important as finding similarities.

Nor is comparison meant to substitute for case studies of regime change. What it does do is to mesh the diverse approaches discussed above. Obviously, each one is most likely to be successful when informed by the others. If comparisons had been developed, it might have been possible to interpret more accurately events in Eastern Europe. Regardless of past efforts, it seems that examination of other cases helps develop a better understanding of the possibilities and probabilities faced by this part of the world.[63]

Despite discrepancies, there are notable points of convergence in the transition literature. Most authors ask the same type of questions and support their response with the same sort of evidence. There has been a shift from functional to genetic questions. Moreover, most scientific inquiry commences with the conscious or unconscious perception of a puzzle. Also of note is the fact that most scholars have adopted a narrow definition of democracy, viewing it as a political system separate from the economic and social system to which it is joined. This raises the question of whether the two systems can be separated from each other.

A major problem is that, within the political science literature on regime transition, there is no common language for inquiry. Scholars define salient terms and concepts, such as transition, consolidation, liberalization, democratization, to cite a few, quite differently. Obviously, dialogue is difficult without a common understanding of terminology. Another characteristic of the transition literature is that, although it is fertile in description, it is impoverished in terms of generating testable hypotheses focusing on historical contingency and the variety of causal paths to democratization. Bunce observes: 'What is offered ... is not ... a theory of democratization – a series of "if, then" claims that can be tested – but rather an approach to the analysis of democratization; that is, a statement about what should be analyzed and how.'[64]

As is evident from the above presentation of selected representative models used to study regime change, there is no consensus on theory in the political science transition literature. In fact, Remmer has referred to '... the current state of theoretical disarray'.[65] There is no agreement on how to conceptualize about the players and the historically-fashioned field on which the game of regime change is played. The principal models presented above are based on diverse methodologies and research designs and utilize different variables for the purposes of explanation. The strength of one model is a shortcoming of another. The structuralist school enjoys an advantage in terms of explaining the causality of regime collapse and the consolidation of new systems. But it is weak, as noted above, in dealing with the timing of collapse and transitions. Conversely, those in the process-oriented camp have been able adequately to deal with the time dimension and the choices related to the search for a new regime. They have not been successful, however, in the prediction of regime consolidation.[66] Victor Zaslavsky posits that: 'In all likelihood, the Russian case will prove an ideal testing ground for weighing the role of structural conditions against the wills and skills of political actors in bringing about democracy'.[67] Only time will tell.

Overcoming the present theoretical disorder will not be an easy task. There are obstacles to be overcome. Remmer presents three in particular. First, she notes that, even though democratization in the last two decades represents an international phenomenon, theory, for the most part (as mentioned previously), is based on domestic political choices and outcomes. Second, theories have been discarded because they were found to be no longer valid, but efforts to generate new ones have been complicated by a wide range of conjunctural conditions, among other things, affiliated with regime change. Third, as noted above, political democracy has recently come about in an environment of dramatic economic recession.[68] It has been difficult to deal with these characteristics of the democratization process because of disciplinary traditions and ossified ways of conceptualizing political democracy.

Comprehensive theory generation is not an easy task because of traditional intradisciplinary relationships. Scholars in two subfields of the discipline of political science – comparative politics and international relations – tend to be compartmentalized. As a result, the work of comparativists, attempting to identify causal patterns, revolves around the concept of the nation-state and neglects, for all practical purposes, international variables. The reverse holds in the case of scholars in the field of international relations. Established disciplinary boundaries account for the lack of integration of variables from both worlds.

This impasse must be overcome. Autonomy and separation can no longer be tolerated. The interdependence of the principal factors noted in this discussion should be recognized. Historical legacies, national structures, the international environment and alternative policy choices all influence the outcome of democratization. In refining the analysis of regime transitions attention must be paid, first and foremost, to this notion and should be the starting point for future endeavours. This might seem a platitude, but it is quite evident from a review of the transition literature that this concept has not received appropriate consideration. Much has been accomplished, but there is still a great deal to be done. The road to be travelled has many bumps. Overcoming them will require the effort of researchers with complementary talents, abilities, and experience in both the theoretical and practical arenas.

Notes

1. Anatol Lieven (1995), 'Present at the Cremation', *New York Times Book Review*, 26 November, p. 6.
2. David Remnick (1995), 'Restoration Tragedy – The Communists: Russia's Comeback Kids', *The New Yorker*, 18 December, pp. 7–8.
3. Giovanni Sartori (1965), *Democratic Theory*, New York, p. 124.
4. Seymour M. Lipset (1963), *Political Man: The Social Bases of Politics*, Garden City.
5. Gabriel Almond and Sidney Verba (1963), *Civic Culture: Political Attitudes and Democracy in Five Nations*, Princeton.
6. Herbert Kitschelt (1992), 'Political Regime Change: Structure and Process: Driven Explanations', *American Political Science Review*, **86**, (4), pp. 1028–34.
7. Seymour M. Lipset (1959), 'Some Social Requisites of Democracy: Economic Development and Political Legitimacy', *American Political Science Review*, **53**, (1), pp. 69–105.
8. Ibid., p. 104.
9. Dankwart A. Rustow (1970), 'Transitions to Democracy: Toward a Dynamic Model', *Comparative Politics*, **2**, (3), pp. 337–63.
10. Karen L. Remmer (1995), 'New Theoretical Perspectives on Democratization', *Comparative Politics*, **28**, (1), pp. 103–22.
11. Rustow, 'Transitions to Democracy', note 9 *supra*, p. 342.
12. Ibid., p. 343.
13. Barrington Moore, jr (1965), *Social Origins of Dictatorship and Democracy*, Boston, p. 5.
14. Dietrich Rueschemeyer, Evelyne Huber Stephens and John D. Stephens (1992), *Capitalist Development and Democracy*, Chicago.
15. Ibid., p. 284.
16. Robert D. Putnam (1993), *Making Democracy Work: Civic Traditions in Modern Italy*, Princeton.
17. Geoffrey Pridham (1994), 'The International Dimension of Democratisation: Theory, Practice and Inter-Regional Comparisons' in Geoffrey Pridham, Eric Herring and George Sanford (eds), *Building Democracy? The International Dimension of Democratisation in Eastern Europe*, London, p. 26.
18. Eric Herring (1994), 'International Security and Democratisation in Eastern Europe', in ibid., pp. 87–118 and Richard Sakwa (1993), 'Russia, Communism, Democracy' in Stephen White, Alex Pravda and Zvi Gitelman (eds), *Developments in Russian and Post-Soviet Politics*, 3rd edn, London.
19. See Giuseppe Di Palma (1991), 'Legitimation from the Top to Civil Society: Politico-Cultural Change in Eastern Europe', *World Politics*, **44**, (1), pp. 49–80; Andrew C. Janos (1991), 'Social Science, Communism and the Dynamics of Political Change',

ibid., pp. 81–112; Terry L. Karl and Philippe Schmitter (1991), 'Modes of Transition in Latin America, Southern and Eastern Europe', *International Social Science Journal*, **43**, (128), pp. 269–84 and Sakwa, 'Russia, Communism, Democracy', note 18 *supra*.
20 Samuel Huntington (1991), *The Third Wave: Democratisation in the Late Twentieth Century*, Norman, Oklahoma.
21 Adam Przeworski (1991), *Democracy and the Market: Political and Economic Reforms in Eastern Europe and Latin America*, New York, p. 99.
22 Gerardo L. Munck (1994), 'Democratic Transitions in Comparative Perspective', *Comparative Politics*, **26**, (3), pp. 355–75.
23 Sakwa, 'Russia, Communism, Democracy', note 18 *supra*, pp. 306–7.
24 Rustow, 'Transition to Democracy', note 9 *supra*, p. 346.
25 Kitschelt, 'Political Regime Change', note 6 *supra*, p. 1030.
26 Przeworski, *Democracy and the Market*, note 21 *supra*, pp. 98–9.
27 Terry L. Karl (1990), 'Dilemmas of Democratisation in Latin America', *Comparative Politics*, **23**, (1), pp. 1–21; Karl and Schmitter, 'Modes of Transition, note 19 *supra*; National Research Council (1991), *The Transition to Democracy: Proceedings of a Workshop*, Washington, DC.
28 Karl and Schmitter, 'Modes of Transition', note 19 *supra*, p. 270.
29 Ibid.; National Research Council, *The Transition to Democracy*, note 27 *supra*.
30 National Research Council, *The Transition to Democracy*, note 27 *supra*, p. 32.
31 Guillermo O'Donnell, Philippe C. Schmitter and Laurence Whitehead (eds) (1986), *Transitions from Authoritarian Rule: Prospects for Democracy: Vol. 4. Tentative Conclusions about Uncertain Democracies*, Baltimore.
32 Kitschelt, 'Political Regime Change', note 6 *supra*.
33 Remmer, 'New Theoretical Perspectives on Democratization', note 10 *supra*, p. 117.
34 Giuseppe Di Palma (1990), *To Craft Democracies: An Essay on Democratic Transitions*, Berkeley.
35 Przeworski, *Democracy and the Market*, note 21 *supra*.
36 O'Donnell, Schmitter and Whitehead (eds), *Transitions from Authoritarian Rule*, note 31 *supra*, p. 37.
37 Przeworski, *Democracy and the Market*, note 21 *supra*, p. 51.
38 Adam Przeworski (1993), *Economic Reforms in New Democracies: A Social-Democratic Approach*, Cambridge, Mass.
39 O'Donnell, Schmitter and Whitehead (eds), *Transitions from Authoritarian Rule*, note 31 *supra*.
40 Karl and Schmitter, 'Modes of Transition', note 19 *supra*.
41 Helga A. Welsh (1994), 'Political Transition Processes in Central and Eastern Europe', *Comparative Politics*, **26**, (4), pp. 379–94.
42 Huntington, *The Third Wave*, note 20 *supra* and Karl, 'Dilemmas of Democratisation in Latin America', note 27 *supra*.
43 National Research Council, *The Transition to Democracy*, note 27 *supra*.
44 Welsh, 'Political Transition Processes in Central and Eastern Europe', note 41 *supra*, p. 391.
45 National Research Council, *The Transition to Democracy*, note 27 *supra*, p. 38.
46 Peter Gowan (1995), 'Neo-liberal Theory and Practice for Eastern Europe', *New Left Review*, (213), p. 38.
47 Ibid., p. 5.
48 Jeffrey Sachs (1995), 'Consolidating Capitalism', *Foreign Policy*, (98), p. 53.
49 Victor Zaslavsky (1993), 'Russia and the Problem of Democratic Transition', *Telos*, (96), pp. 26–52.

50 National Research Council, *The Transition to Democracy*, note 27 *supra*.
51 Huntington, *The Third Wave*, note 20 *supra*.
52 Kitschelt, 'Political Regime Change', note 6 *supra*.
53 Gabriel A. Almond (1989), 'Review Article: The International-National Connection', *British Journal of Political Science*, **19**, part 2, pp. 237–59.
54 Pridham, 'The International Dimension of Democratisation', note 17 *supra*, pp. 7–31; and Geoffrey Pridham, Eric Herring and George Sanford, 'Introduction', in Pridham, Herring and Sanford, *Building Democracy?*, note 17 *supra*, pp. 1–6.
55 Ibid.
56 Remmer, 'New Theoretical Perspectives on Democratization', note 10 *supra*, p. 118.
57 Beverly Crawford (1992), *Markets, States and Democracy: The Transformation of Communist Regimes in Eastern Europe and the Former Soviet Union*, Berkeley.
58 John Pinder (1994), 'The European Community and Democracy in Central and Eastern Europe', in Pridham, Herring and Sandford (eds), *Building Democracy?*, note 17 *supra*, pp. 119–43.
59 Philippe Schmitter and Terry L. Karl (1994), 'The Conceptual Travels of Transitologists and Consolidologists: How Far to the East Should They Attempt to Go?', *Slavic Review*, **53**, (1), pp. 173–85.
60 Remmer, 'New Theoretical Perspectives on Democratization', note 10 *supra*, p. 108.
61 Schmitter and Karl, 'The Conceptual Travels of Transitologists and Consolidologists', note 59 *supra*.
62 Kenneth Jowitt (1992), *The New World Disorder: The Leninist Extinction*, Berkeley; and Valerie Bunce (1995), 'Should Transitologists Be Grounded?', *Slavic Review*, **54**, (1), pp. 111–27.
63 Russell Bova (1991), 'Political Dynamics of the Post Communist Transition: A Comparative Perspective', *World Politics*, **44**, (1), pp. 113–38.
64 Bunce, 'Should Transitologists Be Grounded?', note 62 *supra*, p. 123.
65 Remmer, 'New Theoretical Perspectives on Democratization', note 10 *supra*, p. 104.
66 Kitschelt, 'Political Regime Change', note 6 *supra*,
67 Zaslavsky, 'Russia and the Problem of Democratic Transition', note 49 *supra*, p. 47.
68 Remmer, 'New Theoretical Perspectives on Democratization', note 10 *supra*.

4 Dancing on the Edge of the Chasm: The Struggle for Survival in the Former Soviet Union

Derek Braddon

Introduction

As a source of interregional tension and a catalyst for potential international conflict, few factors weigh as heavily as the struggle for economic survival and progress. Over the last decade, the former Soviet Union (FSU), has seen its position as a relatively stable superpower command economy disintegrate and has experienced rampant inflation, unprecedented levels of unemployment and industrial bankruptcies, declining living standards and a devastating collapse in domestic output and trade. Confronting, simultaneously, such an array of extreme economic problems and associated social and political tensions, most of the republics which comprised the FSU are struggling to transform their economies into more market-oriented, globally-focused economic systems. The task they have to undertake, however, is significantly more than simply to rebuild shattered economies. Ultimately, in an increasingly competitive global business environment, the objective must be to create from the ruins of the old system new world-class market economies that can truly compete on the international stage. At present, the fundamental aim of economic survival has been pursued through the implementation of policies which involve deep and prolonged austerity, widespread economic and social inequity generating, in turn, increasing political disaffection at least in the short term – all significant contributors to growing interregional tension.

This chapter reviews the transition to market forces within the FSU – a topic of considerable conjecture[1] – and then surveys the performance of a sample of FSU republics under their various reform programmes. The degree to which economic interdependence in the region, remains long after political independence has been achieved is noted. The analysis then focuses increasingly upon Russia as the key economy in the region, and its performance under market reforms is evaluated against the backdrop of a sharp contraction in its military expenditure.

Analysts surveying the reform process currently underway in the economies of the FSU republics present a mixed picture of progress and achievement.[2] On the one hand, some economists consider that the transition to a market-based economic system may be neither appropriate nor successful, given the parlous state of many market-based economies in the West. Indeed, in so doing, some have questioned the entire theoretical base of market economics. For example, Paul Ormerod has commented:

> The world economy is in crisis. Twenty million people are unemployed in Western Europe – America faces two severe deficits – and vast tracts of the former Soviet empire are on the brink of economic collapse. In this grim context, orthodox economics seems powerless to help. Teams of economists descend on the former Soviet Union proclaiming the virtues and necessity of moving to a free market system as rapidly as possible: systems of greater purity than those contemplated by Ronald Reagan and Margaret Thatcher. But despite governments in the former Soviet bloc doing everything they are told, their economic situation worsens.[3]

Others, however, doubt whether the problem lies in the reforms being insufficient or obstructed and contend that new urgency needs to be given to the drive towards market liberalization, financial stabilization and privatization.[4] Some recent reports (such as that from the IMF in December 1995) present a far more optimistic picture of the current situation and market reform process, commenting: 'The economies in transition are increasingly seeing the fruits of their adjustment efforts. Many former Soviet bloc countries are enjoying their best economic times since the late 1980's.'[5]

Indeed, taken out of context, the IMF's cautious optimism appears to be justified. Considering recent economic performance in Russia, for example, with a new counterinflation strategy put in place during 1995, monitored on a monthly basis by the IMF in return for a $6.5 billion standby credit, the Russian economy appears more stable now than at any time this decade.[6] On the basis of recent economic indicators, Russian economic performance in the spring of 1996 seemed to be significantly improved on that of just one year previously. Such economic improvement was used as the justification for an IMF agreement to a further standby credit facility of $10.2 billion for Russia in March 1996. In exchange for this, the Russian government have agreed to reduce tariffs and taxes on oil and gas exports, close some existing tax loopholes, and continue to consume US frozen poultry worth some $500 million annually. Commentators have suggested, however, that this most recent standby credit from the IMF to assist Russia's transition had more to do with the preference in the West for the re-election of the Boris Yeltsin administration in the June 1996 elections. Western governments are also currently concerned about Russian objections to the potential enlargement of NATO, the Russian engagement in the brutal and destabilizing war in Chechnya, the sale of nuclear technology to Iran, and Russian rhetoric about the future restoration of the old FSU boundaries.

During 1995–96, the federal deficit has declined from 9.2 to 3.2 per cent of gross domestic product (GDP); official foreign reserves (frequently viewed as a symbol of economic stability and potential) increased over the first half of 1995 from $2 billion to $10 billion, the highest level since the reform programme began; and the monthly inflation rate has declined from around 20 per cent early in 1995 to around 5 per cent later in the year. In the view of pro-market reformers, the prime reason for improved Russian economic performance, measured by such indicators, has been the extremely tight fiscal stance adopted by the government during this period, supplemented by the new spirit of economic enterprise, released as a result of new market freedom.

Intensely deflationary measures, supplemented by the decision to 'peg' the exchange rate in a band of 4300 to 4900 roubles against the dollar, resulted in the monthly inflation rate falling from 18 per cent in January 1995 to 5 per cent by the end of the summer 1995. In general, Russian prices are now much closer to world prices. The standard economic indicators, therefore, reveal – at least superficially – distinct improvement.

The price paid for this limited and somewhat fragile 'success', however, can be measured in two ways: first, in terms of the adverse effects of recent economic policy on society and the economy in the course of a single year (together with the tensions generated by such adverse economic impacts); and, second, by the cumulative effects of the reform measures adopted since the start of the decade and the damage inflicted upon the Russian economy as a consequence.

Looking first at 1995, the scale of austerity imposed on the Russian population has been such that sales decreased by 8 per cent against 1994 levels in the first half of 1995 and, while industrial output stabilized and showed a slight increase in 1995 for the first time this decade, investment (critically) fell sharply by some 20 per cent compared with that achieved in 1994. The unemployment rate continued to increase in 1995, reaching 7.6 per cent by the summer, up from 6 per cent in the previous year. At the start of the reform process, many Western economists saw sharply increasing unemployment in Russia as a key transfer mechanism, demonstrating clearly the market-driven movement of labour from old declining sectors into new expanding activities. Experience since 1991, however, has cast serious doubt on the effectiveness of this transfer mechanism across the FSU and especially in Russia.[7] The austerity measures may have had a beneficial impact upon inflation but their impact on living standards, public opinion, social security,[8] rising tension and, inevitably, the popularity of the Yeltsin administration has been anything but beneficial.

Furthermore, the fragility of the perceived improvement in economic performance – for which such a high price has been paid – is only too clearly revealed in the occasional, but dramatic, upheavals that shake the foundations of the newly emerging economic system in Russia. This was, perhaps, best shown by the interbank market crisis that suddenly developed in August 1995 when ten Russian commercial banks found themselves unable to meet scheduled payments and the overnight interest rate rocketed to 1000 per cent from a previous level of 60 per cent. Only by the central bank injecting immediate financial liquidity to keep the system solvent were these interest rates reduced to 400 per cent and, later, to 170 per cent. Dismissed by some commentators as an inevitable phase in the restructuring of the Russian banking system, upheavals such as this suggest that the economic gains of recent years, frequently offset by significant associated medium-term economic damage, may lack resilience in the face of chaotic conditions in newly created markets.

The situation is altogether more serious, however, when comparing the current condition of the Russian economy with that pertaining at the start of the reform process. The scale of economic disintegration in Russia since 1992 has been little short of remarkable. Between January 1991 and the end of 1995, real industrial production in Russia fell by almost half. Although not entirely comparable, this decline may be considered significantly more intense than that experienced by the United States during the worst years of the Great Depression and represented a massive and potentially cataclysmic contraction in economic power. Inevitably, despite employment policies designed to retain workers, the impact of such industrial decline has had a devastating effect on employment. Officially measured unemployment increased from about 500 000 in early 1992 to almost 2.5 million by September 1995. The perceived weakness of the rapidly disintegrating Russian economy was clearly revealed in the dramatic and sustained depreciation of the rouble against the dollar on the Moscow Interbank Currency Exchange. Nominal depreciation has been particularly severe since January 1994 with the exchange rate moving from about 1250 roubles to the dollar to over 4500 roubles by October 1995. Compared with the last quarter of 1991, the average real wage has declined extremely sharply, effectively falling by half early in 1992 under the initial shock of reform, and then losing about a further 20 per cent of its value by late 1995. Under the impact of intensely deflationary measures during much of the reform process, inflation fell from a dangerously high rate of 38 per cent per month in early 1992 to some 5 per cent per month late in 1995. However, the descent in the inflation rate was not smooth. Towards the end of 1992, inflation increased again to a monthly rate of 25 per cent, falling again to about 20 per cent per month in early summer 1993, before exceeding 25 per cent again in the autumn of 1993. As recently as the spring of 1995, the inflation rate was again approaching 20 per cent, necessitating the implementation of the monetary stabilization programme administered by the IMF.

Economic Crisis in the Former Soviet Union

After the failed coup in August 1991, 15 FSU republics began programmes of economic reform which differed considerably in terms of content, approach and speed of implementation.[9] In most cases, the principal consequence of economic reform has been a prolonged period of serious stagflation. Armenia and Georgia suffered a cataclysmic collapse of output due in part to civil war; the Baltic States saw their output halved and inflation increase sharply; some other republics suffered a similar decline in output but with less severe inflation.

Table 4.1 reveals the extent to which the problems of rampant inflation, negative GDP growth and currency depreciation have affected a sample of FSU republics since the adoption of their respective reform programmes.

Table 4.1 Post-reform annual peaks in economic measures in FSU

	Inflation (%)	GDP contraction (%)	Exchange rate (1994)**
Azerbaijan	400+	−20	182
Belarus	1 000+	−20	24 000
Estonia	30+	−26	14
Georgia	2 000+	−35	250 000
Latvia	30+	−36	0.6
Lithuania	1 100+	−30	4
Moldova	3 000+	−30	4
Russia*	1 300+	−20	31 000
Ukraine*	50+	−30	4 500

* indicates the average monthly rate at the peak.
** measured in units per US$ as compared with a figure for all republics of 0.56 for 1991.

Table 4.1 clearly indicates the extent to which the economies of FSU republics have been ravaged by the impact of the reform process. Most – especially economies which depend significantly upon military expenditure such as Russia, Ukraine and Belarus – have experienced extremely sharp and prolonged contraction in national output. Again, most have experienced devastating rates of inflation as excess demand and the impact of price liberalization have jointly taken their toll. The consequences for post-reform living standards have been only too clear. In Russia, for example, the real wage (taking an index number of 100 for December 1994) declined from 175 in 1990 to just 78 by early 1995.

The Main Stages of Russian Economic Transition

Under the initial phase of economic reform, the Russian economy experienced significant decline in key industrial sectors through a combination of reduced government orders, the 'shake-out' effects of newly released market forces and consequent price adjustment. The production of weapons, low-quality consumer goods, obsolete industrial equipment and agricultural goods all diminished sharply. For the first time, employees in traditionally 'secure' occupations encountered the real threat of unemployment, weak industrial enterprises had to confront the prospect of bankruptcy, and government had to contend with a sharp and sudden collapse of tax revenue. The Yegor Gaidar reforms of 1992 were rapidly implemented but were far from comprehensive. Key prices in the economy were allowed to adjust in a fairly free fashion and the rouble was made convertible. But serious privatization was delayed until 1993. Energy prices, however, remained heavily subsidized for some time, and the private ownership of land remained a contentious issue. This internal economic contraction was exacerbated by the devastating collapse of intra-FSU trade, following the demise of the trade relationships within the Council for Mutual Economic Assistance (CMEA).

For such a tightly knit economic community such as the FSU, interrepublic trade was extremely critical to economic progress[10] and, consequently, the collapse of CMEA trade was devastating. Those republics experiencing the most serious consequences of the collapse in trade were Estonia, Lithuania, Latvia, Armenia, Moldova and Belarus. In each of these republics, total trade exceeds the value of 50 per cent of GNP and FSU-based regional trade constitutes over 40 per cent of GNP.[11]

The system of centralized decision-making within the FSU had given government ministries in Moscow virtually total control over the location, content and price of production as well as its distribution. As a result, economic decision-making became formalized in a series of vertical relationships stretching from a central ministry down to a factory, on to another ministry and eventually down to the end user of the product. No single republic was genuinely self-sufficient in terms of independent sources of supply to meet its requirements.

This bureaucratic structure – with its vertical linkages binding together ministries and factories across a vast geographic area – collapsed with the demise of the Soviet Union, leaving in its place some informal horizontal linkages (principally in the defence industries) and a wave of new trade barriers (import and export tariffs, permits and other bureaucratic obstacles to trade). These constraints serve only to hamper interrepublic trade and provide a potential source of new friction between economies at a critical stage in their transition.

Decades of dependence on a supply system that was genuinely transrepublic cannot be adequately replaced over a short timescale and its collapse leaves in its wake unfulfilled expectations, mutual recrimination and the potential for economic disruption which, fuelled by resurgent nationalism at republic level, can act as a catalyst for wider conflict of a political and ultimately military nature. As A. Kennaway has noted, this is

> ... leading to wars that extend beyond trade into armed conflict. This is visible in the southern republics which are fighting each other in tribal conflict but also accuse Russia, with some justice, of interfering on one side or another side and acting to damage local economies. This is especially true when it comes to exports of oil and gas.[12]

The high degree of economic interdependence between Russia and its FSU partners is well illustrated by the case of Belarus. Despite the republic's declaration of independence in 1991, its independence remains political rather than economic. Belarus depends critically upon Russia and other FSU republics for imports in a range of key raw materials and products, including oil, gas, electricity, power cables, medicines, copper, aluminium, wood pulp and commercial fish products. In particular, its economic survival depends on the maintenance of oil supplies from Russia, natural gas from Kazakhstan and electronic components from Ukraine and Moldova.[13]

In essence, the release of market forces was effectively destroying the 'old' economy in order to free resources for new production opportunities and exports. In the case of Russia, the economic situation became so serious during the early 1990s that 'Entire industries and company towns have closed or have stock-piled unwanted goods, failed to pay wages and have run up impossible debts'.[14] As a result, a somewhat chaotic set of economic conditions emerged with the agricultural sector in serious decline, heavy manufacturing industries pleading for government financial subsidies to cover almost US$50 billion of unpaid bills, the critically important armaments industry confronting massive cuts in orders and the traditional industries reducing workers' hours, cutting pay and defaulting on debts.

Eventually, however, the release of market forces, together with the widespread implementation of privatization policies, encouraged the emergence of a 'new' economy, albeit a relatively small and extremely fragile one. During the period 1991–94, it has been estimated that some 70 000 state enterprises were privatized, compared with an estimate of about 8000 privatizations for the entire world between 1981 and 1989. In addition, some 18 000 new companies were created and, by 1994, about 90 per cent of small and medium-sized enterprises in Russia were operated under some kind of private ownership. By 1994, two-thirds of employees in the core industries were privately employed and some 80 per cent of the service sector was privately owned. By that time, over 3000 commercial banks were operating across Russia, and foreign direct investment was increasing, amounting to about $500 million per month.

The Critical Role of the Defence Sector

The Economist Intelligence Unit reported: 'In defence, as in most other industries, the collapse of the Soviet Union in late 1991 was followed by a chaotic period when factories were left to their own devices. Many stood idle or went bankrupt. Arms production shrank by two-thirds.'[15] While attempting to implement a rapid and wide-ranging economic transformation from command to market economy, Russia and several of its FSU partners has also had to contend with the deeply destabilizing effects of military rundown following the end of the Cold War. The impact of both the end of the Cold War and the collapse of the Soviet Union on the global arms industry has yet to run its full course but, without question, it has already had extremely adverse consequences for production and employment since 1990. Global defence procurement budgets peaked in 1987 at almost US$1000 billion with an estimated 16 million people employed in global defence industries and some 32 million people employed in armed forces and paramilitary groups. Following the perceived end of the Cold War around 1990, the decline in global defence expenditure (already under way) accelerated sharply, particularly in the United States and the FSU (especially Russia). In the United States, following an expansion in Department of Defense budgets of 54 per cent between 1980 and 1985, defence expenditure (procurement and research and development) peaked in 1985–86, taking 6.6 per cent of real GNP. This share of GNP had declined to some 3.6 per cent by 1996. The decline in US procurement funding has been particularly severe. Weapons procurement in the United States fell by almost two-thirds in real terms in the decade after 1985. Consequently, the defence industry labour force was reduced significantly from around 1.35 millions in 1989 to about 800 000 in 1994.

In the states comprising the FSU, the reduction in defence expenditure also continued apace. Evidence suggests that the Russian defence industry, in particular, has experienced a more severe contraction than that of the West although, given the right conditions, the potential scope for conversion in that country could be considerably greater. Estimates suggest that the Russian defence budget which stood at around US$52.5 billion (at 1985 prices) in 1991 had fallen to US$29 billion by 1993.

Given the recognized problems of tracking and accurately measuring defence expenditure in the member states of the FSU, military production estimates may provide a better guide to the severity of the Russian defence cuts. Compared with 1990, even by 1992 Russian tank production had almost halved (from 1300 to 675); artillery production had fallen from 1900 new weapons to around 450; military aircraft production had declined from over 600 aircraft to some 170; and submarine and surface ships output had decreased from 20 to 8 vessels.

Estimates by Novecon, the Moscow-based economics agency, suggest that defence production in Russia fell by a massive 33.4 per cent in 1993. Of greater concern, perhaps, was evidence that the performance of those companies which had enthusiastically pursued Mikhail Gorbachev's *konversiya* strategy, switching resources into civil rather than military goods, fared even worse with a drop in production in 1993 of some 35.6 per cent. In part, this reflected the coincident decline in consumer demand for goods, especially for commodities such as tape recorders, video equipment and vacuum cleaners – the very products on whose market potential the success of the *konversiya* strategy depends. Through 1994, the position of the military-industrial complex (MIC) in Russia, according to Viktor Glukhikh, Chairman of the Russian State Committee for the Defence Industries, 'remained critical' with funding available at one point during that year to finance the construction of just 17 aircraft and 7 per cent of their naval requirements. Other estimates suggest that, in 1994, the Russian Defence Ministry cut its orders for new equipment by an unprecedented 67 per cent and that, in Western accounting terms, some 70 per cent of all Russian defence industries would have been declared insolvent. In the period May 1993 to May 1994 alone, military employment declined by 16 per cent, while hidden unemployment in that sector exceeded 30 per cent. Critically for long-term economic regeneration, Izyumov *et al.* suggest that the decline of the MIC is having a damaging impact upon labour skills:

The qualification and technological potential of the defense complex is decreasing rapidly. Some enterprises are already unable to produce the complicated, high-tech articles they had previously manufactured. Some even lack the skills to produce spare parts for the weapons they had previously sold.[16]

Traditionally, the principal symbol of the economic power and potential of the arms industries in the FSU was the formidable success achieved in the global arms market.

Earnings from arms exports, although notoriously suspect, have undoubtedly fallen catastrophically during the 1990s. Against a possibly optimistic estimate of US$20 billion for the value of the Soviet Union's annual arms exports in the mid-1980s, Rosvooruzheniye (the Russian arms exports agency established in 1993) estimates arms export sales for 1995 will amount to some US$2.5 billion, although this level is some 40 per cent higher than that of the 1994 low point.

Overall, the last decade has witnessed a dramatic change in the fortunes of the Russian MIC and in its capacity to generate economic growth. As Izyumov *et al.* put it:

> ... probably no other part of the Russian economy and society has suffered more casualties than its former pride, the military-industrial complex (MIC). Having entered Gorbachev's *perestroika* at the height of its might and privilege, the MIC now finds itself disgraced, isolated, underfinanced and shrinking beyond recognition.[17]

Such a dramatic decline in the fortunes of the key industrial sector, right at the heart of the Russian economy, carries with it considerable implications at the regional level, where declining income and employment opportunities – in stark contrast to the period when the MIC was a dominant economic force – may prove to be an additional source of regional tension and instability, both within Russia and more widely across the FSU republics where military production was concentrated. Some 760 significant defence facilities within the FSU have been identified, including production enterprises, science–production associations, research institutes, design organizations and military-related 'closed' towns. Of this total, some 75 per cent are located within Russian territory, a further 14.5 per cent in Ukraine, and the remainder distributed across the other republics. Within Russia, the most defence-dependent regions in terms of defence-related employment are considered to be the north-west, the Urals, Volgo-Vyatka and the Volga regions. Sharpening the focus of regional concentration to the *oblast'* level, the most vulnerable, in absolute employment terms, to the contraction in military expenditure are Sverdlovsk, Leningrad (city), Moscow (city), Nizhnii-Novgorod (*gor'kii*), Moscow (*oblast'*), Perm', Samara (*kuibyshev*),

Novosibirsk, Tatarstan (*tatar ASSR*) and Udmurtiya, where the concentration of defence plants in, for example, Izhevsk, Votkinsk, Sarapul and Glazov is particularly high, accounting for some 85 per cent of the republic's total industrial output and some 60 per cent of total employment.

Within Ukraine, major end-product weapon production is located in Kiev, Khar'kov, Dnepropetrovsk, Lugansk, L'vov, Nikolaev and the Crimea. Kazakhstan has not only important production facilites in its northern region but, in addition, some 7 per cent of its territory was used as weapons testing sites under the FSU regime (including nuclear testing facilities at Semipalatinsk and space–missile test facilities at Baikonur). Overall, some 40 per cent of the former FSU territory was occupied by the defence ministry for weapons testing purposes with considerable regional impact.[18]

Defence Restructuring, the New Industrial Revolution and Global Competition

At the national and corporate level worldwide, rapid and uncoordinated economic transformation is taking place at an unprecedented level and pace in a vortex of changing technologies, shifting markets and ever more intense competition. At the national level, the drive towards global *laissez-faire* through the widespread adoption of an economic and political ideology which favours minimizing government intervention and the widespread release of market forces has both fuelled this remarkable economic revolution and provided the momentum to drive it forward. As has already been illustrated, the global economy is having to adapt rapidly, and with limited government support, to the sharp decline in defence expenditure – a crucial element of aggregate demand in many industrialized and non-industrialized nations.

The defence industrial base, then, is clearly confronted with a prolonged and substantial reduction in defence expenditure. To adapt rapidly and effectively to the new environment, most Western prime defence contractors are pursuing a number of important corporate responses which comprise: action to increase their share of a declining military market through enhanced efficiency and cost reduction; focus upon core business while completely restructuring their subcontract and supply base; and development of collaborative ventures to share costs and risks across industry, both horizontally and vertically; and, wherever possible, expansion of civil business, utilizing relevant defence technology and other operational aspects. Furthermore, in the Western nations, many prime defence contractors have either merged or sold operating divisions to reduce overheads. In the latter category, companies such as Ford, IBM and General Electric have sold defence activities to more specialist defence organizations such as Loral and Martin Marietta. It is argued that the industry is now entering the 'fourth and final phase' (a term coined by Norman Augustine, Chief Executive Officer of Martin Marietta) in which large defence companies with different attributes merge in an attempt to reduce costs even further. Recent examples of this phenomenon include mergers in 1994 between Northrop and Grumman and between Lockheed and Martin Marietta. The strategy here is to reduce central organization and research and development costs while enabling the new organization to spread the risk of potential project cancellation or cutback over a greater range of weapons systems.

In the United States, and to some extent within the EU, governments are pursuing a policy with respect to the defence industry rundown which could be termed 'social Darwinism'. As a result, the struggle to survive in the declining defence market is likely to intensify, producing significant, rapid and uncoordinated individual corporate strategic decisions. Indeed, a recent study by the US Office of Technology Assessment came to the conclusion that defence industries that had neither the capacity to diversify (or to market 'dual-use' technologies) nor to find new markets for their particular products or services would be forced out of business or to seek corporate partners to remain competitive and financially sound.

The architects of the post-1945 global economy constructed an international economic framework built upon such key structures as the mixed economy, global integration through a fixed exchange rate regime, a commitment to full employment and free trade and the widespread implementation of policies of macroeconomic management. In the 1990s the new global system has been constructed upon a very different set of values and structures. Economic integration across the world is now to be achieved through global business interaction, unfettered wherever possible by government intervention, with growth and prosperity often being pursued within self-protective trade blocs. Attempts to construct a global macroeconomic management process to replace outdated and ineffective national macroeconomic management programmes have proved singularly unsuccessful, especially in times of international economic recession. Hence, to survive and prosper in the evolving world economy, governments need both to recognize and encourage the revolution in global business organization and management that is currently transforming the shape, content and *modus operandi* of the corporate sector.

In industry more generally, throughout the world, the key to corporate success in the new business environment is now for companies to reinvent themselves in a manner which makes them more fleet-footed, efficient and flexible. Key elements of this new industrial revolution include the adoption of flexible manufacturing systems, utilizing computer-aided design and manufacture, just-in-time inventory systems, cross-functional project teams, organizational reform through strategic alliances and the development of new partnership sourcing arrangements. The most successful companies continually drive forward this process of 'corporate reinvention', choosing constant proactive radical change. In essence, to survive and succeed, they have to constantly redesign their business, create and access new markets and effectively alter the rules of the world trading game to suit their own ends.

In this process, key concepts like 'boundarylessness, speed and stretch' are the keys to corporate – and, ultimately, national-trading success:

> Boundarylessness refers to the ability to work up and down the hierarchy, across functions, and geographies, and with customers and suppliers. Speed achieved by eliminating ... layers of management (creating) an organization quick to seize opportunities and change with the market. ... Stretch is the setting of ambitious, long-term goals ... always setting the bar higher, encouraging employees to take risks.[19]

Companies as established and successful as Shell, General Motors, Ford, Toyota, Samsung and Boeing recognize only too clearly the need to adapt themselves to meet new market demands and appreciate the considerable period of adjustment and learning required for future business success.

It is this extremely challenging global business environment, then, that confronts the newly emerging economies of Russia, Ukraine and elsewhere as they pursue their transition strategies. To enjoy a genuine economic transformation, such reconstruction must take on board the requirements of the evolving global business environment already outlined and, eventually, needs to identify and acquire the means to compete with the best players in the international trading game. The challenge is unprecedented and, some would argue, has yet barely been addressed.

In this context, one of the most important aspects of the debate about the reconstruction of the Russian economy focuses upon the role of international business linkages. Foreign investors have yet to show the level of interest in becoming involved directly in the rebuilding of the Russian economy necessary genuinely to transform that system and increase its chances of gaining real global competitiveness.[20] There are, however, some promising examples emerging. For example, in the spring of 1994, Russia announced the establishment of a joint venture with China to assist Beijing develop its socialist market economy, while helping to facilitate a Chinese version of *konversiya*. This important joint venture brings together companies including Xing-Yui-Ju in Beijing, Yuilang Trading in Hong Kong, Impex in Nizhiny Novgorod and the Institute of Applied Physics at the Russian Academy of Sciences in Moscow. It will attempt to convert electro-optic defence equipment and technology for applications in the global commercial laser and optical products market. The development of such international partnerships, together with a new policy initiative designed to construct and extend interfirm linkages in these transition economies, must take absolute priority within the evolving economic reform strategy in the FSU republics.

Notes

1. L. Balcerowicz (1994), 'Common Fallacies in the Debate on the Transition to a Market Economy', *Economic Policy*, 19 December.
2. V. Barta and C.M. Schneider (1994), *Stabilisation Policy at the Crossroads? An Interim Report from Central and Eastern Europe,* Laxenburg: International Institute for Applied System Analysis.
3. P. Ormerod (1994), *The Death of Economics,* London.
4. D. Kaufman (1994), 'Diminishing Returns to Administrative Controls and the Emergence of the Unofficial Economy: A Framework of Analysis and Application to the Ukraine', *Economic Policy*, 19 December.
5. International Monetary Fund (1996), *IMF Survey*, 4 March.
6. *Economist Intelligence Unit Country Report: Russia*, 4th quarter, 1995; *Russian Economic Trends*, 21 March 1996.
7. R. Layard and A. Richter (1995), 'How Much Unemployment is Needed for Restructuring: the Russian Experience', *Economics of Transition*, **3**, (1), March.
8. V. Mikhalev (1996), 'Social Security in Russia under Economic Transformation', *Europe–Asia Studies*, **48**, (1), January.
9. O. Havrylyshyn, M. Miller and W. Perraudin (1994), 'Deficits, Inflation and the Political Consequences for Ukraine', *Economic Policy*, 19 October.
10. C. Senik-Leygonie and G. Hughes (1992), 'Industrial Profitability and Trade among the Former Soviet Republics', *Economic Policy,* 15 October.
11. B. Eichengreen (1993), 'A Payments Mechanism for the Former Soviet Union: Is the EPU a Relevant Precedent?', *Economic Policy*, 17 October.
12. A. Kennaway (1993), 'Economic Problems of the FSU and Some Suggestions for their Solution', RMA Sandhurst: Conflict Studies Research Centre.
13. Ibid.
14. *Financial Times*, 11 November 1994.
15. *Economist Intelligence Unit Country Report: Russia*, 4th quarter, 1995.
16. A. Izyumov, L. Kosals and R. Ryvkin (1995), 'The Russian Military–Industrial Complex: The Shock of Independence' in J. Di Chiaro III (ed.), 'Conversion of the Defense Industry in Russia and Eastern Europe', Proceedings of the BICC/CISAC Workshop on Conversion, April.
17. Ibid.
18. For further discussion, see J. Cooper (1991), 'The Soviet Defense Industry and Conversion: The Regional Dimension' in L. Paukert and P.J. Richards (eds), *Defence Expenditure, Industrial Conversion and Local Employment,* Geneva: International Labour Office.
19. R. Salazar, (1995), 'Leading Corporate Transformation', *World Executives's Digest*, August.

20 For an analysis of recent foreign direct investment in the FSU, see K.E. Meyer (1995), 'Foreign Direct Investment in the Early Years of Economic Transition: a Survey', *Economics of Transition,* **3**, (3), September.

5 Energy in the Former Soviet Republics

Victor Gilinsky

Introduction

Since the break-up of the Soviet Union, energy issues have had a special importance for the successor republics. Energy is the lifeblood of economic activity and, for the lucky states that can produce more than they need, energy exports are an important source of income. This brief review of the post-Soviet energy picture emphasizes strategic rather than the commercial issues, although the two are, naturally, related. The most important questions have to do with oil and natural gas and, to some extent, nuclear energy.

The former Soviet Union, taken as a whole, is rich in energy resources. Less than a decade ago, the Soviet Union was the world's largest oil producer. The oil and gas deposits are not, however, evenly distributed among the new republics. This was of little importance in Soviet times but it becomes a cause for tension when new political boundaries define the energy-rich and energy-poor. Russia is the region's dominant producer of both oil and gas, with most of its production coming from the single West Siberian region. The other important oil-producing countries are Kazakhstan and Azerbaijan, while the other important gas-producing countries are Turkmenistan and Uzbekistan, with Kazakhstan likely to be important in the future. Other countries in this region, such as Ukraine, come into the strategic picture either because they have no energy and are hungry for it, or because critical transport routes cross their territory.

The demise of the Soviet Union and its replacement by independent states has changed the equations for producing energy and transporting it to markets. The end of state monopoly control and the opening of vast areas for exploration by the international oil industry was described by *Petroleum Intelligence Weekly* as one of the most stunning events in the history of oil. On the other hand, the introduction of political boundaries into what was once an integrated energy system has created enormous complications and sources of conflict. For example, 90 per cent of Russian gas exports go through Ukraine, something the Russians did not care about before, but now find worrisome. Similarly, Azerbaijan and Kazakhstan, two promising oil producers, are both landlocked and finding it difficult to get Caspian Sea oil to market through regions of hostility and war.

Energy issues have been made more problematic by the background of economic decline in most of the post-Soviet countries. Energy consumption and production is sharply down, and it is not clear how far it will drop before the situation improves. Russia still consumes a great deal of energy – nearly 10 per cent of the world total or about 33 quadrillion British thermal units (million billion Btu) per year, in contrast to US consumption of about 85 quads; in other words, about 210 million Btu per capita per year in Russia compared with 320 million in the United States. Russian energy consumption is more than double that of the United States *per unit of economic output*, as best that can be measured, which suggests that making more efficient use of energy should receive a high priority.

A word about the world context. Most world energy projections foresee an overall marginal shift in the pattern of energy use from oil towards gas (and coal as well, although not necessarily in the former Soviet states). The shift towards gas is bound to be beneficial to the region's gas producers, although transportation issues have yet to be worked out. Oil, however, is still the world's primary fuel. World oil consumption of about 68 million barrels per day is equivalent, on an annual basis, to about 25 billion barrels per year, of which the Organization for Economic Cooperation and Development (OECD) countries consume about 41 million barrels per day. By 2010 world oil consumption may increase to perhaps 90 million barrels per day, with most of the increase coming in Asia. The projected Asian increment is larger than the entire current US consumption, and this is bound to affect relationships throughout the entire region.

The discussion in this chapter is organized around the main energy sources: oil, natural gas, coal and nuclear energy (which has a strategic importance out of proportion to its small contribution to electricity production). Gas makes up nearly half of the region's energy production and is consequently the region's most important fuel. Oil makes up perhaps a third, and remains the chief world fuel. For that reason, let us start with oil.

Oil

Russian oil, or what was then Russian oil, played an important role in twentieth-century history. Over 100 years ago, oil from Baku broke the US oil monopoly, then centred in Pennsylvania. At the turn of the century about half the world's oil came from the Baku region and Tsarist Russia was then the world's largest producer of oil. When oil itself became a vital transport fuel it took on major strategic importance. During the First World War the oil-poor Germans tried to get Baku's oil and failed. Lord Curzon later said, 'the Allied cause had floated to victory upon a wave of oil'.[1] Baku oil was one of Adolf Hitler's strategic objectives in attacking the Soviet Union in 1941. The oil diverted him from other objectives at two crucial moments during the Second World War. When the German armies approaching Moscow in the critical months of 1941 asked for reinforcements from those heading for the Caucasus, Hitler made his famous remark, 'My generals know nothing about the economic aspects of war'.[2] Again in 1942, Hitler headed for the oilfields of the Caucasus. His dream was to continue to Iraq and Iran. At a critical moment in the battle for Stalingrad, Field Marshal Fritz Erich von Manstein begged Hitler to divert forces from the Caucasus but only triggered a harangue from Hitler who told him, 'It's a question of the possession of Baku, Field Marshal, unless we get the Baku oil the war is lost'.[3] By the time the German forces were moved it was too late to save those trapped at Stalingrad. Ironically, in the Caucasus the German army ran out of oil before it could reach its goal, only reaching Grozny.

After the Second World War, Soviet oil production shifted to other regions, notably the Urals and West Siberia, although Azerbaijan remained the key producer of oil equipment. After the spectacular increase in oil prices by OPEC in 1973, the Soviet Union gained the opportunity to earn large amounts of hard currency. Arguably, Soviet revenues from oil and gas exports in subsequent years kept the Soviet system afloat for many years longer than would otherwise have been the case. In the late 1970s, the US Central Intelligence Agency began to predict a drop in Soviet oil production. This is said to have alarmed Soviet leaders who pressed for high production no matter what, leading, as a result, to the mismanagement of the oilfields and contributing to the present deterioration in output. Perhaps it would have happened anyway.

In any case, in the 1980s the Soviet Union was the largest oil producer in the world at about 12 million barrels of oil per day (a barrel is about 170 litres; there are about seven barrels in a ton of oil, the exact figure depending on the type of oil). By comparison, during this period the United States produced about 10 million barrels per day and Saudi Arabia only about 5 million. Naturally, the Soviet Union was a major exporter and, at the time of its collapse, exported nearly 3 million barrels of oil per day. If we include shipments to other Soviet republics, Russia then exported about 6 million barrels per day. The Soviet Union was also a major exporter of gas: Russian gas exports were about 6 trillion cubic feet (Tcf), also about equally divided between other Soviet republics and other countries. President Ronald Reagan was so concerned about the political consequences of Western overdependence on Soviet gas that, in 1985, he tried and failed to scuttle the Russian pipeline to Europe. In retrospect it appears that he need not have worried; the Russians were only too glad to export. During and after the collapse of the Soviet Union, the plundering of Russian oil and gas for export by new private interests is said to have played a large part in creating the new, monied political/business class in Russia.

The Soviet system was gargantuan and inefficient. It fostered excessive economic specialization, almost as if to ensure that no region would be self-sufficient. Refineries were generally not where the oil was, nor were drilling equipment factories. In spite of all this, the system was integrated and it worked, however inefficiently. With the break-up of the Soviet Union the system broke down into its component parts, some of which worked and some of which did not. From an integrated command system there resulted a fragmented free-for-all with 'immense underlying problems'.[4] The oil industry especially was hobbled by lack of investment and severe shortages of equipment, most of which had previously come from Azerbaijan. On top of everything else, oil and gas producers have faced delinquent payments from consumers.

Since the break-up of the Soviet Union, the oil production in its successor states has fallen by nearly half. In 1994 production was about 7 million barrels per day, with Russia producing about 6.4, Kazakhstan less than 0.5 and Azerbaijan about 0.2.[5] Estimates for 1995 production suggest that production has fallen again, perhaps to less than 6 million barrels per day for Russia. Exports are still apparently about 3 million barrels per day, an amount made possible only by the dramatic drop in Russian oil consumption to about an equal figure.[6]

The Russian oil industry has undergone some restructuring. Starting in 1993, the state-owned oil monopoly began to split into independent, vertically integrated oil companies which control production, refining and distribution networks. The two largest firms produce about 1 million barrels per day each (larger than, say, Texaco's production), with the rest divided among many firms. The Russian oil industry is thus made up of a number of state-owned and private oil companies.

Most of current Russian production, perhaps 70 per cent, comes from Tyumen Province in Western Siberia. This is an enormously rich area that also produces most of the gas. The Volga–Urals region ranks second in oil, producing perhaps a quarter of the total. Other regions include the Arctic and the Far East, especially offshore Sakhalin Island, which is an important new area for exploration, as is the promising area of the Caspian Sea. The Russians have not divulged the extent of oil reserves, but estimates range up to around 100 billion barrels. It should be noted that Russian and Western methods of estimation differ significantly in terms of assumptions about the proportion of oil that is recoverable, with Russian estimates being higher. Russians emphasize technical feasibility and typically assign recovery rates of 40 per cent. Western estimates take commercial constraints into account and typically assign rates of about 33 per cent. The recovery from the Tyumen Region now averages around 20 per cent. Tyumen may be roughly on a par with Mexico, Kuwait, or even Iraq or Iran.[7] In any case, it holds larger reserves than those of any country outside of the Middle East. So far, the Russians have mainly exploited the large reservoirs that contain about half the oil, but there are still many untapped smaller reservoirs. Altogether, the area is relatively unexplored and further large finds are possible. So far, about 40 billion barrels have been extracted from this region.[8]

The West Siberian fields are the key problem area for Russia's crude production.[9] The fall in Russian oil production is mainly concentrated in several of the producing associations in Tyumen. The main reason is said to be the previous short-term focus of the central planners – an overemphasis on production from the large fields and insufficient investment in smaller and medium-sized fields. The oil industry is also generally inefficient. While the technical level of the workforce is high, the equipment is inferior and in short supply, and producers lack adequate financial incentives.

The region has interested foreign firms. The oil is there, and the West has the money and technology that are needed to get it. However, as the West sees it, while the geological and technical risks are low, the financial and political risks are high. Among other concerns, Russian law covering oil and gas is complex, to say the least, as is the tax scheme. The Western oil companies remain entranced by the possibilities, but the pace of investment is low. Most of the foreign efforts involve applying enhanced recovery schemes to existing oilfields.

One aspect of Soviet centralized planning and economic specialization was that Tyumen province has almost no refining or processing capacity. Russia's two dozen refineries are decades old and considered relatively unsophisticated. Refinery throughput is about half of what it was in 1990. Ukraine has the second largest refining capacity, but that is used only at about one-third capacity because the Russians now favour their own refineries.

The Russian pipeline system now runs at about 60 per cent capacity. It was built to bring all oil from the Soviet periphery to the centre. Now that they are independent, the Azeris and Kazakhs seek ways to get their oil to market that do not leave them under Moscow's thumb, but that is not so easy. The most interesting aspects of the pipeline situation concerns the manoeuvring connected with getting oil from the Caspian Sea region to open water.

The region around the Caspian Sea is the area that has created the most excitement about new oil production. The Caspian fields are probably not so large as those in West Siberia, but may be more promising commercially as the international companies find it easier to deal with Almaty than with Moscow.[10]

Kazakhstan is almost as large as Europe. It has less than 20 million people, most of them concentrated in the east whereas the oil is in the west. Kazakh production is projected to be in the range of 0.8 million barrels per day in 2000 and nearly double that in 2010.[11] Some of the most promising North Caspian offshore regions are still off-limits, partly because of fears that drilling would harm the area's caviar industry, but also because the Kazakhs want to gain experience in the business before cutting deals on their most prize fields. Kazakh reserves are estimated to be in the 2–4 billion tonne range (or over 15–30 billion barrels).[12] To develop this potential will require foreign involvement and foreign technology. That certainly applies to the Kazakh oil in Tengiz and other fields that are in deep and difficult formations for whose development Kazakhstan has signed a multi-billion dollar deal with Chevron.

The estimates of Caspian oil reserves are significantly lower than those for West Siberia, but they are large enough to interest the international oil companies which are circling around waiting for an opening. It is well to keep in mind that all the estimates are very rough and the region is relatively unexplored. To provide some perspective, the Kazakh reserves are in the same category as those of the United States or China. There are rumours that the Caspian fields may ultimately match those of the Middle East but that seems excessively optimistic.

Ideally, the landlocked states (and their customers) would like to have multiple routes for oil so as not to be overdependent on any one country. In practice, no matter what, Russia will be an important factor in extracting and transporting the oil. It is not irrelevant that there is a large Russian population in Kazakhstan that is heavily represented in the oil and gas industry. Kazakhstan is landlocked and, for the present, depends on pipelines to Russia established during the period of Soviet control.

Russia is important here for several reasons. It controls the only existing pipelines out of the region and may control access to future routes. It also borders on the Sea, and will not be left out, calling into question Azerbaijan's legal right to enter into development contracts in the Caspian on the basis of historical arrangements in the area – specifically, the treaties which the Soviets signed with Iran in 1921 and 1940 which Russia considers binding on the new republics. There is also the question of the legal definition of the Caspian: is it a 'sea' or is it a 'lake'? Under international law, resources around a sea are partitioned according to each country's territory. In the case of a lake, consensus is required for development. Since Russia borders a segment of the Caspian Sea that is poor in oil and wants to have as large a share as possible, it insists on the 'lake' definition. Russia is joined in this view by Iran. Azerbaijan maintains that the Caspian Sea is indeed a sea and Kazakhstan agrees quietly, so as not to offend Russia. Turkmenistan has agreed with Moscow under pressure.

The Azeri reserves are estimated to be about 5 billion barrels, roughly equivalent to Norway's or Britain's North Sea reserves. But the Caspian deep offshore region has been little explored and these estimates of Azeri potential may increase substantially. Most of current Azeri production comes from a shallow offshore field in the Caspian being developed by Russian firms. Reserves in this area are estimated at about 500 million barrels. Western firms with more deep-water experience are carrying out exploration in deep water. Azeri production has been hampered by lack of access to adequate technology for deep offshore drilling and development. The cheapest way to get the heavy oil gear needed for extraction into the Caspian area is by ship via the Don and Volga and the connecting canal (rail transport through the Caucasus is apparently much more expensive). This gives the Russians another point of leverage.

After several years of negotiation, in 1994 the Azeris signed a multi-billion dollar development contract with a consortium of oil companies, with the principal participation of Western oil companies. Iran was specifically excluded as a result of US pressure, a circumstance that no doubt helped the Iranians to conclude the Caspian was not a sea but a lake requiring consensus for development. Total reserves in the three fields which the consortium will develop are estimated at 3–5 billion barrels (about one-half US yearly use). Azerbaijan hopes to achieve production at about one million barrels per day by about 2003.

There is currently no export pipeline for future production from the Kazakh or Azeri fields. The discovery of the huge Tengiz field in the Northern Caspian region and the possibility of offshore Azeri fields has inspired interest in a variety of new pipeline schemes. Without new pipelines there will not be development. All the countries in the region, including Turkey and Iran, are angling for a role, and a seemingly unlikely outsider – Oman – is involved, too. There are four options whose fluctuating fortunes make it unclear which will be chosen initially. Probably more than one route will ultimately be developed. As mentioned, Turkey and Iran would both like to see Caspian oil shipped through their territory.

One possible route to Turkey – to a Turkish Mediterranean port – is through Armenia. Since Armenia and Turkey have not been the best of friends and neither have Armenia and Azerbaijan, the political problems are obvious. Armenia now occupies about 20 per cent of Azeri territory and the

Azeris are blockading Armenia's energy supplies (which is one reason the Armenians have to run their dangerous nuclear reactor). Despite this, Armenia is trying to establish good relations with Turkey to make a pipeline of 1000 kilometres possible.

A second option is to send the oil south to Iran for shipment either from a Persian Gulf port, or through Iran to Turkey for shipment from the Turkish port of Ceyhan. Here the problems are again political – US hostility towards Iran remains an important factor in Caspian Sea oil and US pressure on the consortium probably precludes this option. Yet another possibility would be an oil swap with Iran. Azeri oil could be shipped to Iran for use in the Iranian North, with Iran exporting equivalent amounts from Gulf ports.

A third option is to run a pipeline through Georgia to the Black Sea or on to Turkey. Here war and political instability in Georgia are a problem. Despite this, there has been talk about various schemes, including initial rail shipment of oil through Georgia – to test the route, so to speak – as well as a pipeline to the Georgian port of Batumi. A hundred years ago Russian oil, developed by the Nobel brothers, found its way to European markets through Batumi. The Rothschilds financed a railway that operated until brother Alfred's dynamite helped to blast a pipeline through the most difficult terrain. To carry the oil on from Batumi, Maurice Samuel, the founder of Shell Oil, then invented the oil tanker.

A fourth option, and the one with the most push behind it, is to run a pipeline up through Russia to the Black Sea port of Novorossiysk. This project involves the Kazakhs, too, in a consortium, and seems to have been organized by agents of the Omanis, of all people. This route is, of course, heavily favoured by Russia, which would apparently stand to earn up to $500 million per year in transport fees. There are two problems: one is that the pipeline would traverse Chechnya, the scene of recent fighting; the other is strong Turkish objection to increased oil traffic through the Bosphorus, although the 1936 Montreux Convention requires the Turks to let the oil through. The Bosphorus already handles 1.6 million barrels per day and it is narrow and crowded. Adding another million barrels a day would mean that tankers carrying over 350 000 tonnes of oil would pass through the Bosphorus every day. One alternative would be to ship Azeri oil from Novorossiysk across the Black Sea to a Turkish Black Sea port and subsequently by land pipeline to the Turkish Mediterranean port of Ceyhan. There is also talk of a pipeline under the Caspian, to provide a path for Kazakh oil and to connect with a future Azerbaijan–Turkish pipeline. All these schemes require some resolution of political and security issues.

Natural Gas

The main energy resource in the Soviet successor states is natural gas and most of that is in Russia, in the same Tyumen region that produces most of the oil. Tyumen is, so to speak, the Saudi Arabia of gas, containing about 40 per cent of the world's known gas reserves. Its known reserves are estimated at nearly 1400 Tcf, or over 50 years of US consumption. Russia currently produces about 21 Tcf (the next producer is the United States at 19 Tcf, followed by Canada at 5 Tcf, Netherlands at 3 Tcf and Turkmenistan at nearly 3 Tcf). Gas has fared much better than oil since the break-up of the Soviet Union, and gas production and exports have held up.

Rather than being split up into competing companies, as was done with the oil monopoly, the gas giant Gazprom has retained its monopoly position as a vertically integrated monopoly. It is probably not irrelevant that Prime Minister Viktor Chernomyrdin was formerly the head of Gazprom (rather like John D. Rockefeller becoming President of the United States!). Gazprom operates Russia's largest fields, with over 70 per cent of the reserves – one-third of the world total – and over 90 per cent of Russia's gas production. It is also a vast enterprise in other ways. To talk about Russian gas is therefore to talk about Gazprom. During the past several years of economic collapse, the organization has maintained a successful operation and, in a sense, is more powerful than ever. It is the largest company in Russia, with over 300 000 employees, and accounts for nearly 5 per cent of Russia's economy. It reportedly has revenues of about US$25 billion (which would put it at about 100th in the '*Fortune* 500' list), and its estimated profits of about $6 billion make it the second, or possibly even the first, most profitable enterprise in the world. It is worth in excess of US$500 billion. In addition to supplying Russia, Gazprom also meets nearly all of Eastern Europe's gas demand (nearly 2 Tcf to Ukraine, 0.5 Tcf to Belarus, nearly as much to the Czech Republic and Slovakia) and meets about 25 per cent of Western Europe's gas demand (about 1 Tcf to Germany and about 0.5 Tcf each to France and Italy).[13]

In short, the Russian gas industry is not in nearly as much disarray as the oil industry.[14] Russian gas production is about 21 Tcf, of which about 2 Tcf leaks out of the system and about 13 is consumed domestically, leaving about 6 Tcf for export by pipeline.[15] Unlike oil production, Russian natural gas production has dropped little, principally because the output from the West Siberian gasfields, which produce 90 per cent of the gas, has remained stable. If these results have something to do with the continuation of the gas monopoly, it raises questions about 'reform'.

Over half of Russian gas use is for electric generation; about one-third is used for industry; and only a little over 10 per cent is used in the housing sector. The rest is used to run the gas system itself. Not only are Russian gas reserves – mainly in Tyumen – enormous, they are also concentrated in shallow, uncomplicated reserves which can be developed with relative ease. This means the gas industry has less requirement for foreign technology. Two of the largest fields have estimated reserves of about 200 Tcf each. Together they could supply the United States for about 20 years. A field in Siberia's Yamal Peninsula is said to have even larger potential and Russian officials say it will produce 6 Tcf in 2010. The plan is to export the gas through a 5000-kilometre pipeline running through Belarus and Poland. About 90 per cent of Russian gas exports to Europe run through Ukraine, a proportion which Russia would like to reduce. Among other things, there were payment problems in Ukraine and apparently, in 1992, after Russia cut off supplies, Ukraine started tapping the pipeline.

The second largest natural gas producer is Turkmenistan, a country of 4 million people, slightly larger in area than California. Production in 1993 was about 2 Tcf, nearly all for export. Proven reserves total over 100 Tcf and estimates go as high as 500 Tcf. Its gas pipelines go to Russia, which leaves Turkmenistan at the mercy of Gazprom, which controls the pipelines and has been sending the gas to Soviet successor states rather than to the West where the reliable paying customers are (some of Turkmenistan's clients in former Soviet republics have apparently not been paying for the gas). Just as Russia is trying to avoid sending its gas through Ukraine, so Turkmenistan is trying to get to hard-currency-paying customers without going through Russia. To diversify transport routes, the Turkmens talk of a pipeline to Turkey through Iran – a US$7 billion project. The difficulty with this idea is that projects involving Iran run into international funding problems because of US hostility. Another idea is to go through Afghanistan to Pakistan, but that depends on peace in Afghanistan. There is also a fanciful project for a pipeline across China with a liquefaction plant on the Yellow Sea for shipment to Japan.

The third producer is Uzbekistan, a country of 23 million people, also slightly larger than California. Gas production is about 1.6 Tcf and consumption is about 1.2 Tcf, leaving almost 0.5 Tcf for export. Reserves may be up to 100 Tcf.

Coal

Coal is still important in the former Soviet states but its role is declining. If anything, the situation in the Russian coal industry is even more critical than in the oil industry. Russian coal production in 1995–96 may have been about 250 million tonnes, which represents a reduction of nearly 40 per cent.[16] As in other sectors, the coal industry is in trouble because customers have not been paying and producers have underinvested. The mines lack modern equipment and mining is inefficient and dangerous. Most coal is produced in Siberia's Kuznets Basin. Labour disputes have increased because of reductions in employment and failure to pay salaries. Perhaps 100 000 miners have been laid off and there are plans to lay off another 150 000. Ukraine is the second largest coal-producing region, at about 130 million tonnes. Kazakhstan's output is very nearly as high.

Electricity

Russian electric generating capacity is about 215 000 megawatts – the equivalent of over 200 large plants. The electric plants have been running at about 50 per cent capacity. At full utilization, they would generate 1840 billion kilowatt-hours. Actual production in 1994 was about 890 billion kilowatt-hours.[17] About 200 000 megawatts are tied together by transmission lines into an integrated system.

Of the installed electric generating capacity, 21 per cent is hydroelectric, 10 per cent nuclear and 69 per cent fossil-fuelled thermal. The 69 per cent thermal plant fraction breaks down into 45 per cent gas-fired, 17 per cent coal-fired and 7 per cent oil-fired. As mentioned, over half of Russian gas consumption goes to fuel electric plants. A much larger proportion of electricity goes to industry than in the United States.

In 1990 Russian per capita use of electricity (nearly 5400 kWh) was roughly equivalent to that of France or Japan, although it was used less efficiently. The figure has now dropped significantly. The most optimistic scenarios used in US–Russian official discussions envision returning to the 1990 level of use by the year 2004. Other scenarios have Russia reaching only 70 per cent of the 1990 level by 2010. The consequences of these possibilities depend on how much is accomplished in increasing efficiency of use. Per unit economic output, Russia seems to use three or four times as much electricity as do Western countries. Almost 80 per cent of the system losses are at low voltages where part of the problem is the lack of metering. One problem is that prices have little effect on patterns of use because many customers have stopped paying their bills. In 1994, apparently nearly half the bills were unpaid (a situation that is difficult for an outsider to understand). On top of that the data are unreliable.

Thermal stations account for about three-quarters of Russian electric output (the rest is hydro and nuclear). The Soviet plan was to rely on nuclear stations, especially in the West, but this plan was derailed by the Chernobyl accident. The country is now left with an aging population of thermal plants.

The needs of the electric system, in order of priority established by an official US–Russian group, are to deal with the pattern of inefficient electricity use, upgrade nuclear safety in a number of nuclear plants (some are not worth upgrading), to upgrade the transmission system, and to refurbish the thermal plants.

The transmission system generally does not meet the planning criteria assumed in the West for coping with possible faults: it does not have the same degree of resiliency and would be more likely to fail catastrophically. The control equipment – the computers and their software and communication equipment – is inadequate and outdated by Western standards. The electric industry is in the process of being restructured. The transmission lines are controlled by a central organization (RAO EES Rossii) that also operates some of the generators. There are 70 regional distribution organizations – the equivalent of utilities.

One of the effects of the break-up of the Soviet Union was that some transmission lines that connected Russian regions now fell in foreign countries (for example, Kazakhstan). To take into account the new economic and political uncertainties, the Russians are planning for higher generating reserve margins.

Nuclear Energy

Russia has 29 nuclear electric units of several types and vintages. They produced a little less that 100 billion kWh, in 1994, or about 11 per cent of the total.[18] Russian nuclear electricity production is apparently down, partly because overall electricity demand fell (you cannot store electricity), but also because some reactors were operated at lower power for safety reasons. Of the 29 Russian power reactors, 11 are of the RBMK type (light-water cooled, graphite-moderated) regarded in the West as insufficiently safe. Of the remainder, four are pressurized water reactors of the older VVER-440/230 type, which are regarded as equally inadequate, two are of a newer VVER-440/213 type and several are of the newer VVER-1000 type. The safety problems are said not to be limited to equipment. There are also reports that the morale of reactor operating staffs is dangerously low because, among other reasons, they are not paid regularly. If this is correct and leads to reduced safety discipline, it is something about which to be genuinely concerned.

Ukraine's nuclear capacity is about 12 000 megawatts of electricity. Nuclear power plants provide about one-third of Ukraine's electricity. There were some efforts by Western states to get Ukraine to close the remaining Chernobyl units by 2000 but nothing seems to have come of this so far. Ukraine, which is apparently trying to extract maximum Western support in return for easing Western fears, wants the equivalent of US$4.4 billion to shut down the two remaining operating Chernobyl reactors. Western interest partly reflects concern for people and partly a sort of nuclear self-interest: Western countries fear that another accident would undercut support for nuclear programmes in their own countries.

Lithuania also runs two of the worrisome RBMK reactors. They are the mainstay of its electricity production and Lithuania is more dependent on nuclear energy than any other country in the world, even France. Armenia, desperate for electricity, has restarted one of its two units, Medzamor unit 2, an older type VVER-440/230, which had been shut down after the December 1988 earthquake.

Any action concerning the Russian nuclear sector has to take account of the power of the Ministry of Atomic Energy and Industry (Minatom) which is virtually a state within a state that once employed upwards of a million people. Minatom has also been aggressively pursuing export opportunities and has signed a contract for completing power reactors in Iran, much to US chagrin. As Russian nuclear weapon stocks are reduced, the ministry will come into possession of an enormous stockpile – the largest in the world – of highly enriched uranium and plutonium. Making sure that these nuclear explosives are not again available to would-be bomb-makers will remain a universal security concern for decades.

The Pre-eminent Implication for International Security

In closing, let us return to the incredibly complex and Byzantine circumstances surrounding the pipelines from the Caspian region with a view to reflecting on the pre-eminent international security aspects. First, these circumstances are not unrelated to the recent fighting in Chechnya and surrounding regions. The Azeri and the Russian governments signed an agreement in January 1996 to facilitate the early Azeri oil output. This will probably go by way of Grozny and Tikhoretsk to Novorossyisk on the Black Sea and then through the Bosphorus. Meanwhile, whole towns have reportedly been flattened by fighting along that route. Assuming that the pipeline gets built, it seems likely that its security will remain a problem for the Russian army. While, it is true that oil companies are used to having their pipelines blown up in remote locations and going back under guard to fix them, the problems here are more serious, and some accommodation with the Chechens will probably have to be made for the scheme to work. That, at least, is how some Western observers see the situation.

An additional route for a pipeline for early oil is through Tbilisi to Batumi, although Georgian instabilities and uncertain financing raise serious questions. This was the original route for Baku oil at the turn of the century. If this second route for early oil does develop, it will allow the later larger flows – the so-called main oil – to go by both routes, too. The smart money, so to speak, is apparently going to invest in both directions. This will apparently include the Russians, although their role is said to be complicated by the vagaries of current Russian decision-making.

Kazakhstan oil will now probably go north around the Caspian and then down to Tikhoretsk and the Black Sea. Chevron, the main developer of the Tengiz field in Kazakhstan, and the Russians, who are interested in providing the transport route, are said to be 'getting their act together'. If the alternative Baku–Tbilisi–Batumi route develops for Azerbaijan's oil, then a second option opens for Kazakhstan's too, by tanker or, later, by subsurface pipeline across the Caspian, although this latter option would be quite expensive. There remains the Black Sea–Bosphorus problem and Turkey's environmental objections (and interest in revenue). Ultimately some land route will have to be found to bypass the Bosphorus, either by going across Turkey or across Bulgaria and Greece, to limit the environmental stress on that crowded passageway.

Other routes could be opened if the US State Department would ease its dogmatic hostility towards Iran. That country's participation could greatly contribute to route diversity and provide direct access to Gulf ports and Asian markets. An enhanced Iranian role now could also help to moderate the Russian role, which will remain a powerful one in any case. Iran will not be kept out forever as Asian markets exert an increasingly powerful pull on Caspian oil. The Great Game has its own rules.

Notes

1 Daniel Yergin (1991), *The Prize*, New York, p. 183.
2 Ibid., p. 336.
3 Ibid., p. 337.
4 Matthew J. Sagers (1993), 'The Energy Industries of the Former USSR: A Mid-Year Survey', *Post-Soviet Geography*, June, p. 345.
5 The figures in millions of metric tons per year are very close to 50 times the million barrel per day figures, so current Russian production is about 300 million metric tons per year.
6 *Energy Information Administration Fact Sheet*, April 1995.
7 Thomas E. Wallin (1992), 'West Siberia: The Key to Russia's Oil and Gas Future', *Petroleum Intelligence Weekly Special Report*, April, p. 11.
8 The world now consumes a staggering 25 billion barrels of oil per year.
9 Sagers, 'The Energy Industries of the Former USSR', note 4 *supra*, p. 355.
10 Helen Ball *et al.* (1993), 'Kazakhstan: The Golden Road to Oil and Gas in Central Asia', *Petroleum Intelligence Weekly Special Report*, April, p. 5.

11 Sagers, 'The Energy Industries of the Former USSR', note 4 *supra*, p. 356. This corresponds to about 40 and 75 million tonnes per year. Note that 1 million barrels per day is about 50 million tonnes per year.
12 Ibid., p. 366. The Kazakhs also have gas reserves of nearly 2 trillion cubic metres, or about 70 Tcf, which is roughly equivalent to three times the US annual consumption: David Hoffman (1995), 'Russia's Economic Colossus', *Washington Post*, 3 December.
13 Ibid.
14 Sagers, 'The Energy Industries of the Former USSR', note 4 *supra*, p. 377.
15 The gas equivalent of the tanker, liquified natural gas transport, is very expensive.
16 International Energy Agency (1995), *Energy Policies of the Russian Federation*, Paris, p. 188.
17 Ibid., p. 205. See also James F. Wilson (ed.) (1994), *Russian Electric Power Sector Update*, Report prepared for the World Bank, Washington DC, October; James F. Wilson and Igor S. Sorokin (1994), *Electric Power Sector*, Report prepared for the Russian Ministry of Economy, Moscow, December; and *Joint Electric Power Alternatives Study: An Investment Program for Russia*, Final Report, Energy Policy Committee of the US–Russian Joint Committee on Economic and Technological Cooperation, June 1995.
18 The more modern energy units are gigawatt-hours (GWh); a large modern nuclear reactor is rated at about 1GW (1000 megawatts) of electric output, which in a year (8766 hours) of full operation would produce 8766 GWh; Russia has the equivalent of about 15 such units operating 75 per cent of the time: International Energy Agency, *Energy Policies*, note 16 *supra*, p. 220. See also *Nuclear Energy Safety Challenges in The Former Soviet Union*, The Center for Strategic and International Studies, Washington DC, 1995.

6 The Present State and Future of Science in Russia

Sergei Kapitza

Introduction

The momentous changes that have occurred during the last few years and are still going on in Eastern Europe and the former Soviet Union (FSU) are destined to have long-lasting effects on the political, economic and social conditions of much of the world. At a time when even the borders of these countries are evolving it is difficult to expect due attention to be given to the present state and future development of science. However, if we take a longer and perhaps a more detached view of what is happening, then the future of science can be seen to be intimately connected with these changes. Societal developments in the short term serve to determine the present state and conditions for science and technology but, in a more distant perspective, science itself will become a crucial factor in the new liberal and democratic world to be.

If we look at the present conditions for Russian science, the significant feature is that most of the state support has disappeared. It has disappeared not only because of the major economic crisis that has hit the country, but because Russia is going through a profound reconsideration of the place science is to have within it. Under the *ancien régime* the hard sciences were largely subservient to the military effort – an effort that, over the decades, had contributed to the build-up of a fearful system of armaments. By means of nuclear weapons to rockets and guided missiles, ships and planes, guns and tanks, science had determined the high level and sophistication of the armed forces.

Admittedly, those in charge of the large military-oriented programmes were generous in their support of fundamental science. There was an understanding of the overall significance of scientific culture, of the general background needed to sustain a level of development for a global power operating on a world scale. But during the last 20 years there has been a systematic decline in support for what is called 'Big Science'. For example, not a single large accelerator or research reactor was commissioned, despite promised support. The once-ambitious space programme has also lost much of its impetus. The large fleet of Russian oceanographic research ships is now stranded because of lack of funds. With the collapse of the Soviet state, the demise of communism as it was practised, and a marked fall in industrial production due to a deep economic crisis, hard science has simply lost most of its bearings and support. On the other hand, the soft sciences are in even greater disarray, for the whole system of ideas that they were serving has gone. Today, literally tens of thousands of teachers of Marxist philosophy, the history of the Communist Party and of political economy have lost their jobs and in many cases a meaningful existence, since the very substance of their studies has disappeared, indicating the scale of the crisis of ideology. In other words, Russian science has to demilitarize the hard, and de-ideologize the soft, sciences.

In the FSU the main body which determined to a remarkable extent the policy and high status of science was the Academy of Sciences which had among its members many scientists of great distinction. Unfortunately, during the years of decay, high standards were often sacrificed for the sake of political expediency. In addition, a marked decrease in the Academy's standards occurred when the newly formed Academy of the Russian Federation merged with the Academy of Sciences of the FSU. It so happens that the Academy, the establishment of Soviet science, has tended to associate itself with those who were opposed to change, be it the *perestroika* of Mikhail Gorbachev or the reforms of Boris Yeltsin. The conservative policies of the scientific establishment have led to a deep split in the academic community, culminating in the organization of a number of alternative societies of scientists, new academies and even new universities. Notable among these is the Academy for Natural Sciences which has striven to unite scientists from a broad spectrum of institutions, including the universities.

At present, the funding for science has been cut. It is reported that funding of the Russian Academy of Sciences, with its huge network of institutes, libraries, observatories and publishing houses, has been decreased by a factor of three to five. As a result of this and of the opening up of new opportunities in business and entrepreneurial activities, many – especially members of the younger and more dynamic generation – are now leaving science. This means that probably a quarter of all scientists may abandon the discipline; a quarter may leave the country and, of those remaining, half could retire and, ultimately, it would not be surprising if the country were to be left with only 20–25 per cent of all scientists now actively engaged in research. This stage has not yet been reached, but such a trend should be borne in mind for the future.

The changes are not only imminent, but even necessary, however painful and drastic they may be. Science in the Soviet Union was overstaffed and top-heavy. For years it tried to develop as a self-contained entity, to a great extent isolated from world science, and this is another reason for change now that the country has opened up. It is under these conditions that we should attempt to formulate the national science policy of Russia, and to define its new priorities.

The Need for Fundamental Science

To better understand the modern demands and challenges we should look at the complex interconnections between modern science and society and the economy. First, let us consider fundamental science – science pursued for the sake of knowledge. Basic science is motivated by the deep-seated need to understand and interpret the world around us and that of humankind itself. On the other hand, applied research is pursued because of its usefulness. Today the profound connections between fundamental science and culture are generally recognized, although these tenuous ties are strained by growing anti-scientific and anti-intellectual forces. The applied sciences, intimately linked with industry, have a direct effect on technology and economic development.

In terms of investment, fundamental science, applied research and development (R&D) and industry can be represented by the ratio 1:10:100. But, thinking in terms of the time it takes to develop a set of concepts in fundamental science, develop a trend in applied research, and to carry its impact further into the industry, then the reverse relationship applies (that is, 100:10:1), for it may take decades, perhaps even 100 years, to develop a tradition in fundamental science or build up a university, ten years to develop a field of applied research, whilst an industrial enterprise can switch over to a new product or model in a matter of a year. For example, the fundamental discoveries in quantum mechanics led, within a generation or two, to the invention of the transistor and then the laser. A century before, the theory of electromagnetism provided the background for the development of the electrical industry and later radio, television, radar and modern communications. Today, perhaps on a shorter timescale, we are witnessing the remarkable impact of discoveries in modern genetics and molecular biology on the practice of medicine and agriculture and on progress in evolutionary and environmental studies. The discoveries in astronomy and cosmology are being made possible by new technology, especially by space technology provided by the aerospace industry. These novel methods and facilities are used for observing the earth and have resulted in a virtually new way of looking at planetary phenomena. Thus, fundamental sciences, in close cooperation with modern technology, have a continuous and very profound effect on our understanding of the world, on our well-being, and on our civilization.

As has been indicated, fundamental science has a long development timescale. The long-term factors that affect the development of fundamental science can be appreciated if it is realized that only now, some 40 years after its defeat in the Second World War, has Germany regained its position in the field of science – a tradition that, to a great extent, was destroyed during the years of Nazi rule.

Today, the industrial impact, and even the general impact, in applied sciences of the newly emerging countries of Asia and the Pacific is far greater than their contribution to fundamental research. The difficulties in establishing a regional or national tradition in basic science has even led to the notion that such attempts ought not to be made, since fundamental research is pursued nowadays as a global intellectual enterprise. In so far as this is true, this does not mean that, in a developed scientific community, fundamental research should not be pursued, for it is part and parcel of our modern culture and directly contributes to higher education as long as it is practised on a national basis. It is for this reason that any discontinuity or serious stoppage in the development of science in Russia may have long-term effects and should be of immediate concern both for the scientific community and the country as a whole.

The current economic reforms in Russia are significantly affecting industry and also, to a great extent, applied research. The law of supply and demand can, and should, determine the new pattern of development and here we may expect rapid and profound changes – changes which will also affect the huge military–industrial complex of the FSU. The transformation to a market economy is principally a change from a military-oriented command economy of the recent past. Thus military defeat in the Cold War – a war obviously never fought outright but whose economic consequences remain with Russia – dictates the reforms. It is in this state of turmoil that fundamental science has become lost. In the first place fundamental science cannot, and should not, be carried out according to direct market forces. However important are the responsibilities of science and scientists in the way they conduct their business, no short-term book-keeping and direct monetary control can really estimate the immediate output of fundamental research. Calculating the efficiency of fundamental science has to be done on a long-term basis – in decades at least. It is well known that the balance is much in favour of science, but this happens not because it was designed to work that way, but because the power of knowledge has an immense multiplying factor. While an invention, the result of applied science – of R&D –

leads to percentage, or even tangible, gains the discoveries of fundamental science open new fields of human endeavour. That is why basic fundamental science should be supported by the state and by society, and the public should be fully aware of this. The level and accomplishments of basic science should primarily be assessed by the world scientific community and society at large and seen as a an important part of modern culture.

The main way in which fundamental science has such a profound effect on our civilization is due to the extent to which the following generation is exposed to the ideas and concepts of new science. This should be of the utmost priority for science in the service of society. It should be seen as the most significant part of the new long-term contract between science and society that now has to be negotiated and pursued as the result of the new set of social conditions in the countries of the FSU. Formerly serving the grandeur of the country, as expressed in large and seemingly impressive projects or in sheer military might, science in Russia now has to redefine its mission.

What, then, should we do with Russian science? First, it should be integrated to a much greater extent with the universities, with training the next generation of scientists and engineers, doctors and lawyers, teachers and statesmen. It is this new generation that is to be the real instrument of reform, the main hope for the future. The continuity of teaching, and of training, of this next generation should have the highest priority, both for science and the country.

New Departures

At times of decisive transformation of society, when there is a challenge to the existing system, new educational institutions tend to be founded. During the French Revolution the *Grandes Ecoles* were established. After the Russian Revolution and under the pressure of industrialization in the 1930s the present system of technical institutes was set up, institutionalizing to a great extent the separation of research and teaching. After the Second World War, with the post-war demands for high technology and armaments, the now-prestigious Moscow Institute for Physics and Technology was founded. Its development was due to a suggestion by leading scientists of Russia and it received full support of the Party and government. It became a very successful, though singular, example of the uniting of teaching and research, with special emphasis on educating future scientists and engineers with a thorough course of physics and mathematics, taught by the best talent available. Today this experience can, and should, be used for new departures in tertiary education. For example, an important development has been the setting up of teaching departments at a number of science centres around Moscow in order to expand the graduate training capacity of these specialized scientific institutes.

More than ever Russia has to sustain and develop its tradition of higher learning. Apart from oil and gas, the Russians' minds are arguably their greatest asset. Of all that was great and good in the Soviet system we should certainly include the longstanding traditions of education, a respect for knowledge and the status of science. Russia must now learn how to gainfully employ this important asset. It is here that we can hope for links to be forged between the newly emerging enterpreneurial class and science and technology. The communist regime never really managed to properly develop and employ the intellectual potential of society as the most dynamic and progressive factor in the modern world. Instead, the Marxist idea of the supremacy of the working class interpreted in a dogmatic way, subservient to the political interests of the ruling party, contributed to the collapse of the Soviet state. Probably in no field was this so evident as with computers and information technology.

Unfortunately these positive attitudes towards science and technology are under great pressure. A successful profiteer may become a millionaire in a day, then squander his money in a night. A taxi driver gets ten times more money than a doctor or a university professor. Administrators, even of the Academy of Sciences, are much better off than the scientists themselves. Science as a cultural phenomenon, and science and technology news, have vanished from newspapers and TV, the public mind. Anti-scientific trends are rampant; astrologers and quack doctors flourish. To a great extent these are symptoms of the profound crisis through which the country is passing.[1] Equally, it certainly reflects a deep-seated new resentment towards science. Have not its proponents said time and again that Marxism is the only true scientific system of ideas on which to build a Brave New World? Have not the scientists, especially the physicists, promised utopia from nuclear energy, culminating in Chernobyl? Have not other less prestigious projects failed to deliver, be it the imminent prospect of fusion energy or the expected arrival of high-temperature superconductor technology? How should we now assess the success of space exploration, after the initial spectaculars? And what are we to do with the mess in the Russian environment?

Here it should be said that Chernobyl was more the result of the social and psychological unpreparedness of Soviet industry and society to enter the nuclear age, rather than that of defective technology; that the early promise of thermonuclear energy and room-temperature superconductors was made, or rather implied, by the world scientific community. We should admit that these questions should be addressed not only to Soviet and Russian science, but to the broader global constituency of scientists – issues and promises that sooner or later will have to be resolved. For in a certain sense the crisis in Soviet science, and even in the former Soviet Union in general, is a phenomenon that reflects in an amplified way some of the critical problems of the world as a whole. This point of view is not fully appreciated and even less pursued; it deserves to be taken more seriously.

Integration with World Science

The next priority of Russia's science policy should be that of integrating its science into world science. In applied science matters will take their due course as Russian industry becomes gradually integrated into the world economy. One can only hope that, in this process, Russia will cease to be an exporter of commodities and arms and will manage to develop its high technology and knowledge-based industries for more benign purposes. The integration of Russian fundamental science into world science cannot happen immediately, however, for the separatist traditions are deep-rooted, having been cultivated for decades. Here, again, the foremost priority should be to provide opportunities for the younger generation to access world science as soon as possible. At the beginning of the Gorbachev era there were at least 25 000 students from the People's Republic of China studying in the United States. Discussing this matter during a dinner in Washington, I mentioned these figures to the Soviet Ambassador and asked him how many Soviet students and scientists were currently in the United States. Less than 100 came the answer. This message was delivered to Gorbachev. His reaction was immediate and supportive, but not much happened – at present there are reportedly 40 000 Chinese students and still only a few thousand Russians!

Today much is spoken about the brain drain. Despite all the surrounding publicity the figures are not yet alarming. The departure of some scientists should partly be seen as a way of normalizing the connections and ties between Russian science and the world at large, for it is necessary to compensate for these decades of self-imposed isolation. In the international exchange statistics in Table 6.1 we can see the trends and development in Russian science. Hopefully, with the stabilization of the political situation, priorities will be redefined and we shall see the return of scientists to the country. The figures in Table 6.1 were provided by the International Department of the Academy of Science. They are self-explanatory and reflect the decline of research activities, especially in fundamental science, in Russia. The Academy accounts for 10 per cent of all scientists.

The crucial issue is that key members of the academic community are leaving, books on science are ceasing to be published, and the continuity of

Table 6.1 Exchanges and travel by scientists of the Russian Academy of Sciences

Purpose of travel	1991	1992
Attend conferences	6 956	5 058
Exchange collaboration	1 506	628
By invitation	8 451	7 357
Expeditions	329	112
Contracts (long term visits)	467	881
Accompanying persons	1 262	1 597
Total	18 971	15 633

research and teaching is being lost. For example, the revised volumes of the world-famous *Course on Theoretical Physics* by Landau and Lifshitz have been stranded for more than two years in the Publishing House of the Academy of Sciences due to lack of funds. Many senior members of that remarkable school of physics have also left, and here the continuity of an internationally recognized tradition may be broken.

There can certainly be no objection to the worldwide traffic of scientists. But consider this analogy. When a football superstar is transferred from one club to another, many millions are paid, demonstrating to the world the significance and real value of that individual, but when a great professor is invited abroad, nobody ever thinks of compensating the institution that trained and nurtured for years a scientist of distinction. Can we expect, in such circumstances, to generate in the public mind the strong image of science, or the willingness to support the sources of such very special talent?

Today the image of science and the status of scientists needs to be cultivated and developed to a much greater extent than ever before. Russia's painful lesson sends a message to many other countries that the decline of science is being considered by some as an imminent global phenomenon. I do not share these gloomy expectations, although unfortunately scientists themselves often engage in doom-mongering. In most cases this is a rather primitive exercise in modern pseudoscientific eschatology. Good as brainteasers, these messages often generate despair rather than hope, and demoralize rather than help confront the real issues of the world and of our civilization.

Since the Age of Reason science has promised much. Now it seems that the Day of Reckoning has come and it is probably high time for the world scientific community to start to show less complacency and more fortitude in assessing and defining its priorities. In developments challenging Russian science this exercise has to be taken much more seriously than ever before. Can these new priorities be worked out by the old and conservative academic establishment, or are new leaders to emerge? To what extent can the management of science be left to scientists themselves? Can one paraphrase the old maxim that war is too important a business to leave to the generals? In no way should it be thought that I favour the introduction of administrative control of science; in Russia we have a good deal of very unfortunate experience in such matters. But today's critical situation does demand new ways of resolving the complex issues facing the scientific community. To what extent such decisions could be assisted by international advice is a very important question. An external authority could probably help to overcome the vested interests of the 'old boys' club' that up to now has been running Soviet and now Russian science not without some success.

Many question the authoritarian manner in which much of Soviet science (and not only science!) was governed, and how to extend the new democratic concepts to science administration. This is not an easy matter, but one that has to be faced and resolved in one way or another. Probably a new governmental means of administering funds, similar to the National Science Foundation in the United States, or Germany's *Deutsche Forschungsgemeinschaft*, should be envisaged, separating advice and decision-making. Of the greatest importance for such an agency would be the implementation of a new scientific policy to be worked out both by the scientific community and, hopefully, by parliament. This could be expected only with the election of a new legislature.

Help from Outside

It is only proper to mention the help and assistance being provided to Russia by the world scientific community. Much has been done to provide for the continuity and availability of scientific publications, since most library funds in Russia and the former republics have been cut off. The initiative of publishing and distributing at a reduced price *Nature Monthly,* thus opening up a significant channel of communication with world science, is very much welcomed. Grants to individual groups of scientists are of great help, as is support to schools of excellence that are so much in need of protection. Funds for travel are important, especially for young scientists. Of the assistance to Russian science coming from foundations the support by the Soros Foundation in the United States is worthy of special mention.

These contributions are significant at a time of change and frustration, when the fragile body of science could so easily collapse. But a long-term science policy cannot be sustained by such means; some even believe that this help may undermine the structure of Russian science, or rather what is left of it. In providing support for individual scientists and science projects it is very easy to upset the all-important balance between the distinct group and the host institution that provides much of the infrastructure and the intellectual tradition of a good centre of research. Of all centres of study the universities have a more permanent nature than any other institution. Today we see how mission-oriented centres of research – centres that could even be considered to have once been centres of excellence but now to have fulfilled their purpose – have great difficulty in finding support and a socially acceptable means of existence. This is best illustrated by military research establishments. Finally, it should be borne in mind that only the country itself can, and should, really define the priorities and manage its science.

In the foreseeable future the greatest loss is likely to be experienced by experimental research, since it is more costly than purely theoretical work, the latter always having been strongly represented in the FSU. The long-term and serious lag in development of Big Science has already been mentioned. Should the state continue to support these large laboratories which now, by any standards, have lost time, staff and much of what they had to offer? On the other hand, large-scale projects need to be chosen on the basis of their significant contribution to national goals and the international community of science. Here again, new priorities have to be defined. Unfortunately, the pressure of former commitments, of the vested interests of the large, and often still powerful, groups and the tradition of continuity make it all the more difficult to make the right decisions and then carry them out.

Due to lack of hard currency the former obligations of Soviet science towards international institutions and learned societies and projects, now taken over by Russian science, are all frozen. International financial assistance and help would be most welcome to meet these payments and debts. Funds now offered for technical assistance might be allocated to international institutions for the support of research by Russian scientists and scientists of other countries who cannot at present find the means at the national level.

Keeping up Morale

In times of difficulty and strife, morale factors become important. Of all the reasons for the loss of will and morale on the part of scientists, the lack of appreciation of their work and even their place in society probably ranks highest. The change in values now taking place in the country is having a significant effect on the attitudes of the younger generation. Anti-intellectual trends seen in media freed from censorship and responsibility towards society, coupled with expressions of rampant nationalism and anti-semitism, add to the frustration and despair felt particularly by the young and most promising generation at the postgraduate and post-doctorate level, forcing them to leave science or the country. These issues and the public attitude of society towards science are usually not taken into account, but they are of great importance. Recently, on the initiative of the Academia Europaea, 20 prizes were granted by an international jury to young scientists of the FSU, in a move to support the next generation at a decisive time in their careers. One of the real responsibilities of the senior generation and of the world community of scientists is to recognize this mood, for, while the state of the body may be repaired by money, the spirit is much more elusive. Yet it is crucially instrumental for the success and future of science.

Nuclear weapons laboratories are of special concern, and it is perhaps there that some of the fundamental difficulties of converting the research branch of the military–industrial complex can be best seen. Right from the outset these institutions were off-limits – beyond limits in terms of money and resources and also off-limits in terms of contact not only with world science, but even with the majority of their colleagues at home. Now they are open to the world; they have to redefine their priorities, and find new ways of employing the very special talents of their scientists and engineers, the great resources at their command. This is no simple matter because of the very high degree of compartmentalization of such mission-oriented research establishments. Another factor that has to be recognized is that of the high average age at these institutes, which only serves to make changes even more difficult to accomplish. It can only be hoped that this challenge and ensuing changes will not lead to an intellectual dimension in nuclear proliferation. The sense of responsibility developed amongst the staff of scientists and engineers at these remarkable centres of research now becomes a duty with regard to global, rather than national, security in the issue of nuclear weapons proliferation.

Service in the Newly Independent States

The break-up of the Soviet Union into a number of independent republics, and the new policies pursued by Eastern European states, has led to new conditions for the development of science. After the euphoria of independence, when scientists in the newly independent republics were often the most vocal spokesmen for the new freedoms, many have now to face the facts of life. For example, the heads of state of two former republics of the Soviet Union were professors of physics – President Stanislav Shushkevich of Belarus and President Askar Akaev of Kirgizstan. If support for science is low in Russia, things are often even worse in many of these newly independent countries, and much rethinking and reorganizing is needed. The initially severed professional ties with Russia are now gradually being repaired and much has to be done to redefine the connections in the Russian-speaking world in terms of training students, granting degrees, publishing books and journals and organizing joint conferences – in other words, in support of the infrastructure of science. Science may, and should, become an integrating factor for these states, and here international professional organizations have a special mission. For example, the former Union of Scientific and Engineering Societies has been reconstituted as an Association of such societies of the new republics of the FSU. In a similar way recently the Physical Society of the Soviet Union has been transformed into the Euro-Asian Physical Society, following the concepts of the European Physical Society. To what extent these new international organizations will manage to unite scientists in parts of the world so divided by nationalism has yet to be seen.

Although each of these countries has problems unique to its own situation, many of them derive from the way things were organized in the Soviet Union and copied by its former allies. Probably here the crisis of the academies is one of the common features. In Germany, for example, the former East German Academy of Sciences has been disbanded, whilst in other countries profound changes are being found necessary. The financing of science through foundations, directing funds to specific projects and individuals rather than supporting institutions is assuming greater importance. In this case internationally available expertise becomes a significant factor in assessing research projects. The greater independence and objectivity of outside expert opinion may introduce common standards of excellence with reference to world science which in turn may lead to the development of personal and institutional ties and the identification of new priorities in national science policy.

Conclusion

However varied are the conditions in these newly independent countries, the case of Russia is of special significance. It is here that the challenge of reform is most acute, not only because in this country the policies that must now change were pursued for 70 years, longer than anywhere else, but also due to the sheer scale and complexity of the society in this current state of great turbulence. However painful and even traumatic these changes are, we have to see them in the context of a profound social transformation, the true magnitude of which only future historians will be able to measure.

Note

1 *Scientific American*, August 1991.

7   The Kremlin's Chechen Policy
Ruslan I. Khasbulatov

Introduction

The small Dagestani town of Kizlyar gained immediate world-wide publicity owing to a terrible tragedy: early in the morning of 9 January 1996 an armed detachment of 200 to 250 men led by Salman Raduyev, a son-in-law of the rebellious Chechen President General Dzhokhar Dudayev, stormed the town. The rebels destroyed the local aerodrome with three helicopters, dispersed the town police, then seized the hospital and filled it up with some 2000 townsfolk. All the detainees as well as the hospital staff and the patients – about 3000 people in all – were declared taken hostage by the rebels who put forward the following political demands for the Russian authorities to meet: stop the hostilities against the Chechen people, remove the Doku Zavgayev collaborationist regime, and withdraw Russian troops from the whole of the Northern Caucasus.

The demands resembled those already made by another group of Chechen rebels under the command of Shamil Basayev who also seized a hospital in Budyonnovsk, in Russia's Stavropol Region, in June 1995. On that occasion Russia's Prime Minister, Viktor Chernomyrdin, was pressed by Russian and world public opinion into negotiations with Basayev that resulted in the liberation of the hostages, a ceasefire, and the opening of negotiations between Russian and Chechen delegations. The talks led to an Agreement on the Cessation of Hostilities, reached on 30 July 1995, under which the parties agreed to resolve the conflict through negotiations thus implementing the Agreement.

Yet seven months later, this additional terrorist act on the part of Chechen rebels resulted in the loss of numerous human lives. What made it possible? Why is there no peace in Chechnya? What caused this new aggravation of the situation? These are the questions that will be addressed in this chapter.

The Evolution of the Kremlin's Chechen Policy

As soon as the hostages were set free in Budyonnovsk in June 1995, peace talks began between the Russian and Chechen delegations, mediated by a group of observers from the Organization for Security and Cooperation in Europe (OSCE). They proved hard-going but were nevertheless successful. The peak of the process was reached in late July 1995 when the aforementioned Agreement was signed – essentially a classical 'treaty on the cessation of hostilities' as has occurred over the centuries-long history of wars. But a grim fate awaited the Agreement. It was immediately attacked, first by the Russian Ministers of Defence and the Interior, then by all sorts of 'political experts', and later by Parliamentary politicians in Moscow. The alleged 'unilateral concessions to the Chechen side' were the main subject of criticism. Poor Arkady Volsky, who had spared no effort to have the conflict resolved peacefully, was forced onto the defensive under endless accusations of having committed all but treason. He was really a sorry sight on the television screen. Soon rumours spread that he was being 'recalled' from Chechnya (as if he occupied an important governmental post!).

Having agreed on a set of military issues, the negotiating sides failed to make any progress over the following two months, in the political sphere at least, to consolidate the success achieved. And from September 1995 a clearly dangerous tendency developed in Federal policy, namely to break off talks with the Chechen side, accusing it of breaching the Agreement of 30 July as a result of having an unconstructive approach to the talks, of having procrastinated and of having violated certain provisions. It has to be recalled that the Agreement focused on the renunciation of hostilities, the cessation of the military conflict, the withdrawal of Russian troops beyond the frontiers of the Chechen Republic (in keeping with the established schedule) on the one hand, and the simultaneous disarmament of the resistance units and their disbandment on the other. The units on the Chechen side were to be replaced with local self-defence groups under the jurisdiction of the rural authorities. At the beginning, everything proceeded quite smoothly, especially so when cash was offered for the arms surrendered. Later, the process started 'misfiring' – funds were exhausted and the resistance fighters arriving to surrender their arms had to go back to their bases with their 'wares' in hand, having waited for many hours in vain for Russian military representatives. After a widespread propaganda attack by the mass media, with the Federal side incessantly accusing the Chechens of reneging on their commitment to surrender arms, the process came to halt. The last straw was a conflict over the 'self-defence groups' – the Russian side questioned their legitimacy though they had been provided for by the Agreement. Later on, it became clear that the new issue was not at all accidental: the intention to undermine the Agreement itself was slowly beginning to take shape. As for the notorious self-defence groups, they were necessitated by the situation: widespread crime forced the rural population to take control of their own defence.

But the Chechen side did not understand the Russian side's reason for revising this provision of the Agreement and accordingly reacted by assuming an unyielding, if formally justified, position and by insisting on the honouring of this obligation. In fact, this reaction played into the hands of the Russian side which was looking for a pretext to break off the talks and renounce the Agreement.

Quite unexpectedly for Moscow and his own command, General A. Romanov resolutely opposed these dishonest manoeuvres. He must have gone through painful hesitations before reaching his conclusion on the necessity to resolve the crisis exclusively by peaceful means. Outwardly, the act would look both strange and unexpected, given the fact that he had been actively involved in the 1993 Kremlin putsch against the Parliament and the Constitution. Possibly, it was the realization of that sin and guilt that pushed him to a firm belief in the necessity honourably to carry out his peace-enforcement mission. Romanov was a man of action, possessing enormous capabilities for reaching that or any goal. As commander of the task force, it was he who rejected military-political gambling. Most likely, becoming such a peace-oriented general-politician could not have failed to strain his relations with the Interior Minister. And how 'timely' the attempt on his life was – on 6 October 1995, the day he was due to meet me! That assassination attempt gave cause for the final breaking-off of the Russian–Chechen negotiations – though the Federal authorities dared not denounce the Agreement of 30 July. Besides, the cause of the Agreement, providing for the permanent deployment of two Russian brigades of unspecified strength on Chechen territory, was to Russia's advantage (again from the formal point of view, though, as a matter of fact, such deployment has little to commend it because, strategically and tactically, Chechnya is of little value and many provisions of this type are misinterpreted). Around this time, I tried to convince Aslan Maskhadov that the Chechen side should insist on resuming the talks because Russian society had constantly been made to believe that it was the Chechen side which was not willing to proceed with the negotiations but was trying to break them off. Then on 12 October, Sandor Meszaros, the chief of the OSCE mission in Grozny, announced that the Chechen side was ready immediately to resume the negotiations and insisted that the Russian side fulfil its previous commitments. But the negotiations never resumed. The Federal authorities adopted another bloody scenario: the newly-bankrupt collaborators were to be replaced with a member of the old guard compromised over five years previously and now declared all but 'the

Saviour of the Nation' – though the people of Checheno-Ingushetia had previously known him as the Republic's chief communist. Moscow recalled its bankrupt protégés from Chechnya and sent in a new ruler – Zavgayev who had headed the Republic's Party Committee for over 20 years before being ousted in disgrace in the summer of 1991 when he supported a coup d'etat aided by Moscow. Zavgayev reanimated the mythical 'Supreme Soviet of the Chechen Republic' (before September 1991 there existed the Supreme Soviet of the Checheno-Ingush Republic) and convinced Moscow that negotiations with the warring Chechen side were pointless. He then suggested a policy of 'fait accompli' that was intended to mean his 'election' – under the control of the Russian occupation authority – as the head of the Chechen Republic while repudiating the negotiating mechanism and ignoring the warring Chechen forces.

All of this demonstrated the Kremlin's new political course. It reaffirmed the Federal authorities' renunciation of the policy they had undertaken to pursue in the aftermath of the Budyonnovsk tragedy; that is, a peaceful settlement of the conflict, whose guarantor Boris Yeltsin had proclaimed himself to be. It was a totally new course aimed at the rejection of any attempts to find common language with the Resistance Movement, at strengthening the positions of the puppet regime and at its legitimization. The election farce of 17 December 1995 in Chechnya was declared by Moscow as a 'legal election' though less than 5 per cent of voters participated. Occupation troops and ballots cast by representatives of the Zavgayev administration made up the 'rest'. The population felt deeply hurt by such an unconcealed insult to their opinions. It provoked the Dudayev supporters' actions in Gudermes and, probably, in Kizlyar.

The Chernomyrdin–Zavgavev Accord

A special role in legitimizing Zavgayev was to be played by a so-called 'Agreement on Basic Principles of Interrelations Between the Russian Federation and the Chechen Republic' – an idea stolen from my Peace Plan. But I had suggested signing such a document between the conflicting sides – a logical measure had the Federal authorities wanted peace. Such a Treaty (or Agreement) would have laid the foundation for a complete termination of the war and the beginning of a peaceful process of recovery in Chechnya. But an 'Agreement' between the Federal Government and its former clerk was almost tantamount to an 'agreement between the head and tail'; given the hostile attitude of the majority of the population towards the 'representative of Chechnya', its effect was similar to that of gasoline used to extinguish fire.

People are not as stupid as they are thought to be in the Russian corridors of power. They immediately realized that the signatories' intention was to strengthen the position of the 'head of the Republic' on the eve of the election of 17 December – which had been organized especially for him in the hope that none of the other candidates would be able to contest the election effectively with less than a month for the whole campaign. They thought: 'What if Ruslan Khasbulatov wins? God forbid!' They did not even count on their 'election-rigging' capacities.

The publication by a Moscow newspaper, *Vek* (Century), of a draft Treaty between Russia and Chechnya which I had written back in October and agreed with many influential republican public organizations, including the Resistance leaders, was another factor that pushed Moscow to an 'agreement'. No doubt, the publication of my draft treaty impelled Moscow to make significant concessions in the signed 'Agreement' regarding the powers of the Chechen Republic – though it will hardly be able to enjoy them because the accord is doomed to fail. Nevertheless, the effect in Chechnya was quite the opposite to the one hoped for by those who had drafted and signed the 'Agreement'. Even Zavgayev's supporters, after they learned about that 'historic document' from a television broadcast on 8 December, said: 'While some fought Russia for Chechnya's freedom others, working on the President's staff and servilely persuading the authorities to send troops to their home republic, signed an "agreement" with them. It is an insult to people, their feelings, and their national pride. It is nothing less than the humiliation of the people.' So, instead of promoting Zavgayev's image, the 'Agreement' aggravated overall tension in the Republic which exploded with new hostilities, including those in Gudermes.

What was the intention of the 'Agreement'? First it *de facto* abrogated the 30 July 1995 Agreement on the termination of hostilities signed with the warring Chechen side; second, it consolidated the new Federal course of denying the warring Chechen side a military-political status; and third, it 'substantiated' the total refusal of the Federal side to hold political negotiations with the resistance. In general, we witnessed here a complete revision of the political realities recognised during the Budyonnovsk crisis. This led to the preponderance of such terms as 'bandits' and 'terrorists' in the vocabulary of the high-ranking military. But those 'terrorists' enjoy the support of the majority of their people. And they control nearly all of the Republic – forcing the newly elected 'head of the Republic' and the representative of the Federal President to live at the airport in Grozny under the protection of forces who constitute almost an army brigade.

I have warned both the Chechen provisional authorities and the Russian leadership that the enforced and falsified election of the head of the Chechen Republic, with the warring Chechen side ignored and outlawed, will not bring about peace and stabilization, but will rather aggravate tension and possibly cause a new war and increased terrorist activities. That was why, on 9 December 1995, I refused to participate in the election of the head of the Republic; also why I called for its postponement, for the resumption of Russian–Chechen negotiations (which had been at a standstill since the previous September) and for the determination of a future date for the election of legal authorities of the Republic.

Fighting in Gudermes

My worst forecasts came true. Early in the morning of 14 December 1995 a Resistance battalion led by Dudayev's son-in-law, Raduyev, overran a contingent of Russian troops and entered Gudermes. Although the Russian force was quite impressive – some 1000 heavily-armed men and officers – it was completely destroyed. It could offer resistance only at the railway station and around the commandant's office building. The Russian troops found themselves encircled. Soon, in turn, Gudermes was tightly blockaded by Federal troops. Then mechanized support units from Grozny rushed to the rescue but, in the environs of Gudermes, they were routed and dispersed, with up to 100 men killed and wounded and some 20 persons missing. After such a defeat, the Federal command subjected the town to air and artillery attacks and reinforced the blockade.

Tall central buildings were turned into fortifications and weapon emplacements. Communications with the outside world, including Grozny, were disrupted, and reporters were kept outside the city limits. The Federal military command was afraid lest people should learn about still another inglorious war which they had unleashed; and this not for the sake of the 'unity and integrity of Russia' but with the sole purpose of installing in Grozny a puppet whose only merit consisted in handing out generous bribes to the political and military bureaucracy involved in decision-making on Chechnya. According to refugees, the corpses of Russian soldiers were left lying all over the streets exposed to sniper fire. During the course of a week, the centre of Gudermes was heavily bombed and shelled, and over 300 local residents were killed or wounded. People moved to the suburbs, but those who were unable to break through the blockade hid in basements during assaults. Gudermes is a very important town in Chechnya. It is the biggest transport junction through which both the only railway and roads as well as the pipeline for Caspian crude oil pass. Had the Resistance set itself the task of holding Gudermes and done so for quite a long time, then, from the viewpoint of Russia's interests in the region, that would probably have proved catastrophic. However, there is nothing to corroborate the claim that the battalion that seized Gudermes was defeated and forced out. More likely, the Resistance military command did not intend to hold the town. At all events, after a number of abortive attempts to break into Gudermes, the Federal command started planning a new operation for its seizure. Apparently, this was the most 'successful' combat operation in the history of Russia's interior troops – not counting the 'successful seizure' in April 1995 of Samashki, where there was no armed enemy in sight. The exact number of losses among Russian men and officers, including those killed in the approaches to Gudermes, has been kept secret. This is quite easy because a great number of 'contractual servicemen' were not registered among those 'killed' or 'taken prisoner'. But by official estimates, the total number of men killed during one week in the battle for Gudermes amounted to nearly 100. The town residents cite another figure – 300.

Having seemingly accomplished their immediate mission of demonstrating that the Zavgayev puppet regime was not able to consolidate its positions in Chechnya, even with Russia's powerful military support, the Resistance units left Gudermes unhindered. In fact, this operation again showed that if the Kremlin is interested in peace, it should adopt the course of seeking negotiations with the warring Chechen side. It should return to the policy that led to the signing of the Agreement of 10 July 1995 on the termination of war, strictly observe its provisions and meet its obligations on political issues. There is no other way. No Kremlin puppet can rule Chechnya any more.

Tragedy in Dagestan

In the early morning of 9 January 1996, Raduyev's Chechen unit stormed the Dagestani town of Kizlyar close to the Chechen–Dagestani border. Then 2000 local residents were herded into the hospital and declared, along with doctors and patients, to have been taken hostage. The leaders issued political demands: the Chechen Republic had to be recognized as independent and all Russian troops had to be withdrawn from the Northern Caucasus. Obviously, no one was going to meet these demands and the generals immediately busied themselves with preparations to destroy Raduyev's group. The Dagestani leaders played an active role in preventing the deaths of the 3000 hostages and did not let the generals attempt to solve the problem as they had in Budyonnovsk in June 1995 when they stormed the hospital. The Dagestani leaders resolutely denounced any suggestions of such strong-armed tactics; despite the insult to their people, they would not let a war with Chechens be unleashed on their territory. The conflict was virtually settled within 24 hours: almost all 3000 hostages were set free and the 'terrorists', holding just over 50 persons, boarded buses and – as agreed with the Dagestani and the Federal military authorities – headed for the Chechen-Dagestani border.

The fighters planned to cross into Chechnya in the vicinity of the village of Pervomayskoye, 300 metres from the border. But when the first three buses with fighters crossed the bridge over the border-line river, one of the accompanying helicopters fired a machine-gun burst in front of them. The fighters returned to Pervomayskoye where they captured and disarmed over 30 Federal soldiers. Several hours later the village was tightly encircled by Federal troops and preparations began for the destruction of the fighters. The Dagestani authorities did their utmost to get the hostages free peacefully, but this time their attempts proved futile.

On 14 January Federal troops attacked the fighters' positions. First they were subjected to gunship and artillery fire, then they were stormed by Armoured Personnel Carriers carrying paratroopers from elite units. The battle raged until 16 January. Official reports asserted that nearly all the fighters were dead, though some of them had been taken prisoner, and – what is more important – that the 'terrorists' had shot their hostages. During the three days of fighting between Federal troops and Raduyev's group, the most terrible news was spread, namely that the fighters had killed the six Dagestani elders who had come to negotiate with them. Later, this news was disproved. Speaking on television, the freed hostages said that the fighters had not killed a single hostage but had taken care of them, though they had been exposed to danger from Russian troops, planes and artillery. Over 70 hostages were liberated; it was a miracle they had survived. The fate of over 100 others is not known. They might have died under fire or during the attacks. Raduyev escaped with his men and some hostages.

I suspect that from the very beginning the Russian authorities were probably not interested in the hostages' fate. They wanted to punish the 'terrorists' immediately regardless of the possible deaths of hostages. That was why they employed tanks, planes, artillery and special task-units. By the end of the third day of fighting, spokesmen for the attacking troops broke the news that all the hostages were already dead and that they had begun using the rocket weapon system 'Grad' which spelled death to everyone in the target zone. But later it became known that the hostages were alive. What should one believe? Certainly all this revealed a total inability to conduct properly-planned operations to liberate hostages and – what is more – the inability of a whole army group to inflict a quick and effective defeat on a rebel unit using only small arms.

After Moscow announced its 'total victory' over the 'terrorists', Raduyev appeared on television on 22 January for the first time following the Pervomayskoye battle. He hugged his hostages, saying that he had about 80 of them; they thanked him for having saved their lives at the hands of Federal troops. As observers rightly noted, the spectacle was totally humiliating for Russian society which had been assured by Yeltsin and his commanders of their own sweeping victory. Marshal Mikhail Barsukov, who had revealed his absolute inability to conduct any kind of military operation, then demonstrated his talent to single-handedly aggravate national differences. Speaking on television, he said (quoting an anonymous celebrity) that, to a man, Chechens were thieves, bandits and robbers.

On 24 January the Resistance leaders received a Dagestani delegation in the village of Novogroznenskoye and handed over to them all Raduyev's hostages (42 people in all), some from Kizlyar and others from Pervomayskoye. But about 20 militia men from Omsk continued to be held: the combatants suggested exchanging them for their comrades (dead or alive) still held by the Federal authorities.

It is clear that the 'rescue' operation had totally failed. So had the 'terrorist-destruction' operation to which the former had been sacrificed. As never before, the authorities displayed their horrendous inclination for misinformation, lies and insinuations, a situation unheard of even in the worst communist times: state leaders manipulated obvious facts in front of the whole world. And when the true facts become known, they did not blush or bother to apologise. Yeltsin claimed that fortifications had been erected in advance in Pervomayskoye, which thereby could have withstood a siege by a whole army! How could Dagestanis react to that? And what about his words that, from now on, at last, Avars will start cutting Chechen throats. That was the reaction of the person who calls himself the head of state: here his countrymen were encouraged to start killing each other. This shocking truth has altered the attitude of many in Dagestan and the Northern Caucasus towards the events in Chechnya and in the Kremlin.

Events in Chechnya in February and March 1996

In the second half of February 1996 the headquarters of the Federal troops in Chechnya decided to attack the positions of the Resistance fighters in revenge for their failure to destroy Raduyev's group. Several Chechen villages were targeted, including Bamut, Novogroznenskoe and Sernovodsk. The troops killed civilians and destroyed their houses in Arashti in Ingushetia. Next, Russian aircraft and artillery bombed the village of Novogroznenskoe, declaring that the headquarters of the commander of the rebellious general, Maskhadov, was based there. The village was surrounded by more than 600 units of tanks and more than 10 000 soldiers and officers which destroyed 95 per cent of houses and killed about 1000 peaceful inhabitants. These barbarous actions were accomplished after all the combatants had left the village. Then the Federal troops started to bomb and set fire to the resort of Sernovodsk with its population of 15 000. This town was also surrounded by troops and tanks. Only 2000 to 3000 people could get away, the rest being forced to stay in their houses. They have seen all the horrors of war: exploding bombs, their houses being destroyed, their children, old men and women dying.

During those days, namely on the night of 5–6 March, the Resistance combatants seized Grozny and for four days controlled it. Russian troops then started to bomb Grozny and to fire heavy artillery. And again all the victims were civilians. The combatants left Grozny without loss.

Evidently Moscow is not ready to enter into serious negotiation with the Chechen Resistance movement, relying instead on the puppet Zavgayev's government. Orders to force people to get down on their knees will not succeed, but will instead lead to new bloodshed and growing discontent at Kremlin policy among the people of the Caucasus. It seems that the Kremlin has emerged as a perpetrator of state 'terrorism'.

Peace can be assured only by peaceful negotiations between the fighting sides. When will the Kremlin realize this? We have to stop playing with the word 'negotiation', which misleads public opinion, and start real negotiations. It is thus necessary to recognize the Agreement of 30 July 1995 and to start negotiations with the Chechen Resistance combatants.

International Guarantees

It is highly doubtful that the military establishment, which has been firmly controlling the decision-making process, will ever agree to an equitable settlement of the war, (the more they suffer defeat, the more they will be inclined to seek a military solution to conflict). At the same time, the possibility of unleashing new internal conflicts is self-evident. That is why an international legislative basis is needed for settling so-called 'internal conflicts'. I believe most of them could have been avoided, and those that do start could be settled in a comparatively short period of time if the well-known principle of 'non-interference in domestic affairs' would be taken in context with other fundamental principles. It should be stressed that The Hague and Geneva conventions and agreements, which form the basis of present-day international humanitarian law, are rather ineffectual in influencing 'internal conflicts'. At the same time, it is such internal and regional conflicts which will evidently have a major impact on the modern world in the coming decade. Hence it is a matter of urgency that we reconsider the principle of 'non-interference in internal affairs' and introduce the following interconnected principles:

- the principle of settling an 'internal conflict' not by means of using force (military measures), but by peaceful means;
- the principle of internationalizing internal conflict if it is unleashed;
- the principle of making decisions on the basis of majority vote in international organizations responsible for settling internal and local conflicts;
- the principle of the bindingness of decisions made on 'internal conflicts', and the need for the international community to take drastic sanctions should parties fail to abide by such decisions.

The present-day world is unified and interrelated, and it is fragile. The wars and conflicts of the 1990s, no matter what they are called – local, regional, ethnic, territorial, national-liberation or civil – should change the very concept existing in our minds (under Aquinas' categories) of 'just' and 'unjust' wars. Any belligerent party will try to justify the war it is waging. But for a child, perishing in the hell of war, these justifications are of no use at all. Any war is a crime.

An arsenal of international actions and means of influence should be used to prevent wars and to stop them where they start. At the same time it is necessary to reject the principle of 'non-interference in internal affairs' which is based upon nation-state egoism.

What we need is not a 'negotiations game', which is in reality the talk of a master to a servant, but frank, open and responsible negotiations, with relevant international guarantees backing up the obligations undertaken by the parties. We need negotiations between belligerents; the elimination of such words and phrases as 'bandits' and 'illegal armed units', substituting instead 'armed struggle of the people', 'resistance movements' and 'resistance fighters or combatants'. In the Chechen case, we need a group of international observers in Grozny empowered to organize negotiations and guarantee any obligations made by the negotiating parties.

To facilitate the preparatory stage, it would be worthwhile to start negotiations between the same delegations which signed the Agreement of 30 July 1995 and continued them until late September 1995. During the very first Russian–Chechen meetings, it would be useful to raise the issue of the status of the delegations.

It will be necessary to discuss and reach agreement on the following issues:

- working out and signing a joint Political Statement on negotiations as being the only way to solve the Russia–Chechnya crisis;
- publishing a special Declaration of the OSCE to guarantee the obligations assumed by the parties;

- making and adopting a joint Russia–Chechnya Declaration to the effect that the elections held on 17 December 1995 were not legitimate;
- co-ordinating a Draft proposal entitled: 'Basic Principles of Agreement between the Chechen Republic and the Russian Federation' on the status of the Chechen Republic and the period of its validity and its tasks;
- withdrawing all Russian troops from the territory of the Chechen Republic and giving it the status of a demilitarized republic;
- arranging and carrying out Republic elections under the auspices of the OSCE and developing preliminary terms of the procedures;
- demobilizing the combatants of the Resistance units and reintegrating them into the civil community;
- rejecting the use of force or any other forms of pressure so as to prevent military confrontation or settling of scores with individuals or organizations during the transition period;
- arranging to carry out a referendum aimed at determining the Republic's status (or alternatively preparing a draft Agreement and presenting it in a referendum).

Conclusion

I can find no excuse for the 'terrorists'. Using hospitals, women, children and doctors to achieve a political goal is disgusting. Such methods and actions were condemned at the beginning of the century by international conventions, the Geneva and Hague Conventions, which make up contemporary international humanitarian law. After calling for help from the international community, appealing to international law and accusing the Russian authorities of acts of genocide against the Chechen nation, Dudayev should have known that his new 'terrorist' acts would undoubtedly be condemned by the world. And he indeed delivered a deadly blow to his own prestige and the resistance movement itself which is now identified with 'terrorism'. It has lost all the moral advantages it used to enjoy prior to the events at Kizlyar. For, as I see it, the world community was about to intervene in the Russian-Chechen conflict more resolutely. But Dudayev's adventuristic and despicable behaviour has now deprived the movement of all those advantages.

The only way to terminate the war and achieve a peaceful settlement is in returning to the negotiations on which the Russian authorities embarked after the events in Budyonnovsk in June 1995, and which they subsequently abandoned under pressure from the 'war party' which hoped for easy military solutions. But military solutions are never easy. War generates war, hatred, conflict, resistance and 'terrorist' acts. This is corroborated by what has happened in Budyonnovsk, Kizlyar and Pervomayskoye and by the beginning of new hostilities in Chechnya.

It is obvious that the military should be kept away from decision-making on the Kremlin's Chechen policy. The problems of peace and war are too serious to allow the military into this sphere, especially the Russian military which has demonstrated its inclination to wage wars of destruction without giving a thought to motives, reasons, ethics or other humane considerations.

8 The Chechen Crisis: Predictable and Unpredictable Consequences

Alexei Vasilyev

The Russian army is suppressing resistance in Chechnya with a great effort, shedding blood and bearing losses. It will certainly take some considerable time to complete operations in mountain villages. Indeed, the Chechens' guerrilla warfare against Russian troops may drag on for many years.

Chechnya existed for three years as a *de facto* independent state, albeit unrecognized by the rest of the world. In resorting to forcible measures, the Russian leaders were guided by the following simple logic. Chechnya is a part of the united Russian Federation, and the Russian constitution and laws must be effective there. The Dzhokar Dudayev regime, formed illegitimately, contrary to the majority's will, armed itself to the teeth, deploying even heavy armament and aircraft seized from the Russian army. Chechnya exported oil, but all revenues from it were accumulated on the Grozny leader's foreign accounts. More than 1000 criminals of various nationalities, wanted by the Russian militia (police), had found shelter in the republic; 1200 railway trucks of transit trains had been robbed in its territory; prosecutors' offices, militia (police), healthcare systems, education and pension payments did not function. In other words, the Chechen people needed to be saved from the criminal clique who had seized power over them.

The Chechens' logic was quite the opposite: they wanted to live in an independent state. The Chechens fought against Russia in the nineteenth century and in the 1920s, and then suffered Josef Stalin's genocide in the 1940s. Although Dudayev did not enjoy the majority's support, Russia's military action rallied the Chechens behind him against Moscow. The difference between the union republics (such as Kazakhstan) and autonomous republics (such as Checheno-Ingushetia) of the Soviet Union was seen by the Chechens as a mere formality. Why had Kazakhstan, with a Slav majority in its population, been allowed to become independent while Chechnya, with an absolute majority of the indigenous nationality, not been entitled to independence?

Attempts at negotiation failed. The Russians were ready only to talk about Chechen disarmament. The Chechens only wanted to talk about independence. The two parties resembled two butting rams; forehead against forehead. Hard confrontation has cost thousands of lives (including those of more than 2000 Russian soldiers) and has led to enormous destruction and economic loss.

But to fully grasp the social, ethnic and mass psychological background of events one has to turn to the past. By the start of the twentieth century, after having been forcibly included in the Russian empire, the Chechen people had not yet formed as a nation; the country had no developed class movement and considerable manifestations of *teip* (kin and tribal) relations persisted. This *teip* structure of the society was changing very slowly, despite the territory's involvement in the united economic and sociocultural space of the Russian empire. The decades-old traditions of anti-colonialist struggle formed some specific features of the Chechens' national character, combined with the features of the social and religious organization of society which was characterized by a combination of clan structures and Sufi orders *(tariqats)* – mostly branches of the Qadiriya and Naqshbandiya orders. These structures strengthened military organization in Chechen society during Russia's Caucasian war in the mid-nineteenth century. Together with the country's geographical features (inaccessible mountains), they enabled the Chechens to resist Tsarist Russia's expansion for many decades and to wage armed struggle against the communists in the 1920s. They retained their social structure and traditions even during their exile in Kazakhstan in the 1940s and 1950s, despite humiliation and deformation of their national mentality.

The Sufi orders had to cease legal activities during the Soviet period, but they retained their influence on the peoples of the Northern Caucasian republics. This was possible due to a network of underground mosques, medressehs and presses at their disposal, as well as to numerous faith teachers and literature distributors, who continued to spread the propaganda of Sufism in spite of repression. In the early 1980s the number of *murid* (disciple) group members in Checheno-Ingushetia was estimated at 60 000. (The Chechens and Ingush formed a joint autonomous republic until 1991.)

The Sufi order's activities became more open in the latter days of the Soviet Union – the period of Mikhail Gorbachev's *glasnost* – and many young people came under their influence, although it is certainly true that

Sufism enjoyed a strong influence among them even before *perestroika* began. In 1978 a poll among young believers showed that 51 per cent of respondents belonged to a particular *tariqat*.

The balance of forces between Sufism and traditional Islam, which was in a stable condition in the period of dominance of official Soviet atheism, is changing in favour of Sufism. The spread of *tariqats* is common to both remote rural regions and large cities and industrial centres. Sufi orders have become active in the central parts of Chechnya and Ingushetia, where some towns, such as Achnoy-Martan, Gudermes, Urus-Martan, Noghai-Yurt, Shali, Vedens and Nazran, were centres of certain *tariqats* as far back as the establishment of the Soviet Union. Characteristically enough, the shift of *tariqat* activities to towns is accompanied by their politicization, including the emergence of extremist politico-religious action in their activities. Undoubtedly, the Sufi orders influenced the recent developments, and all, or some of them, support the concept of Chechnya's secession from Russia.

During the collapse of the communist quasi-civilizations, the self-identification of the post-Soviet Islamic nations is based either on nationalism (appeal to national roots), or on Islam, or both. For instance, the nationalist shade dominates among the political movements in Tatarstan, while in Chechnya it is mixed, national–religious, with a manifest Islamic base.

However, in the real-life situation, when such words as sovereignty, national independence, democracy or freedom are pronounced in the specific context of Chechnya, are they anything but a verbal coverage for certain groups' thirst for power and money? In this sense, the picture of developments in Chechnya differs here from that drawn by a part of the Russian and Western media and scholars.

The principal source of combustion for the fire that broke out in Chechnya was the marginalized segment of its people. It should be emphasized that a considerable proportion of the Chechen people were artificially kept suppressed, deprived of jobs, property and habitual residence after their deportation. The semi-literate, declassed elements of the population were therefore predisposed to favour demagogical, populist, nationalist-patriotic and egalitarian slogans and the extreme radicals' aggressive activities.

The intellect behind the masses' 'revolutionary' activities came from the small segment of the national intelligentsia whose professional activities were initially politicized and tended to have nationalist–radicalist shades. They imbibed the theory and practice of classical Bolshevism, while disowning it in words. When imposed upon a deeply deformed and wounded national psychology, the 'national idea' as interpreted by its neo-Bolshevist adherents, acquired a pronounced anti-Russian flavour with a notable share of Vainakh (Chechen) messianism. It became the ideological postulate of the Vainakh Democratic Party, which considers the 'Chechen revolution' the first stage of the so-called 'domino effect'. The ultimate goal of the nationalist–radicalist ideologists is the creation of a Greater Caucasia, led by Chechnya. According to them, the Chechen people's historical mission is to ignite the 'freedom fire' and inspire the 'enslaved peoples' of Northern Caucasia with their example. When those peoples reject the ideals of the 'Chechen revolution', it is treated as a manifestation of their 'backwardness'.

It is not only the alienation and destitution of a sizeable part of the population, or people's political immaturity or lack of democratic traditions (not to mention civil society), but also the application of Bolshevist methods, under the guise of general democratic phraseology, in the struggle for power that has enabled the nationalist–radicalist political forces to pursue their selfish goals. All their actions have been motivated by a thirst for power and lucrative offices in the state machinery – by their efforts to become, essentially, a new officialdom. Evidence for this is backed up by the fact that the staff of the ministries and state agencies was inflated sixfold after the 'revolution'. Government offices were crowded by ill-educated and incompetent employees who had been remunerated in that manner for their services to the leaders.

Dudayev relied upon armed men and a frail conglomerate of rival groupings, each with armed detachments and its own sources of finance. He relied upon privileged *teip* and mafia clans, the newly formed officialdom and the uneducated strata of population with their folklore-mythological consciousness, adherence to the 'national idea' and belief in a charismatic leader. As a matter of fact, the regime that established itself relied largely on force and intimidation. Most likely Dudayev himself also became a hostage to the situation he had created.

Against this background, the Russian leaders initially chose a non-interventionist attitude towards the developments in Chechnya. Boris Yeltsin said once that the republics of the Russian Federation might take as much sovereignty as they wanted. The bloody experience of Chechnya demonstrates the way they may use this sovereignty.

At the same time, renowned Russian politicians, including Ruslan Khasbulatov, then the speaker of the Russian parliament, and Sazhi Umalatova, a leader of the neo-Communist opposition, both of Chechen origin, denounced the actions of Dudayev's followers and called upon Dudayev to demonstrate political fortitude and resign for the sake of ending the protracted crisis in Chechnya which had brought it to the verge of civil war. During the bloody clashes in Moscow between Yeltsin's followers and the parliament, Dudayev supported the Russian president. This did not prevent him from stating that Chechnya would not take part in the election of a new Russian parliament.

Before Moscow's military actions, the result of confrontation in Chechnya was determined by political will, resolve and armed detachments of the opposition forces, and by their ability to attract broad strata of the population. Yet, paradoxically, Dudayev would never be able to seize or retain power without the help and connivance of certain political forces in Russia.

In July 1991 a certain All-national Congress of the Chechen People (OCCP), led by Dudayev, then known to few outside, proclaimed the independence of the Chechen republic. Nobody would have paid this event any attention had the Supreme Soviet of the Checheno-Ingushetian autonomous republic, chaired by Doku Zavgayev, not supported the anti-Gorbachev and anti-Yeltsin State Emergency Committee in August 1991. Taking advantage of the Committee's defeat and Yeltsin's victory in Moscow, Dudayev's men occupied the government buildings and dispersed the Supreme Soviet members, beating them mercilessly with iron rods. The Dudayev coup had the consent and blessing of the Supreme Soviet of Russia, the 'democratic' press and Yeltsin himself. Then the Dudayevists also dissolved the Provisional Supreme Council of three dozen carefully selected pro-Dudaevists. Moscow was preoccupied with the last round of struggle between Yeltsin and Gorbachev and remained aloof.

Perhaps Khasbulatov, who was then gaining in strength, considered Dudayev as his vice-regent in Chechnya, but the latter had plans of his own: to seize all power, establish a dictatorship and achieve full independence. The Moscow 'liberals' and 'democrats' preferred to overlook this possibility, for they were ready to ally themselves with the devil himself to combat the communist regime in Russia. In November 1991 'elections' were rigged, and Dudayev, naturally, became the president. Moscow refused to recognize these 'elections'. Yeltsin proclaimed a state of emergency in Chechnya, but did not resolve to send troops there. By November, all agencies of the federal authorities were wrecked in Chechnya, the KGB office and archives were seized and its agents went over to Dudayev. Military garrisons were blockaded. In the following year Dudayev seized all the weapons of the Russian army units stationed in Chechnya (50 000 units of firing weapons, dozens of units of armoured hardware and artillery) in one way or another. The Ingush, a people akin to the Chechens, then seceded from Chechnya and proclaimed a separate republic as a part of Russia.

Chechnya's 'independence' proved to be of a unique variety, like almost all phenomena in post-Soviet Russia. The Checheno-Ingushetian Republic had always ranked almost bottom among the components of the Russian Federation in terms of socioeconomic development, and almost 90 per cent of its budget revenues consisted of federal allocations (that is, it came from the ethnically Russian regions). As soon as that channel was dammed, the legal sources of people's income dried up. Production fell by 60 per cent by volume in 1992 as compared to the previous year. The recession continued in 1993 and 1994 resulting in a complete collapse of industry chiefly caused by the mass emigration of Russian-speaking people, who had comprised most of the industrial work-force (about 60 000 people in 1992).

Unemployment was very high among the Chechens, especially among the rural population. In the early 1990s excess labour resources formed at least one-third of the employable population of Checheno-Ingushetia. Unemployment grew drastically under 'independence'. The political explosion forced masses of people into the towns and the Chechen capital was soon crowded with excited and armed youths. Some of them formed the backbone of the Dudayev regime's social base.

Dudayev's economic plans proved to be delusionary, to say the least. For instance, he proposed to build a giant water pipeline from Northern Caucasia to the Middle East in order to export drinking water from Chechnya to the Arab countries! Oil extraction fell by more than 200 per cent in 1992 compared to 1980, falling to 1.5 million tonnes. Revenues from it did not return to the Republic. True, oil supplies for processing at the Grozny refinery continued from other regions of Russia, yielding some income, but they reduced inexorably. Petty rackets and bribery at the bottom and large-scale corruption at the top were the 'mechanism of economic regulation' that formed in 'independent' Chechnya. Salary payment at the agencies financed from the state budget ceased almost immediately after the 'sovereignization' of Chechnya. When the police become 'self-supporting', they become a part of the criminal world.

Chechnya gradually became the most important centre for the forgery of banknotes and financial documents in the FSU, flooding Russia. In 1993 alone 9.4 billion forged roubles were seized in Russia, of which 3.7 billion roubles were identified as having their source in Chechnya. According to experts, the sums that have remained in circulation are far higher. Chechen criminal groups participated actively in the misappropriation of 4 trillion roubles, using forged letters of advice and credit cheques. This sum amounted to billions of US dollars.

Chechnya became a staging post for smuggled arms, drugs and other commodities. Aeroplanes belonging to various Russian companies made between 100 and 150 unsanctioned international flights monthly from Grozny airport. Of course, these operations would have been impossible without the support of Russian and, above all, Muscovite mafia groups and corrupt officials. The Russian authorities could control Chechnya's airspace, but chose not to. The very absence of federal control by prosecutors, customs and taxation officials in Chechnya permitted its use as a base and shelter for criminals and made it extremely attractive to the international criminal community.

Arms traders enjoyed more freedom in Chechnya than anywhere else throughout the world. Semi-automatic machine guns and grenades were available at any market as if they were potatoes. The National Guard was reinforced with criminals. There were about 200 particularly dangerous recidivists (a category of criminal including those who have been sentenced three or more times for serious crimes) among those who were released in late 1991 and given arms to defend the 'revolution'. The infamous Ruslan Labazanov, who was among the commanders of the Presidential Guard for more than two years, was just one of the brigands at Dudayev's service. He defected from the President and declared a vendetta on him. Many people in the top echelon of the republican leadership are known for their criminal records.

Former chief of the security service, General Ibrahim Suleimanov, disclosed Dudayev's personal involvement in public funds embezzlement and multimillion accounts in foreign banks. Dudayev appointed a close relation to be director of the Grozny central market, and another relation (with an educational background of two classes at primary school) headed the 'independent' airport of Grozny. His other relatives occupied key offices at Chechen banks.

Trying to lead the all-Caucasian 'struggle for independence from Russia', Chechnya became the main base of the militarized Confederation of Peoples of Caucasia. One of its leaders (the chairman of the 'parliament'), Yusup Salambekov, was simultaneously Dudayev's close associate and a leader of the All-national Congress of the Chechen People. It is noteworthy, however, that the Confederation discharged him from the office of chairman as soon as he switched to the anti-Dudayev opposition. Neither is it chance that the commanders-in-chief of the Confederation's troops – Isa Arsamikov and then Shamil Baseyev – were always Chechens drawn from Dudayev's entourage.

Yet what did Moscow do to prevent, or nip in the bud, the transformation of a 'prodigal son' of the federation into a focus of economic and political instability which was extremely dangerous to Russian society? 'Nothing' would be the wrong answer. The situation in Chechnya proved useful and comfortable for many people in Moscow. Only the very naive would believe that such a large-scale operation might be organized and accomplished within the Russian Federation without the complicity of the state and commercial banking structures. Even train robbery, apparently a purely 'local business', was coordinated from Moscow; the train robbers knew the contents of each truck in advance.

To whose command did Dudayev owe uninterrupted access to deficit quotas for Russian oil products, to oil terminals and to even more deficit oil export licences? Who allowed planes with smuggled cargo to enter Russian airspace on their way to and from Grozny, defying even international organizations' warnings on drugs transport via the Chechen capital? Obviously, the people in question were generously paid for their services. The temporizing policy on Chechnya suited many. The uncertain political status of Chechnya and its equivocal 'semi-isolation' from Russia, which comforted everybody and enabled some people to preserve and amass political capital, enabled some others to extort fantastic incomes and enabled yet others to strengthen their uncontrolled power in Chechnya itself. All this formed the sum of the causes of the creation of a 'free criminal economic zone'.

Some diplomatic efforts were made, and negotiations were conducted for two years from November 1992 to December 1994, when hostilities started. In late 1992, when the Ossetian–Ingush conflict reached its peak, Yegor Gaidar, the acting prime minister of the Russian Federation, met the deputy prime minister of Chechnya, and agreed on the disengagement of Russian and Chechen troops. In January 1993 a Russian delegation, led by the Speaker of the Council of Nationalities of the Russian Supreme Soviet, Ramazan Abdulatipov, and Deputy Prime Minister, Sergei Shakhrai, visited Grozny at the invitation of the Chechen parliament. A protocol was signed then on the preparation of a treaty between the Russian Federation and the Chechen Republic 'on delimitation and mutual delegation of authorities'. But Dudayev toppled all arrangements. He asserted more than once afterwards that 'no political understanding is possible within Russia' and he, the President of Chechnya, would not tolerate a treaty without a clause on the recognition of the Chechen Republic as a sovereign state and a subject to international law.

A psychotic 'beseiged fortress' mentality was maintained in Chechen society. All efforts were directed to training volunteers. Any opposition was declared treasonable. Amid proclamations of a 'pro-Russian conspiracy' and 'national treason' Dudayev disbanded the new parliament, originally elected simultaneously with himself, in May–June 1993. Another victim was the Constitutional Court, which tried to conduct a referendum on the power system in the Chechen Republic. Dudayev banned all opposition parties and their publications and finally ordered his men to open fire on a protest meeting in the centre of Grozny.

The only federal leader with whom Dudayev was ready to negotiate officially was the Russian president. But Yeltsin avoided any contact with the Chechen general almost instinctively. If their meeting had taken place, it would only have strengthened Dudayev's political position, lending him the legitimacy he lacked and thus finally demoralizing the Chechen opposition who were loyal to Russia and hoped for her aid.

After October 1993, when the anti-Yeltsin Supreme Soviet was suppressed by tanks, Yeltsin felt more free to choose tactics towards the regions, demonstrated by the conclusion of a treaty between Russia and Tatarstan. That treaty is not faultless from the viewpoint of constitutional law. But this alleged 'crime against the constitution', salutary to Russia, was successfully committed largely thanks to a series of legal tricks, which enabled the government to avoid the procedure of its ratification by the Federal Assembly.

However, after missing the president's 'move' in the game with Tatarstan, the Russian Parliament or *Duma* quickly learnt its lesson. It now firmly paralysed all attempts to solve the Chechen crisis by direct negotiations with Dudayev. The *Duma* adopted a resolution recommending that the president and government consult all political forces in Chechnya (not only Dudayev) on future negotiations and (most importantly) insisting on elections to the republican authorities in Chechnya and of Chechen deputies to the Russian Federal Assembly as a preliminary condition for the conclusion of any proposed Russian–Chechen treaty. The latter condition ruled out negotiations with Dudayev, who considered himself as the president of an independent state and was therefore not going to elect deputies to the parliament of a 'neighbouring country'.

This really meant that Yeltsin's hands were tied again. It was easy to demand of him that he insist on elections, but how could he implement it? By tanks? Neglect of the parliament's will would amount to derailing the Public Consent treaty, prepared so carefully, and would spoil relations with the increasingly influential governors of ethnically Russian regions, who were already dissatisfied with the concessions made to Tatarstan. Nonetheless Yeltsin did not give up his intention to conclude a treaty with Chechnya after the 'Tatarstan model' even in these circumstances.

In the spring of 1994, however, the situation in Chechnya began to deteriorate. The Dudayev regime became economically and politically bankrupt. More and more people began to support the opposition. An all-Chechen centre of resistance to Dudayev, led by Umar Avturkhanov, was formed in the Nadterechny district. The provisional council, parallelling the official authorities, had formed there in late 1993 and had asked for Moscow's political support. But while Moscow temporized and vacillated, the opposition leaders who staked everything on the armed overthrow of Dudayev acquired more and more influence. Frequent clashes took place between Dudayev's troops and armed men led by the field commanders and by Khasbulatov who resumed active participation in the political struggle. The traditional mechanism of peace maintenance – the fear of bloody revenge – was broken in Chechnya. Severed heads shown to television newsmen in a square and then transmitted throughout the world became a kind of symbol of the coming massacre.

The situation on the border with the Stavropol area also became heated. Moscow received dismaying telegrams almost daily from there. Essentially, the Cossacks demanded the blockading of Chechnya, and their demands almost became ultimatums after four consecutive attempts to seize buses with hostages and to hijack helicopters from Mineralnye Vody to Chechnya. Russian peasants in Chechnya pressed for their villages to be transferred to the Stavropol area.

Since 1993, the anti-Dudayev opposition has included not only the former high-ranking party and government officials but also most of the members of the Chechen parliament, elected in late 1991, and of the Constitutional Court, heads of town and district authorities, leaders of almost all parties and movements, *teip* leaders and Muslim clergy.

Moscow proved unable or reluctant to deal with the Chechen opposition. Another strategy and another approach prevailed. Preparations for a blitz started in September 1994. Why did Yeltsin decide on an extremely risky military expedition after being reproached for three years about excessive concessions to the republics of the Russian Federation, to Baltic states, Ukraine and Georgia? There may be a simple explanation: he was trying to improve his failing reputation by conducting a 'small victorious war'. As early as in the beginning of 1994, many people felt that the 'love match' between Yeltsin and the liberal circles had entered the phase of 'forced cohabitation'. Because Yeltsin was inclined to adopt the position of a patriot who cherishes state interests, it seemed to many liberals that they could very easily do without him. An impression grew that the political forces who had been supporting Yeltsin for three years were seeking a pretext for rupture. Accordingly, he began to dissociate himself from his liberal allies and yield to the growing influence of the forces who understand and cherish only a 'Great Power mentality' and a 'firm hand'.

Dudayev meanwhile had prepared for war for three years. He purchased weapons and erected three defence lines around Grozny, fortified sectors on the way to it and established guerrilla bases in mountains. And once he saw the concentration of a Russian military grouping near Mozdok, he had no doubt that hostilities were imminent.

When the Russian *Blitzkrieg* failed, generals and militant politicians resorted to increasingly reckless actions – first to win a quick and impressive victory, then to seize at least its symbols (the presidential palace in Grozny with a Russian banner hoisted on it) by fighting tooth and nail, without sparing the Russian soldiers, or the enemy's volunteers, or unfortunate civilians. Given an entirely deformed system of political decision-making and implementation and given the loss of national orientation by the media, the failure in Chechnya was preordained. Essentially, two knots of conflict formed – one in Northern Caucasia and another in Moscow.

What does the future hold? Undoubtedly Chechnya will remain Russia's bleeding and festering wound. One may hardly expect that the new Chechen leadership, who are ready to cooperate with Moscow, will be recognized by the majority of the local population. Hatred for the Russians will accelerate the persecution of the Russian population in Chechnya, which will result in the further destruction of modern industries such as mechanical engineering and oil processing and of transport. The increasingly mononational population of Chechnya will support terrorists and guerrillas in their struggle against the occupying Russian troops.

An optimistic scenario of the future is successful economic development, dialogue with the anti-Russian leaders, gradual reconciliation and the elaboration of Chechnya's special status within Russia. Moscow will play on contradictions between the leaders of different regions, supporting its allies. But a pessimistic scenario would be years of creeping war, growing mutual hatred, Chechen terrorist attacks in Russia and anti-Chechen massacres in Astrakhan or Moscow. As for independence, it may be achieved in many years' time but it will be the independence of a tormented and devastated country in full economic dependence on Russia.

Chechnya has borders with other autonomous republics of Northern Caucasia such as Daghestan, Ingushetia, North Ossetia, Kabardino-Balkaria and Karachai-Circassia. The impact of the developments in Chechnya on the situation throughout Northern Caucasia may be of a dual character. On the one hand, mistrust of Moscow and solidarity with the Chechens will strengthen separatism and tension in the region. At the same time, Russian nationalism will strengthen, directed against the mountain peoples. On the other hand, the tragic consequences of a diehard policy – casualties and ruins in Chechnya – will prompt wise politicians to seek compromises and political solutions.

The conflict in Chechnya has had at least one positive aspect: it did not become a religious conflict, a war between the Christians and the Muslims, as happened in Bosnia. It did not exceed the framework of ethnic and political contradictions. Both Orthodox Christian and Muslim spiritual leaders have made peacemaking efforts. This provides a glimmer of hope for a peaceful dialogue in the future.

The Chechen crisis and the attempts to resolve it by aggresion have so strongly influenced the balance of political forces in Russia itself that its consequences will be felt both in the near and far future. Whatever the outcome, Yeltsin seems to be the loser. Had he left the Chechen situation alone he would have been charged with ruining Russia, and with weakness and conniving with separatism and criminality. Now he is reproached for excessive force and the consequent casualties. Corpses of Russian soldiers and the tearstained faces of grieving mothers, shown on television, have become the trump cards for anti-Yeltsin propaganda. Yeltsin was once the banner of the so-called forces for democracy and virtually all 'democratic leaders' of today are his political offspring. But now they are up in arms against him. Their camp is split and confused.

The political opposition, which enjoys a majority in the parliament, consists of communists with their allies and of Russian nationalists. They win one victory after another in regional elections. Their main arguments concern the impoverishment of people as a result of the 'reforms', unemployment, industrial recession, the catastrophic law and order situation and national humiliation. Now Russia's awkward actions in Chechnya, with the accompanying blood and casualties, are added to this list. The only point to be stressed is that the Russian communists have already adopted a Western European-type social democratic programme and their potential return to power will not lead to a cessation of market reforms or a restoration of the Stalinist-Brezhnevist political model. A more likely scenario is one resembling that in Lithuania, Poland, Hungary and Bulgaria, where the communists have returned to power under new names, but are not restoring the earlier totalitarian regimes.

Losing his base among the 'democrats' and having handed his trump cards to the opposition, Yeltsin has to rely more and more on his military ministries and structures – the army, the home guard and counterintelligence. It means a trend towards the strengthening of authoritarianism which is able to flourish legitimately on the soil of the constitution, which was 'tailored' for Yeltsin and gives him more authority than that enjoyed by a US president, making him in effect almost an absolute monarch. However, the struggle is being waged within the military structures themselves. When some competent generals were purged from them and replaced by officers promoted for their personal devotion to their masters, even the purely military aspect of operations in Chechnya became ineffectual in both planning and implementation. It was an additional blow to the army's, and to Yeltsin's, prestige.

Russia's position in the world has also deteriorated. Certainly, at the time of writing, the West is still supporting Yeltsin, since it cannot recognize the independence of Chechnya because similar problems arise in too many countries. Also, it sees no acceptable alternative to Yeltsin. But television reports on the Chechen war create so negative an image among the Western public of Russia and of Yeltsin personally that many political leaders have criticized Moscow for the methods deployed in Chechnya and for the excessive casualties, especially among civilians. The Muslim world's adverse reaction is far stronger. Few people are interested there in the legal details of Chechnya's right to independence or absence of that right. More important is the fact that Muslim Chechens are being killed by Russian 'Christian' troops. This is a very dangerous factor, as Russia and the Muslim world are natural partners and share common interests. And, as has been noted, the war in Chechnya has not in reality become a Christian–Muslim confrontation.

Unfortunately, the world has not become more secure or predictable since the end of the Cold War and the collapse of the communist regimes. The crisis arc has spread from North-west China to the Balkans, or perhaps even further, namely from the Philippines to Senegal. The conflict in Chechnya is just a link in this chain. The failure of attempts to resolve it is an alarm signal to the whole world community.

9 Theories of Post-communist Nationalism

Andrus Park

Introduction

There is a multitude of general and specific factors determining the nature of post-communist nationalism and an attempt will be made here to identify just some of them. Eight specific groups of causes of post-communist nationalism, often mentioned in the relevant literature, may be distinguished:

- the effect of 'unfreezing' after the collapse of the artificial stability, imposed by communism
- the existence of the perceptions of 'ethnic guilt' for imposing communism
- the communist ethnic cleansing and destruction of nations
- the Communist construction of nations, especially the role of the Soviet federal system which was meant to be a propaganda tool but obtained a real political character under *perestroika*
- the ethno-regional differences of sacrifices under the command economy
- the existence of the post-communist social and spiritual 'vacuum', especially the underdevelopment of civil society
- the role of the relative success/failures of the post-communist economic transition
- the role of the conspiracies and special interests of the old and new political elites.

These groups of causes are playing an important role in forming post-communist nationalism, although explanations offered in those terms are obviously somewhat vague and are often not open to strict statistical interpretations. But this seems to be an almost inevitable result of the complexity of the phenomenon of nationalism itself as well as the language employed by social scientists in studies of this kind.

The Concept of Nationalism

The concepts of nations and nationalism are extremely vague and this may be one of the reasons why they can be so successfully utilized by many interest groups. Katherine Verdery has rightly emphasized that 'nation' legitimizes numerous social actions, often having very 'diverse aims'. Because its meaning is ambiguous, people who use it differently can mobilize dissimilar constituencies who 'think that they understand the same thing by it'.[1]

The word *nation* is used here to denote an ethnic group or *ethnos*, members of which have historical roots, a cultural heritage, self-identification, language and an industrial or post-industrial level of socioeconomic development in common.[2] *Nation-state* is here to be understood as an idealized model of a state where a nation is matched with state. There are no absolutely pure nation-states in the world, but some states (for example, North Korea, South Korea, Japan and Poland) come quite close. *Nationalism* here means what is usually called ethnonationalism. As Anthony Smith says, 'unlike the territorial and civic versions of nationalism, ethnic nationalism conceives of the nation as a genealogical and vernacular community'.[3] Various forms of civic nationalism[4] are here described with such words as 'patriotism', 'imperialism' and 'separatism'. I also prefer to use the word 'peoples' to distinguish what is often called a nation in a civic and territorial sense. I also generally agree with those who think that nationalism was born at the end of the eighteenth century,[5] although much in this chronology depends on how we define nationalism.

Nationalist movements are usually 'organizational vehicles for the articulation of arguments over rights, goods, status, power, and other material and political issues'.[6] In my view, nationalism usually nurtures one or many of the following aims:

- To ensure the survival of a given nation; to stress that 'values associated with the nation are paramount and that they are worthy of defence'.[7]
- To create or restore an independent nation-state: 'Nationalism is primarily a principle, which holds that the political and the national unit should be congruent.'[8] If the creation of a nation-state is impossible, then nationalism may attempt to achieve more moderate goals of cultural, economic or political autonomy for a nation within some existing state.

- To pursue policies aimed at maintaining or increasing the dominant political and economic position of a certain nation in a given state. Such policies may vary from a very liberal form (for example, when a government is simply avoiding any interference in ethnic relations, knowing that democratic and market-based self-regulation will benefit the more populous and richer ethnic groups) to nasty cases of genocide and ethnic cleansing.[9]
- To increase the power of a given nation-state and its influence on other states. This aim may take several forms, such as the current Japanese version of 'soft' and largely economic nationalism[10] or the old-fashioned strategy of imperial expansionism, characteristic of Germany under Adolf Hitler.[11]
- To claim the right of a given nation-state to govern over the territories, historically 'belonging' to the given nation and its ancestors, or currently populated by it.[12]
- To underscore the superiority of a given nation – for example, in cultural terms – over others.[13]
- To emphasize generally the importance of the collective rights of nations as distinct from individual rights. Among collective rights, nationalism often interprets the right of self-determination not only in territorial but also in ethnic terms.[14]
- To reject up to a certain degree even otherwise economically beneficial policies if they obviously threaten to erode the cultural identity of a given ethnic group.
- To minimize the power and influence of another nation(s), against which a given nation is mobilized.[15]

As stated above, a particular nationalism is not necessarily committed to all or even to most of these listed goals, although it usually aspires to achieve at least one of them. It may also be true to say that radical nationalism is usually characterized by increased intolerance against dissenting views and by a readiness to sacrifice for the nation: 'When nationalist appeals work, the claims of other identities and the possibility of calculating self-interest are simply not noticed.'[16]

By post-communist nationalism it is intended here to denote the nationalism that has emerged in the post-communist states of East–Central Europe and in the former Soviet Union (FSU). Post-communist nationalism has some distinctive features, connected with the nature of revolutionary transition. Since communism is widely considered as some kind of social illness, as a deviation from the 'normal', mainstream pattern of world development, all ethnic changes under communism are prone to be treated as illegitimate. Moreover, the nationalist parties of East–Central Europe often claim that the post-1989 liberal regimes have betrayed the true revolution. Despite their anti-communism, the national–radical groups often have 'no great love for the Western democracies, distrusting supranational liberalism', are fearful of consumerism, and, at the extreme, also blame the West for 'selling out Central Europe to the Russians and the Communists'.[17] In Russia, on the other hand, nationalism is often nostalgic about the imperial/Soviet past and even more hostile towards the West.[18]

Ethnic conflict, in this context, means a conflict over the rights of a certain ethnic group within a given state or states (including the attempts by that group to create a separate nation-state or pursue other nationalist goals). Ethnic conflicts may be domestic (involving one state) or international (if several states are involved in the given ethnic conflict). As Charles Maynes has noted there have been four traditional methods of solving ethnic tensions: 'ethnic cleansing, repression, partition, or power sharing. Of the four, ethnic cleansing ironically appears the most politically effective, albeit the most morally reprehensible.'[19]

Nationalism: Destructive and Constructive

Nationalism is such a value-laden concept that it is almost impossible to remain completely neutral when examining it.[20] Some authors have noted the positive role of nationalism in the overthrow of communism. For example, Stephen Bowers has written: 'in the revolutions of 1989, nationalism – complete with all its assumptions about the importance of the ethnic community ... was a positive force in helping produce a popular rejection of the notion of East European membership in a Soviet empire.'[21] Others are convinced that nationalism and democracy are irreconcilable. In the words of Steven Burg: 'ethnically based claims to autonomy thus strike at the heart of the process of democratization, since they compete with individual rights-based legitimation of a liberal democratic order.'[22] Nationalism is often perceived as a major obstacle on the road of economic reform.[23] It is also assumed that ethnicity works against social mobility, since ethnicity is a static phenomenon. Given the importance of ethnicity in Eastern Europe, the prospects for economic and social development there 'are seriously limited'.[24] In sum, nationalism may have had a positive role in the overthrow of communism, but its role became controversial in post-communist settings – that is, 'once the revolutions were accomplished, nationalism's role changed'.[25]

My opinion is close to that of George Soros who has said that national feelings are 'ubiquitous' and that they can play a positive role, fostering pluralism in an open society: 'Only when national feelings are exploited for the sake of creating a closed society does nationalism constitute a threat.'[26]

More specifically, most people's estimate of nationalism is intimately connected with their world-view. Obviously, those who share totalitarian or authoritarian values also have their own perception of nationalism. However, for the mainstream, loosely defined as supporting the liberal–democratic world-view (a group to which I belong), the basic problem seems to be whether nationalism is compatible with other more or less unquestionably positive values, such as peace, prosperity and democracy.

There are certainly circumstances in which nationalist movements lead to violence, poverty and dictatorships, but there are others in which nationalism has been conducive to peace, relative prosperity and democracy. Looking at the post-communist scenario, it seems indisputable that nationalism has contributed to the bloodshed and destruction in Bosnia, Croatia, Georgia, Armenia, Azerbaijan, Moldova and other places. On the other hand, it seems equally obvious that the prospects of peace, relative prosperity, and democracy were strengthened in Estonia or Slovenia as a result of these states gaining independence from their former 'centres'. The case of Estonia is especially instructive in comparison with Russia: Estonia carried out a successful currency reform in 1992, achieved macroeconomic stabilization in 1992–93, held its first democratic elections in 1992 and was admitted to the Council of Europe in 1993. In short, it passed almost all the identifiable milestones of post-communist transition long before Russia and, in 1991–93, achieved much of what the local nationalists in 1988–90 were promising when they argued that it was important to get off the sinking 'Russian ship' as quickly as possible. There are also earlier historical parallels: for example, it is unlikely that Finland would have been better off had it not seceded from Russia in 1917 and had it not defended its independence against Soviet aggression in 1939–40.

Three Categories of Causes

With considerable simplification, it is possible to distinguish three very broad categories of causes responsible for the upsurge of nationalism and ethnic tensions in the post-communist countries: general, pre-communist and specific. As indicated above, attention here will focus on the third group – that is, the specific communism-related causes of nationalism. Nevertheless, it is instructive at the outset to briefly discuss the first two categories.

By general causes are meant factors of nationalism that exist more or less universally and are not specifically connected with the pre-communist,

communist or post-communist situations. For example, nationalism historically occurred as a result of industrial revolution, the spread of literacy, urbanization and other general developments.[27] At the end of the twentieth century, there are several clear worldwide trends which make the further growth of nationalism very likely. As Anthony Smith has said: 'there is nothing especially novel about the present period of ethnic eruption and nationalistic conflicts. Given the power of ethnic ties and the force of national identity, we could expect periodic renewals of ethnic nationalisms.'[28] Others have pointed out that 'ethnic strife may be an unavoidable by-product of change'.[29] Liah Greenfeld has stressed rightly that modern economic 'globalization is entirely consistent with nationalism' and that it 'should be remembered that nationalism originally was able to spread only because a degree of globalization already existed'.[30] The communications revolution also contributes to nationalism, since it leads to the growing perception of political and economic inequalities between ethnic groups.[31] Paul Kennedy has also identified something similar, saying that 'the coming of a telecommunications revolution to developing countries could well cause billions of "have-nots" to feel ever more angry at the "haves"'.[32] A similar feeling is also shared by Stephen Griffiths, who says that 'the emergence of the "globalization" phenomenon is, paradoxically, strengthening local and ethnic allegiances around the world'.[33]

It is now almost universally accepted that 'the technology gap between developed and developing world will continue to widen'.[34] It has also been claimed that:

> There will be an unstoppable mass movement of people from South to North, including to Japan. The growing polarization of wealth and poverty makes this an option which no amount of border guards can successfully police.[35]

It is not difficult to see that such unstoppable migration is likely to cause anti-foreigner nationalism in the developed countries. In fact, all three of the trilateral powers – Europe, the United States and Japan – now have 'relations with the developing world on their doorsteps and within their thresholds which have ethnic implications'.[36] There is also a global 'demonstration effect', in which the example of one successful ethnic nationalism stimulates the claims of another.[37] In this connection it is noteworthy that the rising great powers (Japan, Germany and China) are not characterized by the American or British tolerance on ethnic matters. At the same time, as Zbigniew Brzezinski has rightly emphasized:

> ... [the Japanese] national sense of unique identity, the cohesion of its national community, the special ability of its society to generate a shared sense of

direction, and the persistent pursuit of longer-range strategic goals have cumulatively propelled Japan again to the front ranks of world economic power.[38]

The second category includes pre-communist causes – that is, specific historical, geographical and psychological features of today's post-communist countries which were already in place long before communism. These would include, for example, such catalysts of nationalism as the late peripheral industrialization of Russia and Eastern Europe, the fight of many emerging nationalities against erstwhile empires (Russian, Ottoman, Austro-Hungarian), and the specific meaning of blood-relations in the formation of East European nationalisms. Since the Russian and Ottoman empires were considered especially backward, some separatist nationalist movements there were based in relatively more developed areas, whereas in Western Europe separatist nationalist movements often (although not always) emerged in less developed borderlands. Apparently Juliana Pilon is right, saying that by 'contrast to Western Europe, where relative national homogeneity had been achieved before the nineteenth century, East–Central Europe continued to accentuate and nurture differences'.[39] Hans Kohn claimed some time ago that nationalism in East–Central Europe arose not only later, but also generally at a more backward stage of social and political development, than in Western Europe. He asserted that nationalism in this region aimed to redraw the political boundaries in conformity with ethnographic demands and was tinged with pathological, even irrational elements, while the Western nationalism was at least originally 'based on reality'.[40] Anthony Smith also thinks that the 'civic and territorial pattern' of nation largely prevailed in the West (Great Britain, France, Spain, the Netherlands and Sweden). On the other hand, in Eastern Europe and Russia the ethnic, genealogical conception of the nation prevailed, and 'ethnic nationalism aimed at forging nations on the basis of pre-existing *ethnies*'.[41] Several specific features of Russian nationalism also originate from the pre-communist era. For example, Paul Goble has rightly noted that the Russian empire was built 'before the nation at its center was fully consolidated, thus leaving open the question of the boundaries of identity for the metropolitan county and its periphery'.[42]

Specific Communism-related Causes of Nationalism

The Effect of Unfreezing

One of the most frequently mentioned causes of post-communist nationalism is unfreezing: since communist totalitarianism imposed an artificial stability on domestic and international affairs of many countries, it is only natural that long-suppressed animosities emerged powerfully when the whole system was relaxed and democratized.[43] The recurring ethnic quarrels appear much as they were when they were restrained by Soviet power.[44] In other words, 'East Europe's ethnic peace was misleading and was the product, not of genuine harmony, but of brutal enforcement by leaders'.[45] As Barry Posen says, the nationalist preparation for conflict was 'hidden away in the home' in long-repressed multi-ethnic societies such as Yugoslavia.[46] But communist repressions were not enough to eradicate nationalist feelings; they provided only a temporary solution, since those 'repressed only await the day when they can rise up'.[47] Therefore it is not surprising that the newly won freedom was marked by the emergence of vocal nationalism. The collapse of governments which imposed tranquillity in communities harbouring traditional animosities towards each other, has been marked by an outburst of long-suppressed bigotry. 'For many people, racial and ethnic slurs, like pornography, are simply expressions of a new-found freedom.'[48]

The post-communist explosion of nationalism can be also explained within the framework of a wider 'swing theory'. As Kenneth Minogue and Beryl Williams put it:

> The most elementary observation to be made about the Soviet Union in these terms is that after decades of force-fed universalism, the most likely swing would have to be toward the most obviously available particularism. And that, of course, seems to be nationalism.[49]

Responsibility for Communism

From the purely scientific point of view it is meaningless to distinguish more and less guilty nations in communist takeovers. Yet such perceptions of 'ethnic guilt' play an important role in the formation of nationalist ideologies.

The primary and secondary cases of the birth of communism can easily be interpreted in ethnic terms. The 1917 Bolshevik revolution in Russia was undoubtedly the most important landmark in the formation of communist regimes. Certainly in 1917–20 there was a genuine mass support for failed attempts to establish communist dictatorships in many parts of the erstwhile Russian, Austro-Hungarian and German empires. But that support soon dwindled and most of the later cases of Communist transition were determined by the Soviet Union's military power rather than by domestic factors in the relevant countries.

For example, the Bolsheviks garnered 40.2 per cent of the popular vote in Estonia during the Russian Constituent Assembly elections on 12–14

November 1917. But, as the results of the incomplete elections to the Estonian Constituent Assembly on 21–22 January 1918 showed, the support for the communists had by then declined considerably already,[50] and the Bolsheviks were defeated in the war between Russia and Estonia in 1918–20. During the democratic parliamentary elections in independent Estonia in 1920–32 communists were never able to gain more than 10 per cent of seats according to a proportional representation system.[51] The support for communism seemed also to have been quite weak under the mild right-wing dictatorship of Konstantin Päts between 1934 and 1940. In the spring of 1940 there were only 133 members of the Communist Party in Estonia,[52] and there is no doubt that the Soviet regime in Estonia in 1940 was imposed by the Soviet military force and not by the popular consent of the local population.[53] As Henry Huttenbach has rightly pointed out, the fact of the 1940 annexation was later used by the Baltic national movements to give 'legal, historical dimension to their aspirations'.[54]

With a certain simplification we can similarly interpret other instances of communist victory in Eastern Europe and in the FSU as secondary cases – that is, they took place primarily because the Leninist regime triumphed in Russia. The secondary nature of the imposition of communism was most obvious between 1939 and 1945, when Red Army tanks brought Leninist regimes to the Baltic states, Moldova, Poland, East Germany, Hungary and so on. Even when the Soviet role was not so dominant (as, for example, in Yugoslavia), it still played an important background role. Stephen Bowers says rightly that in East–Central Europe the post-war leaders 'were installed in office after having spent the turbulent war years in Moscow where they acquired blatant Soviet orientations on most issues of national development'.[55]

Since the Russians were the dominant nation in the Soviet Union, it is not surprising that the forceful imposition of communism often contributed to anti-Russian nationalist feelings. For example, in the Baltic states communism was often considered to be something specifically related to Russian nationalism:

> The Soviet Bolshevik system declared itself a staunch advocate of mankind's social needs and insisted that brotherhood and equality should reign among all peoples and nations, while in reality it carried out the imperialist expansion policies of the messianic Russian nationalists.[56]

The fact that communism has been so directly linked to Russia may be one of the reasons why Russian nationalism itself has been particularly active in stressing the non-Russian roots of many Bolshevik leaders. The fact that many top communists in the Soviet Union (such as Leon Trotsky,

Joseph Stalin, Lavrenty Beria, Lazar Kaganovich and Felix Dzerzhinsky) were not ethnic Russians and that Marxist ideology originated from the West plays an important role in various conspiracy theories which aim to show that the Russians themselves were subjected to communism as a result of some plot, and suffered more than other nations. As Mikhail Lobanov puts it, Lenin's hostility towards Great Russian chauvinism proved his anti-Russian 'satanic racism'.[57]

Communist Destruction of Nations

In a curious way, the communist system simultaneously destroyed and constructed nations, creating, in both ways, presuppositions for the post-communist nationalism. First, the communist regime in the Soviet Union carried out monstrous terror and genocide campaigns against numerous nationalities. A number of nations (including the Crimean Tatars, Kalmyks, Karachais, Chechens and Ingushes) were deported to the eastern parts of the Soviet Union. Substantial segments of some other nations (for example, Lithuanians and Ukrainians) were also deported. Some quite small nations (like Estonians and Latvians) were put on the verge of extinction first through deportations and later through mass migration from other parts of the Soviet Union and forced Russification. As the Estonian president, Lennart Meri, claimed, 'ethnic cleansing' in Estonia was an 'everyday phenomenon' for 50 years.[58] One of the sources of nationalism among small nations is a self-defence reaction – a perception that there is an imminent danger of extinction. This perception can be traced very well through sociological material. For example, a sociological survey (carried out among ethnic Estonians and ethnic Russians living in Estonia in 1993) indicated that 67 per cent of Estonians thought then (that is, two years after the republic had gained independence) that Estonians as a nation were still in danger of disappearance, whereas 75 per cent of Russians either could not answer the question or thought that there had never been such a risk of extinction.[59]

Tens of small ethnic groups in the north-west and north of Russia, in Siberia and in the far east of the country either disappeared or lost their cultural identity during the Soviet period.[60] Whole segments of the East European nations were also murdered – consider, for example, the killing of Polish officers at Katyn in 1940.[61]

The consequence of such communist ethnic cleansing was to create a nationalist backlash in the name of restoring historical justice as soon as the regime was relaxed. One of the most terrible lessons from the Stalinist legacy for future butchers of nations may be: if you start to implement elements of genocide, you have to go the whole way, since the decimated nations will never forgive the atrocities. While the communist terror left unsurpassed horror stories in the archives of history, it was still not enough to destroy most of the concerned nations completely, inevitably paving the way for a future nationalist revenge.

The communist destruction of nations also took the form of imposing the cultures of dominant nations, most usually that of the Russians. For example, Juliana Pilon stated that 'after the Communist takeover in Romania, the Romanian Academy's linguistic work ... was designed to prove that Romanian was really a Slavic language rather than a modern version of the Latin imposed by the Romans in the first century A.D.'.[62] It was quite clear to the ethnic groups in the Soviet Union that the formation of a new 'Soviet people' could take place most probably at the expense of the 'vitality of the separate national cultures'.[63] Or, as Walter Clemens has stressed, the ideal of national self-determination in the former Soviet Union is driven by the desires to 'cast off the structures of alien exploitation as well as to realize fully the potential of the national culture'.[64]

Communist Construction of Nations

Although the Soviet Union was often (and with justification) called a graveyard of nations, the whole story was not so simple. While destroying nations on one hand, the Soviet regime constructed and created institutional presuppositions for the Soviet Union's disintegration and post-communist nationalism on the other. Here one has in mind not so much the pre-1917 period (when the Bolsheviks were often appealing to the idea of national self-determination to mobilize support for their party), or the early 1920s (when the Soviet Union was created as a very centralized union of Soviet republics), or the period in the 1920s (when Moscow was, to a certain degree, really pursuing the policies of 'nativization' in non-Russian areas and encouraging local cultures).[65] What is referred to is Stalin's willingness, during the years of his absolute domination over the Soviet state and society, to maintain and develop the fictitious Soviet federation. While it would have been apparently possible for him to abolish all the union republics, he presumably preferred to preserve the elaborated set of national–territorial units for propaganda purposes, to demonstrate the successful federal solution of the 'national question' under socialism. Knowing that union republics had no real autonomy, that even the price of cinema tickets or recipes for cakes in local cafes were confirmed in Moscow, it seemed absolutely safe to create parliaments, foreign ministries or academies of sciences for the republics. Under this system the dominant nation – the Russians – had a peculiar position. As Paul Goble has well pinpointed, 'the Russians were offered the choice of being free or being powerful; not surprisingly they chose the latter at the behest of Stalin and thus became the sociological basis of the Stalinist state'.[66]

Although some corporativist arrangements developed after Stalin's death, when the republican communist elites gradually increased their influence in Moscow's corridors of power, the Soviet federation essentially remained an artificial structure until *perestroika*. Once Mikhail Gorbachev began – whether knowingly or due to miscalculation – to weaken the principal centralizing instruments of the Soviet state the fictional republican institutions (such as supreme soviets and foreign ministries) started to take on real functions and act independently from Moscow. The very fact that the Soviet Union in 1991, with amazing speed and relatively little bloodshed, broke into 15 independent states according to their pre-1991 interrepublican borders, underlines the real-political effect of the federal arrangements in the 1936 Stalinist and 1977 Brezhnevist constitutions – arrangements that were considered quite irrelevant during the time of their adoption. In other words, in the long run the Soviet Union would have disintegrated anyway, although it is not difficult to see how much more complicated that process would have been had the Soviet Union been merely a cluster of *oblasts* without any national–territorial autonomies (however phoney).

Sacrifices under the Command Economy

The dwindling command economy system contributed to nationalism in a number of ways but all these were connected with differences in wealth, as well as perceptions that the relative losses of some nations on account of communism have been greater than those of others. In this context, a few features deserve attention.

First, one of the reasons for nationalism was the sharp (and often perfectly accurate) perception of lost opportunities caused by the imposition of an economically backward system imposed by a foreign power (dominated by an alien nation). For example, as a quite comprehensive Estonian–Finnish study states, it 'is a common, if not a very well documented idea, that the standards of living in Estonia and Finland were roughly on the same level in the inter-war period'.[67] At the same time there is 'no doubt that economic development has been faster in Finland than in Estonia, resulting in a higher standard of living and better consumption possibilities for Finns today'.[68] According to some estimates, household income per capita in 1988 was eight times lower in Estonia than in Finland.[69] The lost opportunities concept is important, since the disintegrationist trends in the Soviet Union were spearheaded by the peoples of the Baltic and Caucasus – the most affluent nations in the Union. Theoretically they might have been interested in preserving their relative well-being in the Soviet empire, but in practice they were the most active separatists because they reckoned on much higher living standards after achieving independence – a dream which subsequently seemed much more attainable in the Baltics than in Transcaucasus.[70]

Second, some communist nations felt increasingly that others were living at their expense. Stephen Bowers identified just one aspect of the problem when he wrote:

> Ethnic tension is generated by the perception of many of East Europe's larger ethnic groups that they have carried an undue burden of providing for the development of their nations while the smaller and perhaps poorer groups have become more or less 'welfare' cases. Conversations with Czechs speaking of Slovaks frequently reveal this tendency.'[71]

Smaller and richer nations often had the same feeling. For example, Estonians recurrently attributed their relatively higher living standard to their traditional Estonian–German work ethic, feeling bitterness at being forced to feed Russians, who after all invented and imposed the communist system on Estonia. On the other hand, the Russians themselves often felt that their oil revenues were subsidizing the unproductive economies of Estonia, the other Soviet republics and the Soviet bloc in general. However, when the Soviet leadership tried to use this dependence to contain separatist tendencies, the result was usually exactly the opposite from that intended. For example, in February 1987, speaking in Tallinn, Gorbachev emphasized that, each year, Estonia was receiving from other parts of the Soviet Union goods worth 3 billion roubles, whereas Estonia's own input into 'Soviet economic complex' was worth only 2.5 billion roubles – in other words, in Gorbachev's view Estonia's economy was being subsidized by Moscow to the extent of 0.5 billion roubles per year.[72] Contrary to Gorbachev's probable expectations, this transparent warning about Estonia's economic unviability encouraged separatist drives. In September 1987 Estonian intellectuals published a proposal to introduce 'economic autonomy' for Estonia – that is, a scheme under which Estonia would have obtained a considerable degree of independence and traded with other parts of the Soviet Union on the basis of convertible currency.[73] Allegations of living at another's expense are probably not new in any kind of nationalism but what was specific to communism was the degree to which the tight censorship and distorted price structure made it impossible to make any objective assessments about the real economic relations between the communist countries. In other words, nationalism was fuelled by the same failure of the closed Soviet system to cope with the information-era technology which contributed to many other facets of the Soviet crisis.[74]

Third, the command economy was characterized by excessive demand, subsidized prices, chronic shortages of goods and huge queues. The economy of shortages inevitably created a specific hostility against visitors from other regions who were (partially rightly) viewed as enemies coming to empty the local stores of scarce and cheap subsidized goods. This hostility was usually not extended to visitors from the West, since there were so few of them and the Western system in general was popularly admired for wider reasons. Nonetheless, the command economy was exceptionally efficient in alienating one communist nation from another.[75]

The Post-communist Social and Spiritual Vacuum

Ernest Gellner has well diagnosed the social and spiritual emptiness of the post-communist society:

> Communism has destroyed much of civil society, and the monopolistic organization and faith which replaced it have gone down leaving something which must be as close to a social and moral vacuum as is conceivable in a complex, relatively advanced industrial society. Nationalism is the most plausible and most easily available candidate for filling this emptiness.[76]

Some authors attribute the vitality of nationalism also to the 'emptiness' of the previously imposed official communist culture itself[77] and to the absence of a meaningful tradition of the 'overlapping group memberships in Eastern Europe' that 'might serve to elevate popular consciousness above narrowly defined concerns that correspond to ethnicity'.[78]

The different levels of the development of civil society in an established democracy and in a post-communist state can be illustrated by the relative number of voluntary associations in Finland and Estonia. (A voluntary association is here understood as 'a formation of three or more persons the objective of which is to advance some common interest of its members'.)[79] Voluntary associations can be divided according to their main concerns – such as culture and education, religion, sports, economic and professional, social welfare, hobbies, and issues of war and peace – and in countries like Finland they are officially registered by state. Aili Aarelaid–Tart and Martti Siisiäinen estimated that, at the beginning of 1990s, the number of voluntary associations in Finland per comparable number of population was almost seven times higher than in Estonia.[80]

Whatever is the exact definition of a social and moral vacuum, it is a fact that there was very little perception and articulation of specific (non-ethnic) social group interests during the first stages of anti-communist revolution. Perhaps the picture was slightly different in Russia and Serbia – that is, in the heartlands of the communist geopolitical systems – but the domination of common interests of national liberation was absolutely overwhelming in the areas of classic periphery transitions such as Estonia. Rein Ruutsoo has identified the period 1987–91 in Estonia as a 'movement society', characterized by the 'pre-dominance of large-scale integrative movements'.[81] Nothing exemplifies this phenomenon better than the emergence of Popular Fronts – that is, broad democratic movements which, during their peak, united almost everybody from liberally minded party nomenklatura to half-dissident intellectuals. The birth of the Estonian Popular Front in April 1988 and its death in November 1993[82] are therefore important landmarks in filling the social vacuum.

The Relative Success of Post-communist Economic Transition

A number of old causes of nationalism continue to operate amidst the painful transition to market economy. For example, the feeling of lost opportunities may become even stronger when it becomes increasingly clear how difficult it is to catch up with the advanced Western nations. At the same time it is likely that the hatred of foreign buyers, in its primitive communist form, will almost disappear when capitalism will really establish itself.

A deep economic crisis and the impoverishment of a majority of a population always creates fruitful grounds for extremist agitation, whether fascist, communist or radical nationalist. As George Soros has said:

> Economic prosperity and nationalist dictatorships are inversely related. That is to say, it is in periods of economic crisis, particularly hyperinflation, that nationalism can take such a virulent form. Of course, we all remember that hyperinflation during the Weimar Republic led to the rise of Hitler.[83]

Stephen Bowers has also highlighted that the new post-communist order is experiencing some significant disappointments and that these setbacks frequently promote a greater 'ethnic consciousness as an element of popular anxiety' and ethnic concerns can assume a pivotal role if 'those parties credited with forcing the Communists out of office fail in delivering the economic benefits sought by most voters'.[84]

The main economic causes of nationalism in post-communist settings continue to be connected with dissimilarities such as those between the more and less successful reformers and between the poor and rich social groups. Since the overall economic situation in most of the post-communist countries is harsh, there is, and will be, enough fuel for mutual ethnically flavoured accusations concerning unfair trade, subsidizing, dumping and other similar practices. A special role is played by the post-communist quarrels over dividing the communist-era common property and paying compensation for environmental damage and confiscated assets.

Post-communist nationalism receives an additional boost from the relative success of post-communist economic reform. As already mentioned, the accomplishments of Estonia, Latvia and Slovenia in the post-communist economic reform are likely to increase the national pride of dominating ethnic groups in those states. On the other hand, if the newly won independence leads to mounting economic difficulties (as in the Ukraine, for example), then it may contribute to an easing of the nationalist and separatist passions and pave the way for further integrationist tendencies. In any case, it should be mentioned that the smallness of a state 'by itself need not be a major obstacle to viable independence'.[85]

In some cases, ethnic groups in a state are affected differently by the economic transition. For example, in Estonia heavy industry and the defence industry was staffed mainly by Russians and run for Soviet needs. As Rein Taagepera has written:

> It was an industry based on Russian investment, largely Russian imported labor, management by Russians according to goals set by Russians, and export of most of Estonia's product to Russia. The entire show was called 'Estonian' because the Soviet authorities decided to run it on Estonian soil.[86]

Unsurprisingly, many of those heavy industry giants were unable to adapt to new economic circumstances after Estonia achieved independence, and the people working in this sector paid a relatively higher social price for the transition to a market economy than their compatriots in, say, the service sector or high technology. For example, according to one sociological study, the share of people, belonging in February 1993 to the lowest income group in Estonia (that is, earning less than US$23 per capita per month) was 30 per cent among ethnic Estonians and 41 per cent among ethnic Russians. At the same time 10 per cent of Estonians belonged to the highest income group (that is, earning more than US$77 per capita per month), whereas the comparable figure among Russians was 7 per cent.[87] Such social differences contribute to a certain extent to the development of post-communist nationalism.

A Conspiracy by Political Elites?

Perhaps the most popular theory of post-communist nationalism focuses on conspiracy – by both old and new elites. Serbia's president, Slobodan Milosevic, is undoubtedly one of the principal symbols of the conspiracy by the old communist nomenclature:

Milosevic, who was the head of the Communist apparat, realized that Communism was a dead horse and he changed horses. He mobilized Serbian nationalism by creating an emergency and suspending the autonomy of Kosovo.[88]

The *Washington Post's* Michael Dobbs observes that, for communist *apparatchiks*, nationalism has represented an almost 'miraculous way of hanging on to power following the collapse of Marxist-Leninist ideology. By handing in their party cards and wrapping themselves in the national flag, former Communists were able to acquire new political identities overnight.'[89] Indeed, there seems to be no doubt that ex-communist leaders, such as Boris Yeltsin in Russia or Algirdas Brazauskas in Lithuania, are appealing to nationalism and patriotism in order to attract popular support.

The role of leaders without an ex-communist background in promoting nationalism has also been identified by analysts. Stephen Bowers distinguishes it explicitly, stressing that the manifestation of ethnic politics in Eastern Europe is, at least in part, a result of 'the elites who are replacing the leadership of the old order. Many of the region's new leaders survived the repression of the Communist era as exponents of the interests of their particular ethnic community.'[90]

While the special interests of political elites undoubtedly play a significant role in the birth of nationalism, separatism and other similar trends, the explanations in those terms need some qualifications. First, explanations based on an elite's interests and hidden motives have often strong tautological features. Already it is possible to say by definition that nationalist elites have a vested interest in using nationalism to maintain power. In broader terms every major social development relies on the vested interests of some social groups.

Second, while the old communist elite was, by and large, undoubtedly corrupt, immoral and responsible for many horrors of totalitarian rule, promoting nationalism is not always its special sin. In fact, in many cases the political rivals of the former nomenclature are even more passionate nationalists. It may be different in Serbia and in a couple of other cases, but in a number of instances (for example, in Azerbaijan, Ukraine and Georgia) the former communist *apparatchiks* were, in 1991–93, just more successful than their rivals in exploiting the same nationalist issue. In other words, it is certainly true that in 1991–93 Leonid Kravchuk in Ukraine exploited nationalist feelings, but so did his opponents in *Rukh*. Eduard Shevardnadze appealed in 1993 to Georgian nationalist feelings, but so also did Zviad Gamsakhurdia. During his unsuccessful bid for Estonia's presidency in 1992 Arnold Rüütel tried to present himself as a true nationalist and patriot, but so also did all his opponents. In 1991 Ronald Suny encapsulated succinctly the options for the nomenclature:

For the foreseeable future, nationalism will be the dominant discourse for non-Russians and for the significant number of Russians, as well. Communists will either accommodate themselves to it, as Boris Yeltsin has been trying to do, or be out of the game.[91]

The Future Growth of Nationalism

It seems likely that in 15 to 20 years' time the specific post-communist reasons for nationalism may disappear. In other words, the Stalinist genocides and sacrifices under the command economy will be forgotten, the social cost of transition to market economy will be more or less compensated with the pleasures of capitalist consumerism, and the 'vacuum' will be filled by civil society institutions. But nationalism, in its more general forms, will remain a factor in East European politics for a very long time to come for more general reasons:

> Ethnic conflict is likely to be a permanent feature of the regional political landscape and, perhaps, the most optimistic future is one in which the leaderships of Eastern Europe learn not how to eliminate ethnic strife but how to live with it.[92]

Moreover, nationalism will probably dominate the global scene in the first decades of the next century because of the expectations revolution in the 'global village', the multiplying international migration pressures and the relative rise of Japan, China, Germany and other powers that are not characterized by Anglo–American ethnic tolerance. But this twenty-first-century nationalism – although also characterized by negative and positive features – will have only negligible and remote connections with the specific post-communist form of nationalism.

Notes

1. Katherine Verdery (1993), 'Whither "Nation" and "Nationalism"?' *Daedalus*, **122**, (3), Summer, p. 38.
2. For ways of distinguishing the terms 'nation' and 'ethnic group,' see: Stephen I. Griffiths (1993), *Nationalism and Ethnic Conflict: Threats to European Security*, Oxford, p. 127.
3. Anthony D. Smith (1993), 'The Ethnic Sources of Nationalism', *Survival*, **35**, (1), Spring, p. 55.
4. About civic nationality and nationalism see: Katherine Verdery (1993), 'Whither "Nation" and "Nationalism"?', note 1 *supra*, p. 38; Jack Snyder (1993), 'Nationalism and the Crisis of the Post-Soviet State', *Survival*, **35**, (1), Spring, pp. 5–26.

5   Smith, 'The Ethnic Sources of Nationalism', note 3 *supra*, p. 58.
6   Steven L. Burg (1993), 'Nationalism Redux: Through the Glass of the Post-Communist States Darkly', *Current History*, April, p. 164.
7   Peter Harris (1986), *Foundations of Political Science*, 2nd edn, London, p. 348.
8   Ernest Gellner (1983), *Nations and Nationalism*, Oxford, p. l.
9   About various policies of nationalist domination see Francis Fukuyama (1993), *The End of History and the Last Man*, New York, pp. 266–75.
10 About Japanese 'soft' nationalism see Joseph S. Nye, jr. (1991), *Bound To Lead: The Changing Nature of American Power*, p. 169.
11 Jack Snyder (1991), *Myths of Empire: Domestic Politics and International Ambition*, New York, pp. 92–95; 105–11.
12 Stephen R. Bowers (1992), 'Ethnic Politics in Eastern Europe', *Conflict Studies*, February, p. 7.
13 Ibid.
14 About the modern concept of self-determination see Morton Halperin and David J. Scheffer with Patricia Small, *Self-Determination in the New World Order*, Washington, DC, pp. 1–122.
15 George Soros (1993), *Nationalist Dictatorships versus Open Society*, New York, p. 4.
16 Paul C. Stern (1993), 'Why do People Sacrifice for their Nations?', *The Working Paper Series*, no. 163, Center for Studies of Social Change, New School for Social Research, June, p. 185.
17 Thomas S. Szayna (1993), 'Ultra-Nationalism in Central Europe', *Orbis*, **37**, (4) Fall, p. 547.
18 Andrus Park (1993), 'Ideological Dimension of the Post-Communist Domestic Conflicts', *Communist and Post-Communist Studies*, **26**, (3) September, p. 268.
19 Charles W. Maynes (1993), 'Containing Ethnic Conflict', *Foreign Policy*, (90), Spring, pp. 11–12.
20 The experience of American universities attempting to combine multiculturalism and academic freedom shows how complex and perplexing can be race- and ethnicity-related problems even in a stable capitalist society. See, for example, Majid Tehranian (ed.) (1991), *Restructuring for Ethnic Peace: A Public Debate at the University of Hawaii*, Honolulu, pp. 1–184.
21 Bowers, 'Ethnic Politics in Eastern Europe', note 12 *supra*, p. 23.
22 Burg, 'Nationalism Redux', note 6 *supra*, p. 164.
23 Ibid., p. 165.
24 Bowers, 'Ethnic Politics in Eastern Europe', note 12 *supra*, p. 20.
25 Ibid., p. 23.
26 Soros, *Nationalist Dictatorships versus Open Society*, note 15 *supra*, p. 10.
27 Gellner, *Nations and Nationalism*, note 8 *supra*, pp. 19–52.
28 Anthony D. Smith (1993), 'A Europe of Nations – or the Nation of Europe?' *Journal of Peace Research*, **30**, (2), May, p. 131.
29 Bowers, 'Ethnic Politics in Eastern Europe', note 12 *supra*, p. 5.
30 Liah Greenfeld (1993), 'Transcending the Nations's Worth', *Daedalus*, **122**, (3) Summer, pp. 59–60.
31 Smith, 'A Europe of Nations', note 28 *supra*, p. 131.
32 Paul Kennedy (1993), *Preparing for the Twenty First Century*, New York, p. 63.
33 Griffiths, *Nationalism and Ethnic Conflict*, note 2 *supra*, p. 127.
34 Marvin Cetron and Owen Davies (1991), '50 Trends Shaping the World', *The Futurist*, September–October, p. 15.

35 Immanuel Wallerstein (1993), 'The World-System After the Cold War', *Journal of Peace Research*, **30**, (l), p. 5.
36 Michael Mann (1993), 'Nation-States in Europe and Other Continents: Diversifying, Developing, Not Dying', *Daedalus*, **122**, (3), p. 132.
37 Smith, 'A Europe of Nations', note 28 *supra*, p. 132.
38 Zbigniew Brzezinski (1993), *Out of Control: Global Turmoil on the Eve of the Twenty-First Century*, New York, p. 119.
39 Juliana G. Pilon (1992), *The Bloody Flag: Post-Communist Nationalism in Eastern Europe. Spotlight on Romania*, London, pp. 38–39.
40 Quoted in ibid., pp. 39–40.
41 Smith, 'The Ethnic Sources of Nationalism', note 3 *supra*, p. 55.
42 Paul Goble (1991), 'Imperial Endgame: Nationality Problems and the Soviet Future', in Harley Balzer (ed.), *Five Years that Shook the World,* Boulder, Col., p. 93.
43 See Burg, 'Nationalism Redux', note 6 *supra*, pp. 162–63.
44 Griffiths, *Nationalism and Ethnic Conflict*, note 2 *supra*, p. 127.
45 Bowers, 'Ethnic Politics in Eastern Europe', note 12 *supra*, p. 8.
46 Barry R. Posen (1993), 'Nationalism, the Mass Army and Military Power', *International Security*, **18**, (2), p. 122.
47 Maynes, 'Containing Ethnic Conflict', note 19 *supra*, p. 12.
48 Bowers, 'Ethnic Politics in Eastern Europe', note 12 *supra*, p. 6.
49 Kenneth Minogue and Beryl Williams (1992), 'Ethnic Conflict in the Soviet Union' in Alexander J. Motyl (ed.), *Thinking Theoretically About Soviet Nationalities*, New York, p. 239.
50 Toivo U. Raun (1991), *Estonia and the Estonians*, 2nd edn, Stanford, Cal., pp. 103–4.
51 Ibid., p. 113.
52 Ibid., p. 146.
53 Rein Taagepera (1993), *Estonia: Return to Independence*, Boulder, Col., pp. 58–68.
54 Henry Huttenbach (1990), 'Sources of National Movements', *Nationalities Papers*, **18**, (l), p. 51.
55 Bowers, 'Ethnic Politics in Eastern Europe', note 12 *supra*, p. 4.
56 'Lithuanian Nation: Victims and Losses (1940–1954)', *Revue Baltique*, **2**, (1), p. 45.
57 Mikhail Lobanov (1993), 'Podvizhniki i tushintsy', *Nash sovremennik*, (5), p. 136.
58 *Rahva Hääl*, 9 November 1993, p. 3. One of the latest statistical analyses of demographic changes in Estonia under the Soviet rule is presented in Ene Tiit (1993), 'Eesti rahvastik ja selle probleemid' ('Estonia's Population and its Problems'), *Akadeemia*, **5**, (9), pp. 1847–66.
59 Aksel Kirch *et al.* (1993), 'Estonia: A New Paradigm Between the Estonian Majority and Russian Minority', manuscript, Tallinn, p. 69.
60 See Margus Kolga *et al.* (1993), *Vene imneeriumi rahvaste punane raamat (The Red Book of the Nationalities of the Russian Empire)*, Tallinn, pp. 1–361.
61 See Lavrenty Beria's top secret letter to Jozef Stalin (5 March 1940) and Alexander Shelepin's top secret letter to Nikita Khrushchev (3 March 1959): *Voprosy istorii*, (l), 1993, pp. 17–21.
62 Pilon, *The Bloody Flag*, note 39 *supra*, p. 32.
63 Minogue and Williams, 'Ethnic Conflict in the Soviet Union', note 49 *supra*, p. 240.
64 Walter C. Clemens, jr. (1993), 'Soviet Centrifugalism: Republics as Independent Actors', *Nationalities Papers*, **21**, (2), p. 21.
65 Graham Smith (1990), 'Nationalities Policy from Lenin to Gorbachev' in Graham Smith (ed.), *The Nationalities Question in the Soviet Union*, London, pp. 2–7.
66 Goble, 'Imperial Endgame', note 42 *supra*, p. 94.

67 Olev Lugus (1993), 'Introduction' in Olev Lugus and Pentti Vartia (eds), *Estonia and Finland – A Retrospective Socioeconomic Comparison,* Helsinki, p. 1.
68 Kalevi Koljonen, Urve Venesaar and Mare Viies (1993), 'Consumption' in ibid., p. 213.
69 Robert Hagfors and Toivo Kuus (1993), 'Income – Structure and Distribution', in ibid., p. 328.
70 Clemens, 'Soviet Centrifugalism', note 64 *supra*, p. 21.
71 Bowers, 'Ethnic Politics in Eastern Europe', note 12 *supra*, p. 7.
72 *Tverdo idti dorogoi perestroiki i uqlubleniva demokratii,* Moscow, 1987, p. 29.
73 Taagepera, *Estonia: Return to Independence,* note 53 *supra*, pp. 128–9.
74 One of the excellent explanations of how the new technology contributed to the Soviet decline is presented in Joseph S. Nye, jr. (1990), *Bound to Lead: The Changing Nature of American Power,* New York, p. 121.
75 Andrus Park (1991), 'Beyond Perestroika', *Theory and Society,* **20**, p. 694.
76 Ernest Gellner (1993), 'Homeland of the Unrevolution', *Daedalus,* **122**, (3), p. 152.
77 Minogue and Williams, 'Ethnic Conflict in the Soviet Union', note 49 *supra*, p. 240.
78 Bowers, 'Ethnic Politics in Eastern Europe', note 12 *supra*, p. 21.
79 Aili Aarelaid-Tart and Martti Siisiäinen (1993), 'Voluntary Associations in Estonia and in Finland from the Nineteenth Century to the Present Time', *Proceedings of the Estonian Academy of Sciences. Humanities and Social Sciences,* (2), p. 216.
80 Ibid., p. 231.
81 Rein Ruutsoo (1993), 'Transitional Society and Social Movements in Estonia 1987–91', ibid., p. 211.
82 About the dissolution of the Estonian Popular Front see *Seitse Päeva,* (1), December 1993, p. 5.
83 Soros, *Nationalist Dictatorships versus Open Society,* note 15 *supra*, pp. 4–5.
84 Bowers, 'Ethnic Politics in Eastern Europe', note 12 *supra*, p. 4.
85 Clemens, 'Soviet Centrifugalism', note 64 *supra*, p. 21.
86 Taagepera, *Estonia: Return to Independence,* note 53 *supra*, p. 83.
87 Kirch *et al.*, 'Estonia: A New Paradigm', note 59 *supra*, p. 51.
88 Soros, *Nationalist Dictatorships versus Open Society,* note 15 *supra*, p. 5.
89 Quoted in Pilon, *The Bloody Flag,* note 39 *supra*, p. 36.
90 Bowers, 'Ethnic Politics in Eastern Europe', note 12 *supra*, p. 6.
91 Ronald Grigor Suny (1991), 'The Soviet South: Nationalism and the Outside World' in Maurice Mandelbaum (ed.), *The Rise of Nations in the Soviet Union,* New York, p. 76.
92 Bowers, 'Ethnic Politics in Eastern Europe', note 12 *supra*, p. 23.

10 The Legacies of Soviet Communism
David Carlton

Introduction

The purpose of this chapter is to reflect on what, with increasing perspective, may come to be seen as the principal legacies of the strange and murderous system that prevailed for so many decades in the so-called Soviet bloc. We may conveniently consider the subject under five headings – although there will inevitably be a degree of overlap involved:

- the ideological legacy
- the military legacy
- the legacy of the one-party police-state system
- the imperial legacy
- the economic legacy.

The Ideological Legacy

Here we are concerned with the formal ideology of the Warsaw Treaty Organization (WTO) regimes, namely Marxism–Leninism as, for example, taught in schools and universities. Among its principal tenets were:

- a proclamation that the ultimate destiny of humanity was to see the universal withering away of the state and the abolition of money
- a commitment in the meantime to the 'dictatorship of the proletariat' by a single political party and to the complete common ownership of the means of production, distribution and exchange (it being accepted that, although ultimately inevitable for all, different countries would arrive at this stage at different points in time)

- a commitment to the promotion of atheism.

What, if anything, is now left of this ideology? The answer appears to be virtually nothing. For even those who call themselves communists in the former Soviet Union (FSU) and Eastern Europe are not seeking and gaining votes on the basis of any seriously proclaimed belief in either the desirability or the practicability of this programme. True, they may believe to a greater or lesser extent in a high degree of public ownership, in far-reaching welfare provision and in an extensive role for the state in management of economic activity, but many democratic socialists and social democrats support, or have supported, aims of this kind without being Marxist–Leninists.

The likelihood is, then, that future generations will look back on the Marxist–Leninist era with incredulity. How, they will ask, could hundreds of millions of people have lived for so long under regimes with such unrealistic objectives? How could such extreme chiliasm have obtained such a large measure of apparent support or at least acquiescence? One answer may take the form of a denial that the Soviet-style regimes were really in practice as extreme as hostile contemporaries supposed. Those taking this line will presumably claim that Leon Trotsky's fall signalled an abandonment of any real commitment to Marxism–Leninism and that Josef Stalin and his successors were merely running the system for their own benefit while treating the ideology as little more than a joke. But my guess is that, once the relevant archives have been open for a few decades and a sense of perspective has had a chance to grow, most commentators will be driven to endorse the views of George Kennan, George Orwell, John Foster Dulles and many others who believed that Marxism–Leninism counted for a great deal in the Soviet bloc both in domestic and foreign policy terms long after Trotsky's fall and even after Stalin's demise also. Maybe, indeed, the death in 1992 of Mikhail Suslov, the last acknowledged ideological supremo to have a seat in the Politburo, will come to be seen as the first real turning point – opening the way to the unambiguous ideological apostacy of Mikhail Gorbachev.[1]

But whether future generations decide that, on balance, the role of ideology in the Soviet story was a determining force or largely a joke, the chances are that it will never revive sufficiently as a belief system even to be perceived by any significant number of people to be a major force in human affairs. (Perhaps China, still nominally wedded to Marxism–Leninism, could spring a surprise in this respect but surely not unless it radically alters its present approach to a range of economic policies.)

The Military Legacy

The military legacy of the Soviet experiment is of a very different character and hence likely to influence the evolution of Russia and of the international system as a whole to a degree that would be difficult to overestimate. The fact that the Soviets consistently spent at least 20 per cent of their GDP on arms between 1941 and 1989 means that Russia is, and will remain for the foreseeable future, a military superpower. This is, of course, particularly true with respect to nuclear weaponry and will remain true even if the Strategic Arms Reduction Talks (START) II Treaty is ratified and is implemented in full by 2002. Yet, in most other ways, Russia is now seen to be a country with declining influence and modest medium-term potential.

One consequence of this distorted Russian profile is that Europe will inevitably remain divided into two major military camps – though not necessarily bitterly adversarial ones as during the Cold War. The sheer size of the Russian nuclear arsenal, both in terms of warheads and means of delivery, in comparison with those of France or the UK (or even both of the latter combined) strongly suggests, for example, that the countries on the Western side of Europe will be bound to want to belong to a collective security organization from which Russia is excluded. This probably means that NATO will continue into the indefinite future – with the United States serving as a makeweight to balance Russian military preponderance in Europe. Alternatively, if the Americans insist on abandoning 'extended deterrence' we would surely see the EU developing its own security capability with unfortunate implications for those who wish to see a reduction rather than an increase in the nuclear forces held in Western Europe.

None of this would have been likely if their Soviet predecessors had left the present Russian leaders with a military inheritance commensurate with the country's general economic 'clout'. In such circumstances Russia might have been brought into the Western security system as a second-rank power rather than being perceived as a major potential adversary under future rulers who may turn out to be less benign than Boris Yeltsin.

The Legacy of the One-party Police-state System

In Russia, in particular, the point at issue is whether or not something approaching Western-style liberal democracy can survive into the medium-term future. For the fact is that the revived Russian Communist Party, by purporting to defend the interests of those who have lost, or are likely to lose, their jobs and pensions as the country attempts, however feebly, to adopt market-driven economic policies, still has a significant electoral following. Does this mean that liberal democracy in Russia will be extinguished if communist forces become increasingly influential?

Yeltsin organized the outlawing of the Communist Party of the Soviet Union in 1991 following the attempted military coup against Gorbachev. And, although he has been unable to prevent its re-emergence under Russian constitutional law, he has continued to claim that it was, and is, fundamentally inimical to liberal democracy. Yet it is at least arguable that most present-day communists are no longer anti-democratic nor do they still seriously believe in the Marxist–Leninist ideology. In fact, in 1991 the Communist Party as a whole was not responsible for the attempted coup, and in the preceding years it had presided over a great degree of liberalization and democratization – although not, it is true, over the adoption of Western-style pluralistic democracy. In short, the Communist Party of 1991 was not that of Lenin, of Stalin, or even of Nikita Khrushchev or Leonid Brezhnev. At the time of its dissolution at the hands of Yeltsin it was not therefore universally seen as unambiguously repressive. Hence many who now belong to, and vote for, its Russian successor may be presumed to support something nearer to its Gorbachevian, rather than its Stalinist, previous incarnation. All this is, of course, even more definitely the case in Eastern Europe where reformed versions of former communist parties have achieved much popularity – even winning back office in Hungary and Poland.

Many in the West may have expected the communists to suffer the fate of the German Nazis or the Italian fascists – that is, to have had no significant support in the aftermath of loss of power. But the difference is surely that, in the cases of the Nazis and fascists, the parties concerned had led their countries to catastrophic defeats in war (resulting incidentally in temporary foreign occupation) and, more importantly, were, when they lost power, at their worst in terms of symbolizing repression and violations of human rights. In short, those who wanted to revive Nazism in Germany after 1945 had to contend with the fact that the Holocaust was a feature of the last years of the previous incarnation of Nazism and that Adolf Hitler was there until the end; conversely, those who wished to revive communism in Russia after 1991 had the advantage that Stalin and Stalinism had been at their peak decades earlier and had given way by the late 1980s to *perestroika* and *glasnost*.

The chances are, therefore, that the one-party police-state legacy will prove to be of relatively limited significance to today's communists in Russia and Eastern Europe – although it seems set to be somewhat more difficult to exorcise in Russia than in Eastern Europe.

The Imperial Legacy

The Russian empire in the Soviet era certainly had one unique feature: it was marked by the fact that living standards in at least parts of the outlying empire were higher than in the metropolitan heartland – as any Russian visitor to Czechoslovakia, Hungary and even the German Democratic Republic (GDR) could have testified. There also seems little doubt that Russian subsidies to, say, the Central Asian Republics were exceptionally generous unless understood in terms of ideology. Consequently many in today's Russia feel about all their former possessions and satellites as Benjamin Disraeli once felt about British colonies – namely, that they were millstones around the mother country's neck. Thus, any future attempt by Moscow to recreate Stalin's empire in full would be extremely divisive, to say the least. In any case, at least some of the former WTO states seem likely to be allowed to join NATO, rendering them effectively beyond Russia's reach for the foreseeable future.[2]

However, even though the recreation of the lost empire in its entirety is highly unlikely, we may nevertheless see a considerable re-emergence of Russian influence over much of the 'near-abroad', simply because, after a period of self-assertiveness, some of the relevant states are coming to recognize the economic advantages of a close association with Moscow. Others have regimes which see merit in having Russian support against their Islamic extremist rebels sponsored from Afghanistan or possibly Iran, and yet others are aware of the extreme expense involved in forging new communication links if they dogmatically abandon the traditional ones via Russia in an attempt to avoid 'dependency'. Of course, none of this will be unfamiliar to students of many other newly–independent states. For example, Algeria, for all its early militancy, soon found its way back to a close practical relationship with France.

Where the Russians are concerned, then, we may conclude that a very mixed picture in this respect is emerging. The former WTO countries of East–Central Europe seem to be unanimous in their wish to move unambiguously away from Moscow's orbit. In the distant past they were usually undecided about whether Russia or Germany was the lesser evil, but now, thanks in large measure to the communist experience, they seem clearly to prefer the latter – something made easier by Germany's membership of NATO and the EU. The only limitation on this trend may be the Western reluctance to offer all concerned full integration into the EU and NATO. But should, say, Bulgaria or Romania be destined to be generally cold-shouldered by the West, it would seem unlikely that they would wish to return to full dependence on Moscow.

So far as the states of the FSU are concerned the picture is much more complicated. The Baltic states, for example, will apparently go to any lengths to avoid being pulled into Moscow's orbit. Nonetheless, the presence of Russian minorities in these countries – a legacy from Stalin – and the Western fear of unduly provoking Russia may mean that they cannot entirely rule out future threats from Moscow. On the other hand, Belarus seems eager to move into a relationship of close dependence on Russia. Ukraine, for its part, is deeply split, with its Russian-speaking east and the Crimea attracted to Moscow and its west looking unambiguously towards the West. The governments of the other nine states of the FSU are all, to varying degrees, unable or unwilling to cut off all links with Moscow, and many – especially those with a large minority of Russian ethnicity – are not entirely sorry to contemplate a future in which Russia will occasionally exercise what has been termed a 'Monroevsky Doctrine' in Central Asia and Transcaucasia.

This, then, is the complicated imperial legacy of the Soviet Union. But it is largely also the imperial legacy of Tsarist Russia and, as such, will be of great significance for decades to come.

The Economic Legacy

While entire volumes on this theme are already in print and many more will no doubt follow, only a few theses can be advanced here.

First, the economic disasters that Soviet-style communism brought to all the states under its jurisdiction has apparently ensured a long-term division of Europe into two economic camps which reinforce the military division already mentioned. Only a handful of such states can hope to qualify to join the EU in the foreseeable future, The former GDR has, of course, already been incorporated, although at great cost to the former West Germans (and other West Europeans). For a variety of complicated reasons, Poland, the Czech Republic and Hungary may also be deemed worthy to switch camps, and the Baltic States might soon develop the economic status to follow them – if political–military considerations do not rule this out. But 16 other states, including Russia itself, seem to have been too irremediably impoverished by the Marxist–Leninist experience to be able to make even the slightest case for membership of the EU for decades ahead. Those who think this is too severe a judgement should ask themselves how Western Europeans could otherwise possibly cope with those from the East who, if EU citizens, would surely be tempted to take advantage of their entitlement to live anywhere in the Union. Would there not be floods of migrants arriving from the FSU on every train, just as Albanians attempted to flee *en masse* to Italy? This, then, is Lenin's final cruel legacy to Europe – a Europe no longer divided on ideological lines but on lines of simple wealth and poverty.

Second, we have to face the fact that, in Russia at least, no sustained effort has been made to transform the country into an unambiguously free market economy. Certainly, the term 'shock therapy' can be used with respect to Poland and, to some extent, the Czech Republic but it is becoming apparent that the prescriptions of Jeffrey Sachs and similar theorists have simply not been applied on any serious scale in Russia. Most importantly, the failure to control the money supply has resulted in inflation and repeated devaluations of the rouble. In addition, Yeltsin's government has essentially run away from the task of closing down unprofitable publicly owned enterprises, apart from those in the Moscow and St Petersburg regions.

I am not greatly surprised at this record, since – judging by the suffering and consequent resistance that even modest reform measures have involved – Russian public opinion would probably not have countenanced the degree of dislocation that Sachs' remedies would have entailed. For Russia is not Poland. Its people, after all, have lived under Bolshevism for much longer and have not regarded it as something imposed by a foreign power. Moreover, the old system, for all its faults, did function up to a point and in recent decades brought a degree of stability and predictability into most people's lives.

The ironic outcome may be that Russia (and some of its FSU satellites) will become a bastion of collectivism, corporatism and protectionism in the early part of the twenty-first century. This may well mean that the wealth gap between the two halves of Europe will actually widen rather than narrow. This could have many implications, including some in the area of military security, but space constraints prevent their further exploration here. A final point to consider relates to the impact of the now widely recognized Soviet economic failure on the pace of the current transformation in the capitalist world – that is, on so-called globalization. Perceptions about the Soviets as recently as the 1960s were very different. As Robert Skidelsky has written

> In 1961 the first secretary of the Communist Party of the Soviet Union, Nikita Khrushchev, made an extraordinary speech. He predicted that within ten years the Soviet Union would overtake America in total industrial production, and within twenty-five years would outstrip its rival in wealth per head of population. 'We will bury you', Khrushchev told the West. Nearly half a century after the Bolshevik seizure of power in October 1917, Khrushchev was speaking for a revolutionary state apparently confident of its own future and its dominant position in the future of the world. How far Khrushchev believed what he said is open to doubt. But his truculent rhetoric was taken at face value in the West. When President [John] Kennedy came to London in June 1961, fresh after confronting Khrushchev in Vienna, he told Britain's Conservative prime minister,

Harold Macmillan, 'They are no longer frightened of aggression. They have at least as powerful nuclear forces as the West. They have interior lines. They have a buoyant economy and will outmatch Capitalist society in the race for materialist wealth.' Macmillan agreed.[3]

The effect of these mistaken perceptions by Western leaders may well have been to lead them (and the business elites around them) to sustain and extend collectivism and welfare provision in their own countries, fearing that, otherwise, more extreme collectivists would gain in popularity. The result was arguably the era of social democracy in the West and the concomitant growth in public spending there. It may, moreover, have been no coincidence that the intellectual and political reaction in the West against this trend (associated with US President Ronald Reagan and UK Prime Minister Margaret Thatcher), gathered momentum only when it became obvious to almost everyone that the Soviet system was in dire economic straits.

As for the future, the irony could be that the Russians will continue to cling to collectivism and to run a siege economy while most of the rest of the world dashes towards globalization. Many will wish to offer condolences to the Russian people once it becomes unambiguously clear that they have made such an apparently ruinous choice. But is it not at least possible that the globalization of the rest of the world economy and the end of all protectionism, if these occur, may not turn out to be so very beneficial for great numbers of currently well-paid workers in the Western welfare states? Just because Marxism–Leninism was an abject failure in economic terms does not mean that unbridled free market globalized capitalism will necessarily be seen as an economic success by those currently enjoying life in what may be the closing years of the Western world's social democratic era.

Notes

1. There are several interesting references to Suslov in Georgi Arbatov (1992), *The System: An Insider's Life in Soviet Politics*, New York.
2. See David Carlton (1996), 'Russia and NATO Enlargement' in David Carlton, Paul Ingram and Giancarlo Tenaglia (eds), *Rising Tension in Eastern Europe and the Former Soviet Union*, Aldershot.
3. Robert Skidelsky (1995), *The World After Communism: A Polemic for our Times*, London, p. 1.

11 NATO Enlargement and Russian Policy in the 1990s

Alexander Nikitin

Love/Hate and Jealousy: Russian–NATO Relations from the Early to the Mid-1990s

During the first visit to Russia of a delegation from the NATO Political Affairs Division in early 1992 the Vice-President of Russia, General Alexander Rutzkoi, warmly hugged NATO official General Genschel on the podium of the Petrovo-Dalnyeye conference centre and expressed a historic hope that, in the foreseeable future, the new Russia would join NATO. The audience, comprising Russian and NATO military and political experts enthusiastically applauded. In return a NATO spokesman expressed deep satisfaction at such a prospect. That was a time of early 'romanticism' in Russian–NATO relations when everything seemed possible at a time of collapsing empires, fallen walls and the emergence of new states and alliances.

After the dissolution of the Warsaw Treaty Organization (WTO) NATO was looking for new definitions of its purpose, mission and status. Now that several years have passed it is possible to say that some of the dimensions of this reaffirmation of NATO worked better than others. Doctrinal changes ('no direct enemy', 'no threats but risks and challenges' and 'partnership and cooperation') were important as a turning point, but now many Russian analysts stress that this was a once-only switch and that NATO doctrine is no longer following changing realities in the mid-1990s.

Two other NATO moves were considered in Russia to be significant breakthroughs: first the decision to invite all newly–independent states to join North Atlantic Cooperation Council (NACC) followed by Partnership for Peace; second, NATO's initially experimental, then substantial, involvement in the peacekeeping missions. Both these moves aimed to put NATO at the centre of an all-European security architecture. Both of them have helped

NATO to survive the most uncertain period of the early 1990s when the very preservation of NATO after the end of Cold War had come to be questioned by many Europeans and Americans. But, again, both these moves are losing their meaning and impulse in the second half of the 1990s. Tacitly, but nevertheless quite clearly, the definition of the principal NATO function for the future is a return to a formula which seems comfortingly familiar: namely to deter Russia. But to deter from what? From projecting instability into the West? From imposing its will on the Baltic States or the Ukraine? From concentrating around Moscow a new empire under the cloak of the Commonwealth of Independent States (CIS)?

At the same time NATO's experiment with peacekeeping in former Yugoslavia is perceived now within NATO circles, and broadly by world public opinion, as having been far from successful. Yet, as recently as 1994, the operation in the former Yugoslavia under a United Nations (UN) mandate was frequently referred to within NATO circles as a model for future NATO missions in the next century. Now the attitude is more like that of post-Vietnam in the United States: 'Never again.' Furthermore, NATO officially refuses any forms of involvement (even the sending of observers) in conflict resolution activities on FSU territory – for example, in Tadjikistan, Georgia, Moldova and Nagorno-Karabakh. These functions have been left to Russia and CIS forces with observers from the Organization for Security and Cooperation in Europe (OSCE). And what is the current situation with respect to relations between NATO and various 'cooperation partner' countries? By 1996 those who joined the NACC three years previously on an equal footing found themselves deeply differentiated by NATO policies. The 'best and brightest' – Poland, Hungary and the Czech Republic – have been invited to discuss the final modalities of joining NATO. Bulgaria and Slovakia are kept in the 'waiting room'. The three Baltic States try to work as a group on regional arrangements with Brussels. Romania, Moldova, Slovenia, Macedonia and Albania are left 'on the margins', receiving inarticulate signals that they will not be much welcomed into NATO circles in the foreseeable future. Russia finds itself with essentially worse relations with NATO than before (both Moscow and Brussels having contributed to that). Ukraine frightens Brussels with its willingness to play the 'NATO card' against Moscow. Belarus is not sure what its own self-proclaimed 'neutrality' means and seems to be ready to experiment with involvement in both Moscow-centred and NATO-centred collective security systems. And at the same time three Transcaucasian cooperation partner countries (Georgia, Armenia and Azerbaijan) as well as five Central Asian CIS states (Turkmenistan, Kazakhstan, Uzbekistan, Kirgizstan and Tadjikistan) are being practically pushed out of any NATO-related 'grand design' for security cooperation, and some of them have even stopped sending delegations to NACC sessions.

As a result it has become clear not only to cooperation partner countries but also to NATO countries themselves that NATO as a security organization has relatively little ability to expand its area of responsibilities both functionally and geographically. NATO's ability to play any role in prevention or resolution of regional low-intensity conflicts and ethnic frictions which are becoming one of the principal threats in Eurasia since the end of Cold War is thus far from likely to be decisive. An extension of NATO's security guarantees could be limited at most to Poland, the Czech Republic and Hungary; and even that prospect continues to be the subject of a jealous reaction by Moscow.

Approaches to NATO enlargement existing in Russia among political elites – and it is important to understand that the whole issue of enlargement is not a subject for broad debate among the general Russian public – could be categorised as following the approaches set out below.

The 'Humiliated Great Power' Approach

Spread among nationalistically-oriented politicians, parliamentarians and columnists, this approach attaches 'ideological' meaning to NATO enlargement. It stresses that Russia lost a Cold War and gave up its strength by making many compromises in the international arena – for example, by not 'defending' Russian populations in other newly-independent states from assaults on their human rights. Proponents of this approach are not so much nervous about any 'physical' or 'military' threat that might result from NATO enlargement but rather speak up for the self-affirmation of Russia in the international arena and manifest a syndrome natural to many 'defeated nations'.

The 'Worst-case Planning' Approach

This is mostly characteristic of the professional military who insist that NATO has not changed at all and has preserved all its technical–military capabilities in order to be able to use its military might against Russia or Russian regional interests (which typically are perceived within the limits of the FSU's geostrategic space). From this point of view, NATO enlargement plans are tackled as if they are a purely geostrategic 'march' by NATO closer and closer to the Russian borders. It is suggested that the Russian reaction should consist of military measures such as: relocating significant land forces on the western and Baltic Sea borders of Russia; concluding a defensive alliance with Belarus; and building strong 'new borders'.

'Enlargement is Inevitable but Let's Negotiate Conditions'

This is an approach shared by part of the Russian diplomatic and expert communities. It supposes that enlargement gives Russia an opportunity to impose on NATO certain conditions such as, for example, the non-deployment of nuclear forces on the territories of new members, intensification of confidence-building measures (such as inspections and early warning on troop movements) with respect both to new members and to NATO as a whole. The most important conditions should be of a political nature, involving Russia in the very process of decision-making concerning the NATO 'grand design' and providing for a relationship between NATO and the OSCE which has 'more all-European legitimacy'.

'CIS Military Integration as an Alternative to NATO Enlargement'

Although familiar to the West, this approach manifests a fairly mature trend in current Russian policy and deserves a more detailed analysis. It is now widely recognized in Russian political and military circles that Russian security cannot be provided unilaterally – relying solely upon Russian domestic resources. The collective security paradigm is now back in the Russian strategic planning picture after an intermediate period which saw attempts to build full Russian self-reliance in defence matters. The whole stream of debates around NATO enlargement would not be understood correctly without taking into consideration growing military–political integration within the CIS. The process of step-by-step formation of the CIS collective security system is increasingly perceived in Russia as an 'answer' (or at least a crucial part of the answer) to the need to restructure Eurasian security after the collapse of the Soviet Union and the WTO.

Between 1991 and 1996 the framework of the security dimension of the CIS changed twice. The initial concept of 'common geostrategic space' was based on plans to assure joint ownership and collective command over the undivided military machine of the former Soviet Union. These plans were turned down by the stream of acts of 'nationalization' of parts of the Soviet military heritage by the newly–independent states. Thus, for a while, the CIS's main security task was to assure the peaceful character of the painful process of dividing the army and the huge Soviet military infrastructure. However, already in 1992, a new task was formulated: to develop the military integration of the now independent states towards the creation of a multidimensional collective security system for the CIS. The foundation for the creation of such a system was the Treaty on Collective Security signed on 15 May 1992 in Tashkent by six states (Russia, Armenia, Kazakhstan, Kirgizstan, Uzbekistan and Tadjikistan). Later, in 1993–94, three more states

(Azerbaijan, Belarus and Georgia) adhered to the Treaty. By 1995 the Treaty had been ratified by the parliaments of all the signatory states.

An initial infrastructure of the collective security regional system has now been practically completed. It includes a Council of Heads of States which elaborates and approves basic decisions concerning security matters; a Council of CIS Defence Ministers which coordinates defence and security integration; and a Council of CIS Foreign Affairs Ministers which works on coordinating the external policy of the allied countries. Since 1994 members of these bodies have also been meeting in the CIS Collective Security Council which specifically discusses security issues and conflict resolution matters.

It is important to realize that, after some debate, the concept of the external borders of the Commonwealth was adopted and the Council of Commanders of the Border Guards (as a coordinating organ) was established as a new part of the CIS collective security system. Among other recent developments is the creation of the Joint Air Defence System of the CIS. (Importantly, even Ukraine, which has many reservations concerning CIS integration, joined this joint air defence system.) CIS states have also formed a joint Staff for Coordination of Military Cooperation of the CIS States which is based in Moscow as the highest executive organ in which all states have high-ranking permanent military representatives and where the staff proportionally represents different CIS countries.

More than 100 agreements and documents on military–technical cooperation and conflict resolution matters were elaborated and began to be implemented between 1992 and 1995. Of course, the processes of integration have not been without problems and contradictions. Some CIS states, particularly Ukraine and Moldova, are participating in only a limited number of collective agreements. And almost all countries at different points have violated their financial obligations concerning payments for joint undertakings and quotas of military personnel to be sent to joint peace support missions. But, in general, the collective security integration of the CIS states is one of the most actively developing networks and area of interrelations among the CIS states.

What is a possible future role of the CIS in the structure of Eurasian security? How does it correlate to the role of NATO, the UN, the OSCE and other interlocking institutions? Certainly the CIS does not pretend to any kind of universality: as an interstate integrative union it considers itself, by definition, as only a limited regional pillar of the all-European organizational efforts. However, by the mid-1990s the CIS had already performed its most important initial task, namely that of securing the non-violent 'divorce' of the former Soviet republics and providing a fair division of the economic property, infrastructure and military potential of the former Soviet Union. In the second half of the 1990s the CIS is oriented to changing from being a tool for 'civilized disintegration' into becoming a vehicle for a new stage of integration among the newly–independent states.

The CIS aims at international recognition. This is why the debates around the applicability of the Chapter 8 regulations of the UN Charter are so important to it, since then it would possess important rights and have regional security responsibilities. The UN resolution recognizing the CIS as a regional interstate organization under the UN Charter was adopted in March 1994 but with reservations from certain Western European and Scandinavian countries which denied the right of the CIS to undertake regional peace support operations without preliminary UN Security Council permission. CIS states consider this reservation to be an ideological hangover from the Cold War mentality and an infringement of the sovereignty of the newly–independent states. CIS countries, therefore, insist on recognition of the CIS status in full, including the right of this group of states to undertake collectively agreed measures for conflict prevention and conflict resolution in the relevant region.

In the field of conflict resolution and regional peace support operations the CIS suggests to other European and world institutions a kind of 'division of labour'. Russia is ready to mobilize the collective efforts of the CIS member states to assure conflict resolution and peace support efforts on the territory of the Tashkent Treaty countries. The CIS is ready to do this in practical cooperation with the UN and the OSCE. UN and OSCE observers will be welcomed and are already operating in Tadjikistan, Georgia, Nagorno-Karabakh and Moldova. At the same time if the UN and OSCE are not currently ready, in practical terms, to extend their conflict resolution efforts in the FSU further than continued 'observation', then Russia and the CIS are interested in obtaining from both organizations a mandate legitimizing the CIS efforts to assure stability and conflict resolution on the territory of its states. There are certain similarities between the 'order' for peace support operations in the former Yugoslavia which NATO has negotiated with the UN and OSCE and the comparable 'order' for the peace support operations in the newly–independent states territories which the CIS is ready to implement. Many Russian politicians and military personnel are stressing that the UN and European institutions can no longer 'sit on two chairs' – in other words, continually withdraw from any significant practical conflict resolution efforts for Tadjikistan, Georgia, Nagorno-Karabakh and Moldova while expressing a desire to see these conflicts resolved, and at the same time continually criticize Russian and CIS conflict resolution efforts in these areas. Russia and the CIS are ready for a deeper internationalization of the conflict resolution practices in the CIS and a deeper involvement of the OSCE in particular. Unfortunately, the OSCE efforts in Nagorno-Karabakh and Abkhazia are developing very slowly and the OSCE peacekeeping operation for Nagorno-Karabakh, though announced, has been *de facto* frozen at the planning stage.

Future Relations Between the CIS and NATO

Future relations between the CIS and NATO in the second half of the 1990s have the potential for promoting both conflict and cooperation. For the present NATO tends to avoid any bilateral relations with the CIS as a union and pretends to ignore its growing collective security system formation efforts. Brussels proceeds on the assumption that all relations with CIS states can be organized along bilateral lines. Some diplomats and experts from Russia and from CIS states express dissatisfaction that the NACC mechanism (which is based on collective consultations, multinational transparency and equality of rights and responsibilities for the cooperation partner countries) is increasingly being replaced in practice by individualized relations which inevitably introduce 'segregation' between the cooperation partner countries. The latter are thus prevented from negotiating with NATO in groups – a possible echo of the old formula for 'divide and rule'.

Under such circumstances when many CIS states, including Russia, have a growing feeling of being 'left out of Europe' one of the logical steps for Russia and the majority of the CIS countries in the second half of the 1990s would be to place greater emphasis on the strengthening of security and military integration within the CIS in order to develop their own regional collective security system. That may lead to a new juxtaposition in Eurasia between the NATO-centred and the CIS-centred (or Moscow-centred) security alignments. To avoid the dangers which would inevitably accompany such a split, significant mutual efforts should be undertaken by both NATO and CIS countries and organs. It still seems possible to build into both CIS and NATO structures mechanisms for mutual consultations and for confidence-building and transparency measures. Of course, by many parameters, the NATO collective security mechanism is much more developed and tested than that of the CIS, but both collective security systems are limited, regionalized, experimenting with new functions (peacekeeping and regional conflict resolution) and currently have no clear-cut relations with the OSCE overall mechanism of political consultations. The growing CIS collective security system lacks European international legitimacy (in comparison to the OSCE) just as NATO could not substitute for the OSCE and the UN in their role of highest legitimizing fora arising from a full representation of states.

Some Russian analysts consider that, to certain degree, the future regional role of the CIS in the security field could be compared with the regional role of the Western European Union (WEU): while WEU pretends to be a Western pillar of Eurasian security (and has specific tasks, mechanisms and a self-affirmative mentality differentiating it from NATO and the European Union), in the same way the CIS pretends to the role of an Eastern pillar of Eurasian security. Of course both the WEU and the CIS are insufficient if taken individually but compose important overlapping components of the future European (or Eurasian) security scheme where the OSCE, NATO, NACC, WEU and CIS have specific (partly overlapping and partly mutually contributing) tasks and functions.

The potential of the CIS in the 1990s is weakened mainly by domestic factors concerning developments in Russia and in other CIS member states as well as by the uneven pace of the reforming processes in different newly independent states. But, if under the initiative of Russia, the CIS in a broader or narrower configuration were to be strengthened by the growing reintegrational trends among the newly-independent states in the second half of the 1990s, then this interstate union could become one of the unique and important regional pillars of the multidimensional security, economic and humanitarian organizations of Europe.

12 A Cooperative Security Approach to Addressing Instabilities in Eastern Europe: The Role of NATO

Lamberto Zannier

The end of the Cold War and the consequent evolution of the situation in Europe have brought about a parallel evolution in the role and activities of our institutions. NATO is no exception to this. We face new challenges and instabilities and need updated instruments to deal with them. Therefore, the first contribution that NATO has made to addressing new instabilities has been through its own adaptation to the new political and security environment. For nearly half a century NATO has guaranteed the security of its members and, today, it remains the only organization which can still do so. At the same time, our experience over the past few years has shown that the Alliance is an irreplaceable asset in the search for a new European security order without divisions or unequal zones of security.

This is NATO's ultimate goal. In the last few years, and in landmark summits in London, Rome and Brussels, NATO has adopted new roles and missions in order to be able to achieve this goal. Following NATO's transformation and given the success of initiatives such as Partnership For Peace and NATO's support for crisis management and peacekeeping, the new challenges, considerable as they are, can be mastered only on the condition that the Alliance continues to link Europe and North America in an indissoluble transatlantic security community. The transatlantic link is the source of NATO's enduring vitality and the key to its success in its new, as well as traditional, missions. There can be no bright future for Europe if Europe and North America go their separate ways.

NATO will have four main tasks in the years ahead:

- Bosnia remains NATO's most urgent priority. The troops on the ground serving in the NATO-led Multilateral Peace Implementation Force (IFOR) need constant support and political guidance to carry out their tasks in such a way as to keep the risks low, to keep the chances of success high, and to do the job in the one year foreseen. This is a very time-consuming activity that has required the creation of new mechanisms to ensure proper coordination with all parties involved in this challenging operation.
- NATO also has strategic interests beyond Bosnia. Chief of those is to extend stability eastward. NATO's enlargement is the single most important contribution it can make to the aim of creating a Europe which is increasingly integrated and united. This process is already proceeding steadily, gradually and openly. As NATO moves to take in new members, it will not ignore its cooperation programme with others. Partnership for Peace will be intensified and will act as a permanent bond between allies and partners.
- In parallel, there will be a need to build a strong relationship with Russia. Russia is a great power with an important and unique contribution to make. Russia and NATO have both much to gain from each other, and a permanent framework of trust and cooperation between them must be created. This will be done on the ground in Bosnia; it will be done at the institutional and personal level too. NATO wishes to build a new security architecture, with, not against, Russia.
- Finally, the transformation of NATO will have to proceed further. There will be a need to develop even greater military flexibility through the Combined Joint Task Force concept, and NATO's internal structures need to be adapted further to reflect growing European responsibilities for defence and security.

As a part of its own adaptation to the new circumstances, NATO has also been a driving force in helping develop cooperative processes to overcome instabilities arising from this phase of transition, including those on the former Soviet territory. In this context, it is important to recognize the continuing relevance of arms control, both with reference to the Conventional Forces in Europe (CFE) Treaty and in respect of measures that can be used as a stabilizing tool in the context of a crisis situation, as is the case with negotiations for the implementation of Articles 2 and 4 of the Dayton Agreement on Bosnia-Herzegovina. Also, attention needs to be given to some of the new challenges to European security, particularly in the field of proliferation.

To begin with the CFE Treaty, our starting point should be 17 November 1995 which marked the legal milestone of the completion of the reductions

A Cooperative Security Approach to Instabilities in Eastern Europe   159

period and the achievement of the lower levels of equipment fixed by the Treaty. The most important achievements have been in three main areas: destruction of military equipment; enhancement of predictability and transparency; and the development of cooperation among armed forces. Let us consider each of these in turn.

- **Destruction of military equipment.** Over 40 months, the 30 States Parties to the Treaty have destroyed nearly 50 000 pieces of treaty-limited equipment (battle tanks, armoured combat vehicles, artillery, combat aircraft and attack helicopters), roughly one-third by NATO countries and two-thirds by the other States Parties to the Treaty. In particular, as pointed out by the Russian representative in the Joint Consultative Group in Vienna, Russia alone has reduced a total of over 10 000 treaty-limited items, together with other armaments belonging to the maritime infantry and coastal defence forces. This makes a total of over 11 500 pieces of equipment. The Treaty's implementation has resulted in the destruction of a large proportion of the equipment which constituted the vast overall imbalance of conventional forces that existed at the time of its signature. The achievement and the preservation of these lower limits of heavy armaments represents an important element of stability for the European continent.
- **Enhancement of predictability and transparency.** An unprecedented process of information exchange and verification has taken place to support Treaty implementation. This has involved detailed exchanges of military information on a regular basis, as well as the conduct of thorough verification activities. Over 2300 intrusive on-site inspections of military installations have been carried out, resulting in a very high level of transparency and confidence.
- **Development of cooperation among armed forces.** Implementation of the Treaty has also resulted in an enhanced pattern of cooperation among armed forces. In particular, NATO Allies launched a cooperation programme in the field of verification with the other Treaty signatories, which has promoted a more cooperative military relationship among NATO Allies and all other States Parties. More than 50 on-site inspections have been conducted by joint multinational teams with other Treaty signatories.

Notwithstanding these impressive achievements, however, a number of States Parties have failed to comply fully with their Treaty commitments. First and foremost, Russia has not yet met its obligations under Article V of the Treaty, which sets zonal limits in the flank area. Russia is also accountable for other compliance issues such as those of its forces stationed on the territory of other states – for example, Georgia or Moldova. In the final communiqué of the North Atlantic Council on 5 December 1995, NATO ministers expressed concern about all cases of failure by States Parties to fulfil their Treaty obligations. This also refers to other cases of non-compliance, apart from the flank issue, such as: the problem of naval infantry and coastal defence assets, especially with regard to the former Soviet Black Sea Fleet; delays in the completion of reductions by Belarus; failure to provide adequate notifications of reduction liabilities and to reduce all excess equipment by Azerbaijan and Armenia; the failure by Russia to destroy its excess equipment beyond the Urals by the deadline of 31 December 1995.

The Treaty foresees the possibility of a need to address a range of implementation concerns and establish mechanisms and procedures for finding cooperative solutions to such difficulties. These include, in particular, the activities of the CFE Joint Consultative Group (JCG) in Vienna. The JCG was established specifically to deal with implementation concerns, and all the issues outlined above are under discussion there. The cooperative process foreseen by the Treaty is working. With regard to the flank issue, NATO allies have put forward a proposal with a view to resolving outstanding implementation issues on the basis of a map realignment: the need to work towards such a solution was reconfirmed in a formal decision adopted by the JCG in November 1995. Allies have also presented suggestions to promote cooperative solutions to all other questions of non-compliance, and are engaged in a dialogue with Russia and with the other States Parties to help resolve outstanding issues. While work continues on these issues, a period of intensive inspections began. This 120-day Residual Level Validation Period is a useful tool to monitor the implementation of Treaty obligations. A review of the operation of the Treaty then took place at the CFE Review Conference in May 1996, in order to ensure its future effectiveness. Despite the significant changes that have taken place in the European security environment since the signing of the Treaty in 1990, the Treaty's fundamental aims remain valid. Moreover, it has taken on new significance in contributing to the creation of a climate of trust among former adversaries. In particular, the long-term commitment to maintenance of the reduced force levels and to transparency through detailed exchange of information and the acceptance of intrusive inspections will continue to serve as a fundamental basis for the new European security architecture. For this reason, NATO ministers have reaffirmed their commitment to ensure that the integrity of the *CFE Treaty* is preserved and have called upon all States Parties to fully comply with all their obligations under the Treaty.

The continuing importance of conventional arms control as a stabilizing tool is also underscored by the current negotiations taking place in Vienna as a follow-up to the Dayton Agreement on Bosnia-Herzegovina. A number of ideas put forward by NATO in Vienna, especially those concerning certain stabilizing measures for use in localized crisis situations, have served as a model for a possible package of measures to be applied to Bosnia-Herzegovina. Of course, the experience acquired in developing and implementing the CFE Treaty has also been an important support for the Article 4 negotiations on regional security. In this phase, NATO is ensuring a proper coordination between IFOR implementation and the negotiating tables in Vienna to ensure that arms control measures are fully consistent with the other elements of the peace settlement. Accordingly, NATO has put at the disposal of the chairmen of the two working groups representatives of the NATO military authorities, with the task of acting as points of contact between the negotiations and the IFOR command.

The next broad area of interest to which we must refer is that related to the nuclear disarmament process and the risk of proliferation of weapons of mass destruction (WMD). Following the end of the Cold War, there was a need to reduce dramatically the huge nuclear arsenals that had characterized a security relationship based on a concept of mutual deterrence. In the new political and security environment, where confidence and transparency prevail over the mistrust that had governed East–West relations for over 40 years, large numbers of nuclear weapons have become a liability rather than an asset. In any case, it is imperative to ensure that any regional conflicts or crises characterizing this recent phase in which new regional balances are being sought, do not result in the threatened use of nuclear weapons or of other WMD. Unprecedented progress has been achieved in this area in recent years. Pre-eminent has been the Intermediate Nuclear Forces (INF) Treaty and the Strategic Arms Reduction Talks (START) I and II Treaties. The former's implementation, in particular, is proceeding very well, with the unilateral undertakings assumed on a reciprocal basis by the United States and the Soviet Union (later confirmed by Russia) to eliminate all land-based tactical nuclear weapons. In addition, all tactical nuclear weapons have been withdrawn from surface ships and attack submarines. As a result of these initiatives, 80 per cent of US nuclear weapons have been withdrawn from Europe. All these initiatives have resulted in a drastic reduction of the huge nuclear stockpiles accumulated during the Cold War years.

The dissolution of the Soviet Union has added a different dimension to this process, requiring increased focus on a number of new challenges. The most difficult issue was the achievement of non-nuclear status by those newly–independent states of the former Soviet Union that have pledged to become nuclear-free. This process required, in the case of Belarus, Kazakhstan and Ukraine, additional efforts to provide relevant technical and financial assistance and to discuss the political conditions, including appropriate security guarantees, under which the objective of eventual denuclearization of these countries could be achieved. NATO has been very actively following this process and on a number of occasions has carried out bilateral *démarches* or used the North Atlantic Cooperation Council (NACC) fora to discuss relevant issues with all interested parties. NATO also activated an internal forum to discuss, share information and thus coordinate initiatives of assistance by individual allies on a bilateral basis with Russia and with the relevant other countries concerning the withdrawal and dismantlement of nuclear weapons. Several allied countries have invested a substantial amount of financial resources in projects of assistance, in the conviction that the speedy conclusion of this process corresponds to their own security needs. The United States alone has initially allocated US$800 million of the so-called Nunn-Lugar fund, of which US$175 million has been earmarked for Ukraine. Over time, the US contribution has been increased to US$1.5 billion. Among the other NATO countries most actively engaged in this process are the UK, Germany, France, Italy, Norway and Canada.

This cooperation between NATO countries, Russia and the newly–independent states of the former Soviet Union with nuclear weapons on their territories is mainly concentrated on supporting the process of dismantlement of weapons systems (including transportation), protection, emergency response equipment, the setting up of storage facilities, and the purchase and conversion of fissile materials. Such activities also cover areas such as the establishment of effective export controls, the creation of science and technology centres in Moscow and Kiev and the retraining, resettlement and housing of personnel involved. The main objective of all these activities is to help ensure that the process of dismantlement is carried out in conditions of security and safety and that it does not result in any loss of control or proliferation of materials, equipment or technology, thus creating potential instabilities on the periphery of NATO. Notwithstanding these efforts, there is some concern among allies at the lack of progress in the dismantling of tactical nuclear weapons by Russia. Although this process is based on unilateral undertakings, and therefore Russia is not formally committed to this progress, it has to be noted that the United States has fully carried out its reductions, while there is no indication that Russia will do likewise in the near future.

Events in the former Soviet Union have also had a significant impact on developments in other parts of the world, since the changed international security conditions and their impact on established regional power balances have become a factor that may encourage proliferation. Moreover, the economic situation in Russia and in the other successor states increases the risk of a spread of technologies and/or expertise, from which a number of potential proliferating countries in regions adjacent to Europe could benefit.

In conjunction with the easier access to dual-use and other technologies once considered sensitive, these new developments are a matter for serious concern. For instance, there are today at least a dozen countries possessing ballistic missiles which have the potential of becoming an effective multiplier of WMD capabilities and provide these countries with a deterrent capability, thus altering established regional balances. Accordingly, NATO states consult regularly both among themselves and with their NACC partners to foster a better understanding of the problems involved, to promote the strengthening of the existing regimes and to explore prospects for cooperation in this field. At the same time, we are also aware that these efforts may not always be successful. This is why the proliferation issue figured prominently on the agenda of the NATO Brussels Summit in January 1994, when it was decided to develop an overall policy framework to consider how to reinforce ongoing prevention efforts and how to reduce the proliferation threat and to protect against it. Two groups were established to address the risk to NATO security posed by the proliferation of weapons of mass destruction. A Senior Politico-Military Group on Proliferation was given the task of analysing current developments and of drafting the NATO policy framework, which was adopted at the ministerial meeting in Istanbul in June 1994. The second group, the Senior Defence Group on Proliferation, was asked to examine the defence-related aspects of the proliferation risk.

In the political field, NATO states have exchanged views systematically on the existing non-proliferation arrangements, focusing in particular on the preparations for the 1995 Non-proliferation Treaty Review Conference and on its results, with a view to contributing to improving the effectiveness of existing regimes. They also discussed in detail potential factors determining proliferation and possible instruments available to prevent or respond to proliferation developments. They are now analysing specific factors and instruments applying to individual countries on the periphery of NATO. These consultations do not take place only among the 16 member states. In fact, an important role is played by ad hoc consultations with Russia, encompassing most of the issues figuring on the regular agenda of the group, as well as other topics of relevance, such as the illicit trade in nuclear materials. A third layer of consultations is at the NACC/Partnership for Peace (PFP) level, encompassing all NATO and NACC partners, and aiming to promote common approaches to non-proliferation policies in the Euro-Atlantic area.

In the defence area, NATO states have proceeded first to a thorough exchange of information on the proliferation risks facing NATO, covering countries both on the periphery of NATO and beyond. The assessment of such risks has provided the basis for a common understanding of how the use, or the threat of use, of weapons of mass destruction by potential proliferators could affect NATO's ability to carry out its missions. Following on from this, it would be possible to determine the range of capabilities needed to respond to such threats, for example through the establishment of appropriate response capabilities, including passive and active defences. Most recently, defence issues have also figured on the agenda of NATO–Russia consultations.

The interest in NATO's activities in the field of proliferation and their relative success so far depends in the first place on the interdisciplinary nature of the discussions and on the methodology that has been used. While discussions within individual non-proliferation regimes are of a very technical nature and often result in a slow evolution of the policies adopted by the potential suppliers, the broader approach followed in NATO, taking as its starting point the geopolitical developments (and their security implications) on the periphery of the alliance and beyond, has allowed for a more forward-looking approach to the issue, and has resulted in stimulating reflection in the relevant capitals. Moreover, consultations with NATO's Eastern European partners provides a useful complement to discussions by allowing NATO to compare respective security perceptions and to explore areas of possible cooperation, both political and practical, at the regional level. This is all the more important since, in view of the increasing complexity of the proliferation challenge and the need for developing a responsible and cooperative approach to dealing with this by the international community, the trend towards adopting common approaches by all like-minded countries will, over time, become an essential feature of their proliferation policies.

This leads us to the final theme of this chapter, namely the pursuit of security through cooperation. In fact, disarmament and arms control constitute only one aspect of a more global relationship of security cooperation that encompasses new tools aimed at improving dialogue, addressing instabilities, preventing conflicts and managing crises. As has already been pointed out, NATO has gone a long way towards promoting and supporting the development of these new instruments, while ensuring their evolution within the broader European security architecture in a coherent fashion. Dialogue and cooperation under NACC and PFP, along with enhanced contacts and interaction with the UN and the OSCE, are intrinsic aspects of this development. One concrete example of such cooperation has been the work of the Ad Hoc Group on Cooperation in Peacekeeping, which brings together the 16 members of NATO, all NACC and PFP countries, as well as other OSCE states with experience in peacekeeping, along with representatives of the OSCE and, whenever possible, of the UN. This group serves as a means to share experience and work towards a common understanding of conceptual aspects of peacekeeping and to develop practical cooperation in such areas as command and control, training, communications, logistics and joint exercises. The Ad Hoc Group periodically issues documents representing the common understanding among NACC/PFP members on conceptual and doctrinal aspects of peacekeeping, as well as principles and criteria for participation in peacekeeping operations. Examples have been the 1993 *Athens Report*, defining modern peacekeeping and its main principles, and its *Follow-on Report*, endorsed by NACC ministers on 6 December 1995, addressing the implications of the new multifunctional peacekeeping operations.

The process that led to the finalization of these reports is an example of cooperation in the NACC framework aimed at improving current policies and techniques to control instabilities and crises in Europe. The idea of a Follow-on Report matured gradually as a result of the review of recent experiences in peacekeeping operations, which demonstrated a profound evolution of modern peacekeeping, due to the fact that most operations take place in a difficult environment, often characterized by a break-up of the state authority and by conflicts within states. This imposes a number of additional tasks on the peacekeeping force, including preventive presence, assistance in fulfilling peace settlement agreements, humanitarian assistance, human rights monitoring, and economic rehabilitation activities.

In carrying out these operations, the basic principles and criteria that govern peacekeeping operations – the consent of the parties, impartiality and the limited use of force – still apply, yet may need to be adjusted to allow the peacekeeping force to implement the mandate. Accordingly, it is imperative in these circumstances to make sure that mandates are achievable and realistic and linked to clear political goals: only in these conditions will force commanders be able to adopt a broad range of measures in response to the evolving situation on the ground. While consent of the parties remains a crucial element at the strategic level, it may prove difficult to retain local consent: in these circumstances, the force commanders will have to ensure impartial behaviour by the peacekeeping force but will, at the same time, be allowed to use force to discourage and resist forcible attempts to prevent implementation of the mandate. If we want to be successful in carrying out these operations, we need to make sure that we approach them with the same understanding and on the basis of the same concepts.

With the launching of the NATO-led implementation force operation in Bosnia, this cooperation at the political-conceptual level has become reality. IFOR is a concrete example of how an institution, adapting itself to the new political realities, can play an effective role in addressing instabilities in Europe. In order to carry out the task efficiently, NATO also had to develop new mechanisms to interact and cooperate with other institutions, such as the UN in the first instance, but also with the EU, the WEU and the OSCE, and to work together with other contributing states, including Russia. Operation Joint Endeavour – which involves 32 countries, mostly European, under a single command – will undoubtedly have a major impact on future security cooperation and the development of European cooperative security structures. Most of these countries are PFP partners. NATO cooperation with them on the ground benefits from the training and exercise activities that have been carried out together under PFP. Operation Joint Endeavour is the logical extension of that cooperation, and it is hoped that its success will show the way to durable new security structures, not only in the Balkans, but throughout Europe. Together with closer political dialogue, new patterns of practical cooperation on the ground, along the lines of what is happening today in former Yugoslavia, are among the main contributions that NATO can provide to help tackle future instabilities and crises on the European continent.

13 Instabilities in the Former Soviet Union and Eastern Europe and the Role that OSCE Can Play

Herman De Fraye

Causes of Instability

The main item on the agenda of the Organization for Security and Cooperation in Europe (OSCE) is the elaboration of a security model for the next century. The principle was adopted at the Summit of Heads of State or Government in Budapest in December 1994, and diplomats have been working on it all through 1995 and 1996.

One of the preparatory documents so far produced deals with the enumeration of security risks affecting the OSCE area. The document covers a broad spectrum of risks, ranging from ethnic tensions to criminality and environmental hazards. That may, of course, be consonant with the OSCE's comprehensive approach to security but, in the framework of this chapter, security will be examined more specifically. Here the focus will be on the degree of stability both within and among the states of the former Soviet bloc and on the factors that may affect their stability and, hence, their security. Certainly, such matters as terrorism, organized crime or environmental disasters of the Chernobyl-type can, and must, be addressed. But they belong to another, non-conflictual category than the one to which security has been traditionally restricted.

Which, then, are the factors of instability which may affect the security of individual nations in Central and Eastern Europe?[1] Basically, they can be grouped under four headings:

- political and psychological problems
- ethnic problems
- institutional problems
- economic problems.

We may now consider each of these in more detail.

Political and Psychological Problems

With the end of the Cold War and the collapse of the communist system, people living in the former communist states were initially elated about their newly found freedoms – freedom of thought and expression, freedom of movement and freedom of economic and political initiative. But joy soon made way for confusion and bewilderment when the first tangible effects of the new freedoms appeared to be economic collapse, double-figure inflation, unemployment, widespread poverty, crime and political chaos.

While life under the communist regimes may have been minimally rewarding in terms of personal self-fulfilment and access to material and spiritual quality goods, at least all basic needs, and more, were looked after by the state. People were taken care of from the cradle to the grave. In addition, the communist state provided an ideology which, although undoubtedly a spiritual and intellectual straitjacket, nevertheless gave a sense of purpose to its adherents. Communists were convinced that they were building a new society and new socialist man; they were in tune with the march of history. Indeed, they incarnated history. When the communist regimes disappeared that certitude also disappeared, leaving large numbers of the former communist elite in a state of cultural shock. No doubt, the former *Nomenklatura* consisted of many cynics and opportunists, but there also must have been substantial numbers of true believers – people who were convinced of the moral rectitude and the historic necessity of what their regime was doing. With the collapse of communism, these people lost their intellectual, social and political points of reference. They are the true orphans of the communist system's demise.

What has been said of the elites also applies, in a way, to the population at large. After 40 to 70 years of communist rule and communist education and propaganda, communist convictions and attitudes had seeped down to the person in the street. In a recent interview, Czech President Vaclav Havel relates that, under communism, people had become used to the rigid rules prescribed by a paternalistic state. They protested against these rules and they may have hated them, but they nevertheless adopted the prescribed forms of conduct. Now that these rules no longer exist, people feel insecure.

They still carry with them the schizophrenia of communist times when they thought differently from the way they acted. It will take some time, Havel thinks, before people will learn to take greater responsibility for their own lives and cease to see the state as an enemy rather than the emanation of their collective selves and the vehicle of their common destiny. In the meantime, people may live very volatile political lives, torn as they are between hopes for Western-style prosperity and functioning democratic institutions and nostalgia for order, safety and full employment which the communist regimes did in fact provide.

These psycho-political problems are something that all inhabitants of the former Soviet bloc countries have in common, though in varying degrees. Marxism–Leninism as a means for restructuring society was first introduced in Russia where it persisted as a state doctrine for over 70 years. As a homegrown doctrine, it had the time to sink deep roots in the population. In Central Europe, on the other hand, communism arrived with foreign occupation and served both as its justification and as a means for its preservation. Because of the authoritarian, indeed brutal, traits that Josef Stalin added to the doctrine, Central Europeans tended to reject it as something alien to their European traditions. When they regained their independence, in 1989–1990, their principal concern was to 'return' to Europe and to integrate as quickly as possible in the West's major institutions. For the Russian people, on the other hand, the transition from communism to democracy not only meant the loss of their secular faith, but also the loss of an empire. With the collapse of the communist regimes in Central Europe and the dissolution of the Warsaw Pact and the Council for Mutual Economic Assistance (Comecon), Russia lost the formal instruments of control over its former satellites and, by the same token, the outer crown of its empire. After the aborted coup against Mikhail Gorbachev and the disintegration of the Soviet Union, Russia lost the inner circle of her empire as well. With all 15 former Soviet republics having become independent, sovereign states, Russia suddenly found itself reduced to its geographical dimension of 300 years ago, at the time of the accession to the throne of Peter the Great. It was the last European empire to crumble, and the process may not be yet finished, as indicated by Chechnya's attempt to wrest itself loose from Russia.

History shows that when empires disappear, peacefully or through defeat in war, their disappearance creates a vacuum that often leads, among the successor states and among neighbouring states as well, to a violent scramble for the remains. One of the consequences of imperial break-up is the inadequacy of former administrative borders when turned into international state boundaries which may be recognized by some and disputed by others. Another consequence is the disruption of economic, cultural and human ties between the former centre and periphery, causing tremendous economic loss and severe human hardship. The fact that 20 to 25 million Russians are stranded in the newly independent states, is but one example of the human problems created by imperial break-up. There are of course also countless numbers of Ukrainians and people from the Caucasian and Central Asian republics, as well as millions of people of 'mixed' origin – Soviet citizens in the true sense of the word – who find themselves living in the newly-independent republics with which they have little, if any, affinity. We will return to these aspects later but let us first examine what the loss of empire has done to the Russians themselves.

It has been argued that the Russians have never developed a sense of national identity comparable to, say, that of the French, the Italians, the British or the Germans. The vastness and the openness of the Russian plain, stretching from the Baltic all the way to Vladivostok, and also the fact that Russian history has been one of constant battle against intruders, has resulted in the creation of an imperial, expansionistic mindset. Security could only be gained by continuously expanding borders and by the submission of the very peoples that once had created, or potentially could create, a security threat to the Russian lands.

If Russian identity, therefore, is essentially an imperial one, then the loss of empire causes an identity crisis for which there is little or no historical precedent. It should, then, come as no surprise that the Russian people find themselves in disarray as a result of the triple loss of ideological faith, economic performance and imperial status and prestige.

Serbia, in many ways, shares this Russian experience. Yugoslavia and the Soviet Union were the last truly multinational and multicultural state structures on the European continent. In both cases the dominating core republics ran the federation as it were a greater Russia or a greater Serbia. When the federation broke up, both core republics ended up with large numbers of their co-nationals living in the newly–independent neighbouring states. But the similarities end here. For, by declaring her sovereignty, Russia herself put an end to the federation, whereas Serbia sought to resist to the end the unilateral declarations of independence of Slovenia and Croatia. And whereas Russia has been seeking a peaceful *rapprochement* with the other former Soviet republics in the framework of the Commonwealth of Independent States (CIS), Serbia resorted to war. In a first stage, Serbia sought to keep the seceding republics by force in the federation; later it sought to grab as much land as possible from Croatia and Bosnia in order to realize its second-best goal of a greater Serbia. While from the outset the Serbs were convinced that they were the victims of a German-led, Western conspiracy, the Russians have come to believe something very similar only over a longer period of time. During the electoral campaign leading up to the 17 December 1995 elections, the Western conspiracy theme was played up not only by the ultranationalists of Vladimir Zhirinovsky but also by the communists. Frequently expressed complaints concerned Russia's humiliation – its downgrading and marginalization to a second-rank power to which the West can talk down but which it does not otherwise have to take seriously. Anti-Western sentiments such as these may potentially be one of the biggest security risks for the future in that they may re-create a psychological barrier between Russia and the West which, in time, may become a political or even a military barrier.

At the same time, the Central European former satellites of the Soviet Union have emerged from their 40-year domination by Moscow with a fiercely anti-Russian sentiment which can be equally disruptive for the overall European security situation. These countries may find it difficult to forget that they were cut off artificially from the West for nearly half a century. They have been amputated territorially, left with antiquated economies and with appalling environmental conditions. Their sovereignty had been curtailed by the so-called [Leonid] Brezhnev doctrine, and attempts at liberalization had been brutally crushed by Soviet and Warsaw Pact tanks. Hence these countries may find it more difficult than the existing members of NATO to see the Russians in terms other than 'us' and 'them' and to create a constructive, cooperative relationship instead.

Ethnic Problems

As already indicated, ethnic questions that had long been suppressed by the communist regimes suddenly came to the fore again when these regimes collapsed. As the conflicts in former Yugoslavia and the former Soviet Union have shown, the issue of ethnic tension is the single most important, and certainly the most immediate, cause for armed conflict. That this need not invariably be the case is shown by the Czechs and Slovaks who succeeded in separating peacefully. Yet, the potential for violent solutions is far greater, as the examples of Bosnia, Moldova, Georgia and Nagorno-Karabach demonstrate.

With the exception of Poland, the Czech Republic, Hungary, Albania and Slovenia, all other states of Central and Eastern Europe are confronted with more or less severe ethnic problems. While Albania and Hungary have only small minorities on their territory (Greeks and Slovaks respectively) they do have problems with their co-nationals being a minority in neighbouring states. There are large Hungarian minorities in Slovakia and Rumania and a sizeable group in the Serbian province of Vojvodina as well. Albania, for its part, is rightly concerned about the fate of the Albanian minorities in Kosovo, the Sanjak and Macedonia.

The situation is even more complicated in the former Soviet Union. It has already been pointed out that Russia has up to 25 million of its nationals living in the newly independent states of the CIS. In some of them, such as Latvia and Estonia and even more so in Kazakhstan and Kyrgyzstan, these minorities make up a quarter to one-third or even more of the total population. In other CIS states, such as Moldova and the Ukraine, they live in compact groups in certain areas of these countries where they do constitute real majorities. And Russia itself is an ethnic mosaic, where something like 70 different languages are spoken, ranging from Karelian and Mordovian to Osetian, Bashkir, Buryat and Kabardinian, to name just a few. While in terms of educational and cultural rights, and in terms of overall economic development, it must be admitted that, under the Soviet regime, minority ethnic groups were much better off than in Tsarist times, they were nonetheless subject to various forms of Russification and were, in many ways, treated like second-class citizens. Because Russian was the *lingua franca* of the Soviet Union everyone had to master that language in order to climb the social ladder. Russian was the language of the army and of all other federal institutions, including the central government, parliament, federal ministries and the various organs of the Communist Party of the Soviet Union. It was also common practice to fill leadership positions in the republics with people from the centre (that is, Moscow) and at the same time to invite, or force large numbers from non-Russian areas to take up jobs in the factories of the Urals and Siberia. Some people were even deported collectively, as punishment for alleged or potential collaboration with Nazi Germany. This was the case with the Tatars from the Crimea, the Volga Germans and the Chechens.

The end result of all this is that, today, with all 15 former Soviet republics having become independent states, not a single one is ethnically or linguistically homogeneous. This would be no problem if these states treated their minorities correctly, but it is questionable whether there is a single one among them that does so. The big temptation, as we have seen in the Baltic states, is to drive the alien people out, not necessarily by force but by denying them statehood and by linking all sorts of rights – for example, to education, jobs and housing – to statehood or knowledge of the national language.

In addition problems of borders and territory arise in this connection. Take, by way of example, the conflict involving Armenia and Azerbaijan over Nagorno-Karabakh, and those involving Georgia and Moldova with their respective separatist movements. The Armenians and the Azeris both have within their territory, or surrounded by it, an enclave essentially inhabited by members of the other nationality: the Azeri-inhabited region of Nakhichevan in Armenia and the Armenian-inhabited Nagorno-Karabakh region in Azerbaijan. The situations are not completely parallel because, under the Soviet regime, the Nagorno-Karabakh area was an autonomous 'region' (*oblast*) within the Azerbaijan Republic, whereas Nakhichevan was an autonomous 'republic' surrounded by the Armenian SSR but attached politically to Azerbaijan.

The question of Nagorno-Karabach had been a burning issue between Armenia and Azerbaijan ever since, in early 1988, massive demonstrations in Armenia were held in favour of reunification of the enclave with Armenia. This led to a pogrom in Sumgait and Baku in which large numbers of Armenians were killed. An international conflict resulted in August 1991 when Armenia under President Lev Petrossian declared its independence and included Nagorno-Karabakh within the 'inviolable borders' of the Republic. Azerbaijan responded by suppressing the autonomous status of the province and putting it under direct control of the central government. When Armenian militia in Nagorno-Karabakh started military operations against Azeri regular troops, the conflict escalated quickly into all-out war. The Armenians eventually seized control not only over the totality of Nagorno-Karabakh but also over the area linking this region with Armenia proper and even over substantial parts of Azeri territory south and east of the enclave. Both sides have now reached a stalemate – they concluded a ceasefire in May 1994 – counting perhaps on time and outside pressure to reach a compromise settlement acceptable to both.

What makes the Nagorno-Karabakh conflict so difficult to solve is that it lends itself almost ideally to outside interference. Turkey, which has linguistic and religious ties with the Azeris and a historic animosity against the Armenians, has threatened openly to intervene should Armenia attack Nakhichevan. In fact, ever since the dissolution of the Soviet Union, Turkey has tried to play on its ethnic and linguistic kinship with the peoples of Central Asia in order to carve out of the Soviet spoils a sphere of influence for itself. Turkey's regional ambitions are matched by those of Iran – and to a lesser degree also of Pakistan – which all want to use the window of opportunity, opened by Russia's diminished role, to extend their own influence among the Islamic peoples as much as they possibly can. In addition, Russia has been accused by Azerbaijan of supporting the Armenian side both with weapons deliveries and with military personnel. In a formal sense it was allowed to do so under military cooperation agreements signed in the framework of the CIS but politically it used its presence in order to raise the stakes in case Turkey was tempted to involve itself too in Azerbaijan's affairs.

The conflict between Armenia and Azerbaijan is not the only example of ethnic tensions escalating into military conflict. Georgia is another case in point. When it declared its independence in April 1991, it was already facing a secession movement from the Abkhasians and the South Ossetians, two autonomous regions within the Georgian Republic. Although the

Abkhazians, according to a 1989 census, represented under 20 per cent of the population in the region (against 45 per cent for the Georgians with the remainder being Russians and Armenians), Abkhazia claimed its sovereignty and the restoration of the status of republic which it had enjoyed between 1921 and 1930. In the latter year, Abkhaz leaders claimed, their republic had been illegally annexed by Georgia. In July 1993, the Supreme Soviet of the Abkhaz republic reinstated the 1925 Constitution and hence declared the country independent. By that time, fighting had been going on for several months, causing hundreds of casualties and the exodus of tens of thousands of Georgians. The Abkhaz declaration of independence had been preceded in December 1991 by a similar declaration of independence by the South Ossetian Supreme Soviet. The South Ossetians not only wanted to cut themselves loose from Georgia but sought reunification with their kinsfolk in North Ossetia, just across the border in the Russian Federal Republic. Fierce fighting broke out between the Georgian army and South Ossetian separatists. The latter were supported by volunteers from North Ossetia and (it was claimed repeatedly by Tbilisi) also by troops from the Russian Ministry of the Interior. Now a CIS peacekeeping force, consisting of Georgian, South Ossetian and Russian troops, is supervising a tenuous truce, pending a political solution of the problem.

What has been briefly described here as the travails of the newly independent Republic of Georgia to keep control over her territory, could be repeated almost word-for-word in the case of Moldova. When this republic became independent, it had to face separatist movements both from the Turkish-speaking Gagauz in the south and the Russian and Ukrainian people living in the Dnestr valley, bordering on the Ukraine. The two groups of minorities had been alarmed by the nationalistic upsurge of the Moldavians who in 1989 had made Moldavian (a language very close to Romanian) the official language of the republic. They also reintroduced the Latin alphabet which had been replaced by Cyrillic when the country was annexed by the Soviet Union as part of the Hitler–Stalin pact. The greatest fear of both minority groups was the possible reunification of Moldova with Romania which was indeed one of the foremost aims of the Moldavian nationalists. The issues relating to the language and alphabet, then, were merely seen as first steps towards such reunification.

While an armed conflict with the Gagauz minority in the south was to be averted at the last minute, it proved to be more difficult to impress the much larger Russian minority in the self-proclaimed Dnestr Republic. Indeed, counting on the presence of the Fourteenth Soviet Army in Moldova and on the Russian Kozaks who had come to defend their co-nationals, militia of the breakaway Dnestr Republic engaged in a series of armed clashes with Moldavian security and police forces in December 1991 and in the early months of 1992. Tension increased in the summer of 1992 when Moldovian troops attacked Benderi, one of the strongholds of the Dnestr Republic. The attack was repelled by the combined forces of Russian militia, the Kozaks and elements of the former Soviet Fourteenth Army, now under the Russian command of General Alexander Lebed. While a shortlived joint Moldovan, Russian and 'Dnestr' peace-keeping force failed to stop the fighting and weapons continued to pour in also from Romania, it was scarcely surprising that negotiations over the withdrawal of the Fourteenth Army dragged on throughout 1993. Lebed made no secret of the fact that the Army's role was to protect the Russian minority, but it proved also to be a convenient means of pressurizing the Moldovans to renounce reunification with Romania and to become a member of the CIS. When these objectives were achieved – the first by the cancellation of a referendum on the issue and by the subsequent victory of anti-reunification parties in national elections, the second by the signature of CIS-adherence in April 1994 – talks about withdrawal of the Fourteenth Army could be seriously resumed, particularly because actual fighting had stopped and the breakaway Dnestr Republic had, for all practical purposes, established itself as a political reality. Eventually, in October 1994, Russia and Moldova reached an agreement providing for the withdrawal of the Fourteenth Army over a period of three years.

The conflict over Nagorno-Karabakh and the conflicts in Georgia and Moldavia are but three examples of the way ethnic tensions can escalate into bloody conflicts. The most terrible example, of course, is the war that has been fought in former Yugoslavia between the Serbs, the Croats and the Muslims – the causes of which, evolution and consequences are well known.

The purpose of this section, has not been to give an exhaustive account of all ethnic conflicts arising from the break-up of the FSU. Rather the aim has been to show that ethnic tensions are evident throughout the continent, that they are especially virulent in the countries of Central and Eastern Europe and that, untended, they can become a security risk both for the countries immediately involved and for a larger, regional zone as well.

Institutional Problems

A third factor explaining the state of confusion in the former communist countries, and a source of potential instability as well, is the difficult transition from an authoritarian to a democratic political system.

While a few of these countries (Czechoslovakia, Poland, Hungary and the Baltic states) had varying degrees of experience with democratic institutions before the communist takeover, most of them had none. Besides the lack of experience and tradition with democratic practice, there is also the question of experienced manpower, especially in the successor states of the FSU. Indeed, as has already been pointed out, leading functions in the civil administration, the courts, the military and so on were manned by representatives of the 'centre' – that is, by Russians. Since independence, some of these functions have been taken over by the local elite but many continue to be carried out by representatives of the former imperial power. This may add to the discredit of these institutions in the newly–independent states.

Keeping these two elements in mind, and recalling the time it has taken the countries of Western Europe and North America to construct civil society and a state of law, it is surely not surprising that, five years after the ending of communist rule, the democratization process is still showing serious flaws. Nevertheless, the evidence concerning which people stand for election and the large percentages of electors who actually participate in the elections is a healthy sign of a democratic reflex. The point, of course, is not so much what the individual people think or do. They are critical enough of the authorities and they do not shy away from saying so in public. The same applies to the media which have never before had a semblance of the freedom they currently enjoy. The point is what happens with their vote. Do parliaments, once elected, have real power in the legislative process? Do they control their governments? Are there checks and balances between the different branches of government? Are laws, once enacted, also executed? Do individuals have the possibility of claiming their rights in court? Are the courts responsive to such claims? Are they impartial? These are all questions which are almost impossible to answer for such a heterogeneous group of nations. What seems to be clear, however, is the fact that authoritarian tendencies, as inherited from the past, can still be noticed in a number of cases. They are reflected in the type of strong presidential regimes, like the one in Russia, where parliament, in its relations with the executive, is very weak indeed.

It took the British parliament hundreds of years to wrest from the Crown the legislative and political powers it now enjoys. Maybe it is unsurprising that it will take more than five years before parliaments – and the courts as well – have acquired the independence and the clout to stand up against government and bureaucracy or that the ordinary citizen, who had hoped to reap immediately all the fruits of an open, democratic society, remains confused.

Economic Problems

One of the main causes of the collapse of the Soviet Union may well have been imperial 'fatigue' – that is the growing gap between the demands occasioned by the preservation of its empire and by the confrontation with the West and what it politically and economically could sustain. Indeed, the very beginning of the end was the advent of Mikhail Gorbachev as Secretary-General of the Soviet Communist Party and the launching of his two-track modernization programme, known under the catchwords *perestroika* and *glasnost*. The first was necessary to reverse the downward slide of Soviet economic performance; the second to produce the kind of open, outward-looking society without which no basic reform was possible. *Glasnost* had the additional advantage of inspiring the West to place more trust in the Soviet Union, to spiral down the arms race and, more generally, to give the Soviets the breathing space they needed to reform. However, the lack of a coherent approach to economic reform, indeed Gorbachev's reliance on market-oriented, liberal economists at one time and on conservative, command-type economists at other times, caused the economic actors to become completely disorientated. Yet, through his policies, Gorbachev had set in motion a dynamic which eventually would lead to the independence of the Central European people's democracies, the disappearance of Comecon and the Warsaw Pact and, ultimately, of the Soviet Union itself.

While some Central European states, most notably Hungary, had already experimented with economic reform, the satellite economies were on the whole in a not much better shape than the Soviet one. With the transition from a socialist to a market economy, they had to face more or less the same problems which Russia and the other successor states of the Soviet Union would encounter a few years later. These problems related both to the macro- and the microeconomic level and ranged from the lack of adequate fiscal systems and property laws to the inexperience and the lack of initiative and entrepreneurship of individual players. Economic emergency programmes included the devaluation of the national currency and the easing out of price controls and of subsidies to enterprises in deficit as well as to food, energy and housing. They further included the restructuring of the military–industrial complex and privatization, first of agriculture and the goods and services sector, later on also of larger industrial complexes. The deflationary policies, necessary to obtain needed credits from the IMF, World Bank and the EU, caused much hardship and – a previously unknown phenomenon in socialist countries – unemployment.

The rather dramatic reorientation of trade and investment patterns from intra-bloc to West-oriented relations also did nothing to improve the situation in the short run. Indeed, the loss of traditional Russian markets – for electric appliances from the Baltics or chemical products and machinery from Czechoslovakia, for example – could not easily be replaced by new markets in the West. The low quality of goods on the one hand, and the lack of marketing and sales techniques on the other, made it extremely difficult to penetrate West European markets. The westward reorientation of trade was partly the result of political choice – that is, willingness to underpin newly won independence with solid economic ties with the West – but partly also of purely economic factors. Russian energy deliveries, for example, suddenly had to be paid for at world-market prices and in hard currency. At the same time, Russian importers preferred Western high-technology and Western design over uncompetitive products from their former Comecon partners. Hence these partners had no choice but to try to sell their products elsewhere and to earn the hard currency needed to pay for the vital energy supplies.

The combination of all these factors led to a dramatic reduction in living standards in all the former communist countries. In real terms, per capita GNP during the 1989–94 period fell by an estimated 25–50 per cent on average, and only recently can the first signs of recovery and of renewed economic growth be perceived. The sometimes massive unemployment, the reappearance of visible poverty and, at the same time, the conspicuous consumption of a fortunate few who often acquired their wealth through speculation, corruption or organized crime, have led to frustration and anger among large sections of the population.

These feelings of anger and frustration have swept the communist parties back into power in one former communist state after another. The elections for the Russian *Duma* of 17 December 1995 were but the last in a series in which the communists – whether in a reconstructed form or under their old denomination – have made their comeback. While nowhere they have sought to turn the reform clock back, they do insist on the necessity to slow it down, to keep some elements of a planned economy and to reduce the pain caused by the transition to a market economy by maintaining, or reinstalling, a social safety net. So far, no large-scale social unrest has broken out but unless real improvement can be sensed to be around the corner, hopes for a better material life may not constitute a counterbalance to the frustration and the anger over the present misery for very much longer.

A peculiar aspect of the economic problems, resulting from imperial break-up, is the question of control over energy resources around the Caspian Sea. While until 1991 energy resources were Soviet, whatever the territory of the former Union where they were found, after the dissolution of the Soviet Union the exploitation of these resources became the exclusive preserve of the newly independent states, in this case Kazakhstan, Turkmenistan and Azerbaijan. Kazakhstan and Turkmenistan have little choice but to export their oil and gas via pipelines running through Russian territory. But Azerbaijan does have a choice. Its oil can be piped via a route north of the Caucasus mountain range over CIS territory (Baku-Grozny-Novorossysk) or it can take a shorter route south of the Caucasus through Georgia (Baku-Tbilisi-Batumi). In both cases, the oil will have to be loaded on tankers which then will have to pass the bottleneck of the Turkish Straits. Another option would be to pipe the oil overland to the Turkish city of Ceyhan (in the south-east, close to the border with Syria), either by deviating the pipeline at Tbilisi or even running it through Armenia.

In view of the strategic importance of the oil route and the economic benefits to be drawn from transit rights, the choice of the transport route could be expected to be a bone of contention among the interested parties. One of the first things the Azeri government did was to entrust the exploitation of its offshore oil reserves for a period of 30 years to an international consortium led by British Petroleum but dominated by American interests. After long negotiations with the Azeri and Russian governments the consortium recently decided to split the deal. Most of the first 5 million tons will be transported via the northern route. Afterwards, the southern route via Georgia – which has to be reconstructed at great cost – will be preferred. For the more distant future, the construction of a pipeline to the Turkish site of Ceyhan is being seriously considered. Officially, the preference for the southern route is explained in purely economic terms. Russian transit rights are US$2.12 per barrel; those of Georgia only US$0.43. The geopolitical reasons for the southern preference are, however, equally obvious. The northern route not only passes through Chechnya, a war-ravaged area still in rebellion against Russia, but it also terminates at the Russian city of Novorossysk.

Since oil from the Caspian area may be as important for world energy supplies in the next century as Gulf supplies are at present, the Western members of the consortium surely must have wondered whether it would be wise to transport the oil through Russia whose future relationship with the West is unpredictable. On the other hand, the interest which countries like Russia, Turkey and Iran have shown in the conflicts raging in the area – and perhaps their active involvement as well – must be partly explained by the economic and strategic power game over Caspian oil.

The OSCE as an All-European Security Institution

The successful transition from a planned economy to a market economy and from an authoritarian regime to a democratic one clearly is in the interest of the countries directly involved. But since democratic countries tend to be more peaceful as they prefer negotiated, diplomatic solutions to violent conflict, such transitions are also in the interest of the rest of Europe and of the international community as well. Various strategies for facilitating and speeding up the transition process exist. They include economic and financial aid, the opening up of markets, technical and managerial assistance, cooperation in the field of education, and assistance in the introduction of pluralistic democratic procedures and practices.

Perhaps the biggest contribution to be made, however, would be the creation of a security environment enabling all attention and energy to be focused on the internal restructuring of society. While there is no absolute correlation between the degree of democracy of a given state and the relative absence of outside pressure, it nonetheless stands to reason that a siege mentality – caused by real or imagined threats – will tend to rally political forces around a strong individual or a strong government. In the face of outside threats political divisions are seen as an unaffordable – indeed, as a dangerous luxury – and opposing voices, as a rule, will tend to be smothered. Moreover, in a situation where no enemies, either actual or potential, are perceived, defence budgets can be cut and economic, social or educational outlays increased. On the political side, a more relaxed international environment will also allow more space and freedom for those segments of the population which are not in full agreement with the government. It is in this framework that the OSCE can continue to play a useful role.

During the Cold War, the main function of the CSCE – at the time still the Conference, rather than the Organization – was twofold. The CSCE was meant to be a substitute for a formal peace treaty recognizing the borders and the political realities which had grown out of the Second World War. At the same time, it was also meant to overcome these same realities by instituting a permanent political dialogue between East and West and by introducing a number of confidence-building measures aimed at softening the sharp edges of confrontation. In addition, the CSCE had adopted a series of principles which were intended to introduce a minimum of civilized conduct both within and across the borders of the participating countries.

With the end of the Cold War, the CSCE was up for re-evaluation because its principal function – preventing the East–West confrontation from getting out of control – had ceased to exist. In the euphoria over the nascent New World Order, envisaged against the backdrop of the newly-found cooperation in the UN Security Council and the united stance against Iraq's occupation of Kuwait, a new era of peaceful international cooperation was thought to have set in. At their summit meeting in Paris, in November 1990, the heads of state or government of the CSCE countries formally declared the era of division and confrontation in Europe to be ended. And with the

Charter of Paris, they undertook to lay the groundwork for a cooperative security structure for the new Europe.

It was widely thought that, since the military dimension of security had become a less overriding issue, attention could henceforth be focused on democratic institutions and on economic development and human rights, including the rights of minorities. With regard to democracy, for example, the participating states undertook to 'build, consolidate and strengthen democracy as the only system of government of our nations'. They also declared that 'democracy, with its representative and pluralist character, entails accountability to the electorate, the obligation of public authorities to comply with the law and justice to be administered impartially'. In the economic sphere, the Paris Charter included, for the first time in the history of the CSCE, a reference to the development of market economies and added property rights to basic human rights, mentioned in the Helsinki Final Act.

In Paris, the heads of states or government also confirmed the language adopted a few months earlier by the Copenhagen Meeting on the Human Dimension with regard to national minorities. Key parts of the Declaration adopted at Copenhagen, which are of particular relevance in the context of this chapter, read as follows:

> Participating states will endeavour to ensure that persons belonging to national minorities, notwithstanding the need to learn the official language or languages of the State concerned, have adequate opportunities for instruction of their mother tongue or in their mother tongue, as well as, wherever possible and necessary, for its use before public authorities, in conformity with applicable national legislation. In the context of the teaching of history and culture in educational establishments, they will also take account of the history and culture of national minorities. ...
>
> The participating states, in their efforts to protect and promote the rights of persons belonging to national minorities, will fully respect their undertakings under existing human rights conventions and other relevant international instruments and consider adhering to the relevant conventions, if they have not yet done so, including those providing for a right of complaint by individuals.

With these elements of the Copenhagen Declaration as endorsed by the Paris Charter a few months later, the CSCE had elaborated most of the principles and commitments that would allow the institution to operate in the delicate domain of minority questions.

In July 1991 the Geneva Expert Meeting on National Minorities completed the task by adding the following language to the list of principles:

> The participating states recognize that special efforts must be made to resolve specific problems in a constructive manner and through dialogue by means of

negotiations and consultations with a view to improving the situation of persons belonging to national minorities. They recognize that the promotion of dialogue between States, and between States and persons belonging to national minorities, will be most successful when there is a free flow of information and ideas between all parties. With a view to improving their information about the actual situation of national minorities, the participating states will, on a voluntary basis, distribute, through the CSCE secretariat, information to other participating states about the situation of national minorities in their respective territories, as well as statements of national policy in that respect. Issues concerning national minorities, as well as compliance with international obligations and commitments concerning the rights of persons belonging to them, are matters of legitimate international concern and consequently do not constitute exclusively an internal affair of the respective state.

With the matter of principles and general guidelines thus settled at the Paris Summit and at the Geneva Expert Meeting that came in its wake, the heads of state or government then tackled the institutional aspect of their endeavour. They decided to meet at a summit every two years, and hold a Council of Ministers meeting in between and a Committee of Senior Officials meeting several times a year in order to prepare these meetings and to supervise and coordinate CSCE activities. They further created a political Secretariat (based in Prague), the Conflict Prevention Centre (based in Vienna) and the Office for Free Elections, later renamed the Office for Democratic Institutions and Human Rights (based in Warsaw), thus giving a greater continuity and organizational weight to the work of the CSCE. Last but not least, a parliamentary assembly was created, aimed at securing broader public support for CSCE activities.

Later, in 1994, the CSCE was renamed the OSCE and a Secretary-General, a High Commissioner on National Minorities, and a Permanent Council came into existence. From the changes introduced by succeeding summits, the OSCE has, therefore, emerged as an organization whose tasks, working methods and operational capabilities are now more or less clearly defined. Its main task is to bring about a security environment, based on the comprehensive nature of security, on its indivisibility and on a cooperative approach to it. It seeks to accomplish this task by three different means.

1   It sets the norms for interstate and intrastate behaviour in the military and the human rights sphere.
2   It organizes and facilitates a political dialogue among all the actors in the area, keeping in mind that the security of one state may not cause insecurity for another.
3   It seeks to forestall conflicts through preventive diplomacy, to contain

and try to solve them through crisis management, and to restore a security climate through post-crisis management.

Let us consider each of these aspects in turn.

Norm-setting for Interstate and Intrastate Behaviour

First the OSCE has become *de facto* the major norm-setting institution for the region. Participating states have committed themselves to an impressive body of principles and guidelines not only in the politico-military sphere but also in the sphere of human rights, economic and scientific cooperation, the establishment of democratic institutions and the rule of law. Violation of these principles, especially with regard to national minorities, can give rise to OSCE action. Such action cannot be refused by referring to the principle of non-interference in internal affairs. With the Copenhagen Document of 1990, the OSCE did pioneering work in the field of the protection of national minorities. Neither the UN, nor the Council of Europe had until then focused their attention or reached the necessary consensus on this problem area. The instruments at the disposal of the OSCE are the High Commissioner on National Minorities (at present the former Dutch Foreign Minister, Max van der Stoel), the Office for Democratic Institutions and Human Rights, as well as the system of OSCE missions.

Also in the field of norm-setting, mention must of course be made of the Code of Behaviour in the politico-military sphere. Much of the code has its origins in dispositions of the Helsinki Final Act which were, in fact, confidence-building measures. What has been added since then, principally at the Moscow Meeting on the Human Dimension of 1991, deals with the control of civil authorities over military, security and intelligence services.

Organizing and Facilitating a Political Dialogue

The dialogue function of the OSCE had largely proven its usefulness during the Cold War when it was of vital importance for each superpower correctly to evaluate the intentions of the other. The game was relatively simple then, since there were only two players, with the other countries being more or less relegated to a sideshow. Currently, Russia's relationship with the United States, and with the West in general, remains vitally important even though – for the moment at least – real risks of armed conflict do not arise from that relationship. It does nevertheless make a difference if moves, such as the projected eastward expansion of NATO, are viewed in Moscow as inimical acts or not. Only intensive, prolonged dialogue can tell whether hostile reactions are tactical or reflect real anxiety about new dividing lines or renewed attempts to encircle Russia. Conversely, does Russia's opposition to Polish, Czech or Hungarian NATO membership indicate that Russia wants her former sphere of influence to remain neutral for possible recuperation in its sphere of influence later on? Obviously, the issue of possible NATO expansion cannot be summarized in just a few lines. That would make a caricature of a debate which has been going on for quite some time and in which serious arguments on both sides have been put forward.

The example merely shows how vitally important the political dialogue remains. While generals normally take account only of military capabilities, politicians also have to weigh intentions and other hard-to-measure factors such as fear, mistrust or bluff. The importance of the OSCE as a forum for dialogue, from the summit-level to the virtually continuous discussions at the level of the Permanent Council, can therefore hardly be overestimated. The dialogue function is not only important for the relationship between big powers, it also serves a very useful purpose at a more local level. For example, when the issue of citizenship in the Baltic States came up, with the likely exclusion of large numbers of Russian residents, Russia showed her irritation with hints of trade reprisals and possible delays in the withdrawal of Russian troops. It took the sustained effort and the creativity of OSCE institutions, both at the political dialogue level and that of the High Commissioner on National Minorities, to defuse the issue. The peaceful compromise solution to the Russian minority question in the Baltics shows to what extent the existence of an adequate normative framework, coupled with a multi-tiered institutional system of political dialogue can lead to effective, preventive diplomacy.

Political dialogue not only presupposes that all parties are treated on an equal footing, but also that they are part of the system itself. That was perhaps the big mistake of 1992 when the OSCE membership of former Yugoslavia (Serbia and Montenegro) was suspended because of its aggressive role in Croatia and Bosnia-Herzegovina. This meant that, during the entire war, when dialogue with Belgrade was essential, contacts with the Serb leadership had to take place on a bilateral ad hoc basis, enabling the Serb leaders to play one set of negotiators off against another. A further undesired side-effect of Yugoslavia's exclusion was that, by way of reprisal, the Serb leadership suspended the long-term OSCE missions in Vojvodina, Sanjak and Kosovo. The organization was thus deprived of accurate on-the-spot knowledge about human rights abuses perpetrated against Albanians and Hungarians.

Forestalling Conflicts through Preventive Diplomacy

In discussing the preventive diplomacy function of the OSCE, it is worth recalling that, when the political crisis in Yugoslavia was coming to a head in

1991, the international community was completely unprepared to take timely action. For the OSCE, that may sound rather strange as only a few months before, heads of state or government at their summit meeting in Paris had solemnly declared the OSCE to be a major security instrument for the new Europe. They had added a Centre for Conflict Prevention to its institutions and endorsed the far-reaching Copenhagen principles on the rights of minorities. Yet, no steps were taken when the Serbian leadership under Slobodan Milosevic abolished the provincial autonomy of Kosovo and Vojvodina nor was any serious attempt made to dissuade Croatia from declaring its independence until clear-cut guarantees for the Serbian minority in Krajina had been given. Moreover, once the war had started, the OSCE was eclipsed by the EU, and later by the UN, in the search for a political solution to the conflict. Certainly, it did useful work in the sphere of crisis management, most notably by sending missions to Kosovo, Vojvodina and Sanjak as well as to Macedonia, in order to prevent spillover of hostilities to these areas. But the principal lesson learned by the OSCE from the Yugoslav debacle was that conflict prevention has to be prepared well in advance and that it needs a refined machinery, from early warning to mediation, in order to be effective. This machinery now exists. The OSCE has currently eight missions working in Latvia, Estonia, Tadjikistan, Moldova, Macedonia, Georgia, Ukraine and, most recently, in Sarajevo. Their task goes well beyond fact-finding. In general, the missions will seek contacts with local representatives and further dialogue between the parties concerned.

Accomplishments of the OSCE

Looking at the number of armed conflicts witnessed in the OSCE area since the end of the Cold War, one may wonder whether the institution is equal to its task. European security is said to be one and indivisible, but it clearly means something very different on the Western side of the former East–West divide than it does on the Eastern side. Yugoslavia, Moldova, Nagorno-Karabach, Georgia, Tadjikistan and Chechnya demonstrate this fact. Yet, the very essence of preventive diplomacy tends to obscure the record. It is indeed quite easy to point out the failures – they are there for all to see. But who can tell whether discreet diplomatic action, or cumulative actions over a certain period of time, have been conducive or not to the maintenance of peace? Would conflict have spilled over into Kosovo or Macedonia if UN or OSCE observers had not been present on the spot? Would Ukrainians and Russians have clashed over the Crimea if the OSCE had not offered its good offices? And would Hungary and Rumania have gone to war over the Hungarian minority in Transylvania had the OSCE not existed?

It is one of the paradoxes of preventive diplomacy that its results can only be seen in a negative way – that is, in case of failure. That is perhaps the reason why governments and politicians are so little motivated to engage in it. There is nothing to take credit for. In addition, governments usually tend to react only in cases of urgency or when their immediate interests are at stake. During the opening stages of the Yugoslav conflict, when Milosevic started bullying Kosovo, Vojvodina and Montenegro into subservience, few people in the West would take more than a passing interest in what was going on. Kosovo was far away and perhaps the Serbs were right in tightening control over a restive province. Events have shown, of course, that what happened in Kosovo *did* matter. The subjugation of the province and the brutality with which the Serb authorities gained control over the federal institutions provoked intense fears in Slovenia and Croatia. These republics were probably next on the list. Facing the refusal of the Serb leadership to turn Yugoslavia into a loose federation or confederation, Slovenia and Croatia had no choice but to secede. But, even after the war had broken out, people in the West did not see the necessity, nor indeed the urgency, of taking drastic action. In the words of Christoph Bertram: 'Western governments convinced themselves that it did not really concern them and that all they needed to do was to prevent themselves from being "sucked into the quagmire".'[2] Eventually, of course, they were 'sucked into the quagmire' but, in the meantime, the conflict had taken an enormous toll in casualties, displaced persons, wanton destruction and unparalleled inhuman conduct.

Elsewhere, OSCE governments – apparently, having learned something from the Yugoslav disaster – have reacted faster. The case of the Baltics is a good example of what timely, concerted and purposeful action can accomplish. When in the autumn of 1991 Estonia, Latvia and Lithuania almost simultaneously introduced legislation on citizenship, it became immediately clear that a reaction from their Russian neighbour would be forthcoming. Indeed, the three bills had in common that citizenship of the newly independent republics would be reserved for those inhabitants, and their descendants, who had lived in these countries before their annexation in 1940 by the Soviet Union. Non-national residents could apply for citizenship if they fulfilled a number of conditions such as the length of their stay in the country (ten years in Lithuania, 16 years in Latvia, two years in Estonia), proficiency in the national language, renunciation of dual citizenship, knowledge of the constitution and, in the case of Latvia, swearing loyalty to the Republic. To the Russian inhabitants of the republics, these measures constituted a violation of their human rights, a shameful discrimination and, above all, a profound humiliation. Were they not, after all, the representatives of the former imperial power and, until recently, the real masters of the area? Whereas Russian had been the official language next or above the native language, suddenly it was relegated to non-official, second-class status. The Russian minorities in the Baltics were quick to mobilize support in Russia. By dragging its feet on the question of the withdrawal of Russian troops, the Russian government let it be known that *de facto*, if not *de iure*, both issues were linked.

Although bilateral agreements about withdrawal were concluded in early 1992, and small contingents had started to leave, no definite timetable for the conclusion of the withdrawal had been set. In May 1992, the Russian Under-Minister for Foreign Affairs, Sjelov Koedjajev, stated that the completion of the troop withdrawal depended on the availability of barracks and housing in Russia. But he also said that ratification of bilateral agreements might be endangered by the linguistic and citizenship laws. The formal link had been made. It was probably the good fortune of the Baltic States that they could count on much sympathy among the Western countries, especially in Scandinavia. Under the Swedish presidency of the OSCE, the Ministerial Council, meeting in Stockholm in December 1992, decided to send permanent missions to Latvia and Estonia. These acted in parallel with the High Commissioner on National Minorities and succeeded in convincing the authorities to soften the planned legislation and make it more acceptable to the Russian minorities. As Bertram writes:

> What gave weight to the diplomatic effort was not just appeals for a reasonable compromise, but the concern of the two Baltic governments that failure to reach such a compromise would not only exacerbate relations with powerful neigbouring Russia, but also with major supporters in the West, in particular that it could jeopardise prospects of closer relations with the European Union and the North Atlantic Alliance...[3]

One condition, then, for successful mediation is timely reaction, based on a sense of urgency. Governments have to realize that much is at stake, including their own vital interests. In the case of the Baltic question, it should not surprise us that the sense of urgency was most noticeable among the Scandinavian countries. Geographic proximity, common historic experience, even linguistic affinity (between Estonia and Finland) pushed these countries to set the item high on the OSCE agenda. And they did so long before the issue had gone out of control and before the parties to the conflict had taken positions from which it might prove difficult to withdraw without losing face. Another condition is leverage – that is, a combination of positive and negative incentives which make de-escalation and compromise attractive to both sides. The incentive for the Russians was that, by accepting a compromise, they would prove to be a reliable partner that did not try to bully its smaller neighbours into submission. Failing to acquiesce in a compromise formula would conversely have fuelled Western suspicion of neo-imperialistic behaviour. The incentive for the Baltic governments was the desire to integrate in Western political institutions and the accompanying necessity not to bring security problems into these institutions. That brings us to a final condition – the interplay between various actors on the international scene. Concerted action in this case involved not only the OSCE through its missions and the High Commissioner on National Minorities, it also involved the Council of Europe – which helped redraft the disputed legislation – NATO and the EU. During the consultations leading up to the launching of the Stability Pact, the EU had made it clear to prospective candidates for membership that no applications for accession would be considered unless they had resolved outstanding conflict situations with their neighbours. Of course, the most convincing argument to bring to bear on parties in a conflict is the threat of military force. But, apart from the fact that such a threat must be credible and hence be in line with the aim to be achieved, the OSCE has no military force at its disposal and neither is it entitled to mandate coercive action by someone else. Only the UN Security Council can do so. OSCE action is restricted to the lower level of conflict resolution: early warning, preventive diplomacy, conflict resolution and crisis management.

At the Budapest meeting of 7–8 December 1995, the OSCE foreign ministers decided to engage in an additional task, that of post-crisis management in Bosnia-Herzegovina. The peace-building task includes supervision of the preparation, the conduct and the monitoring of elections, monitoring human rights, the appointment of a human rights ombudsman and assistance to the parties involved both in their negotiations on arms control, confidence- and security-building and in the implementation and verification of resulting agreements. The OSCE has also been invited by the Croatian government to establish a long-term mission there with the objective of assisting central and local authorities in building democracy, protecting human and minority rights and promoting the safe return of refugees. Through these efforts the OSCE will contribute to the peaceful reintegration of the formerly occupied territories. The OSCE failed to prevent the conflict in former Yugoslavia and has been of little help in ending it. But now that the war is over, its big challenge is thus to prove that it can play a useful role in building the peace. In view of the widespread bitterness over the slaughter, the ethnic cleansing and the systematic destruction, building peace between Croats, Muslims and Serbs will of course be no easy task. Ethnic hatred, deep in the hearts of people after four years of war, will see to that. Acts of revenge will be inevitable. The question is to what extent it will be possible to contain them. In fact, the OSCE's task in post-war former Yugoslavia is twofold: it will have to build peace and make democratic institutions work again, but it will at the same time have to engage in preventive diplomacy in order to prevent the conflict from flaring up again. While this may be too mammoth a task for any institution, the OSCE is probably the only one which has the norms, the instruments and the procedures – and increasingly also the experience – to carry it out successfully.

Conclusion

With the end of the Cold War, the risk of a major conflict and of nuclear Armageddon has disappeared, but numerous smaller, potentially very disruptive conflicts have appeared in its place. The New World Order that seemed within reach at the end of the Gulf War, has not materialized. Wars continue to be fought, even in Europe.

The collapse of communism and the disintegration of the Soviet bloc and later of the Soviet Union itself have generated tensions causing instability and potential, or actual, conflicts. These tensions are not only ethnic in origin, even though they are the most immediate cause of instability; they are also political and psychological and have to do with the loss of purpose and, for the Russians, the loss of empire. Finally, the economic plight of the post-communist states and the lack of experience with democratic institutions make these states potentially unstable.

For the Central European states, the choices are clear : their quest for security, democracy and economic development is leading them to seek accession to NATO and the EU. Such accession would undoubtedly satisfy them on all three counts but, to the other emerging democracies which, with the possible exception of the Baltic States, have no prospect of joining either, this would mean creating a new East–West divide. Given the uncertainty of the direction that Russia may take, a feeling of exclusion coming on top of its other predicaments, may strengthen anti-Western sentiments in Moscow and give added vigour to attempts to reconstitute a cohesive bloc of its own. That would bring Europe back to its point of departure – a confrontation between two opposing blocs – the only difference from the past being the eastward shift of the dividing line by a few hundred miles and the absence of irreconcilable ideologies to sustain the confrontation.

The OSCE is one among a number of international organizations which are seeking to transform the previous confrontational relationship between the countries of the former antagonistic blocs into one of cooperation and collective security. While the other organizations have a smaller membership or a more limited scope, the OSCE contains *all* the states of the Euro-Atlantic area and does so on the basis of full equality. Its central task is to bring about a security environment based on the comprehensive nature of security, on its indivisibility and on a cooperative approach to it.

Considering the area as a community of shared values, the OSCE has sought to translate these values in a number of principles and norms of interstate and intrastate behaviour. These cover not only the politico-military sphere but also those of human rights and of economic and technological cooperation. Among the shared values explicit mention is now made of pluralistic, parliamentary democracy and the rule of law, market economy and the rights of property, and, in the sphere of human rights, of the rights of national minorities.

The OSCE organizes and facilitates political dialogue among the actors in the area and seeks to prevent or solve conflicts on the understanding that security of one state may not cause insecurity for another. Preventive diplomacy or successful crisis management presuppose not only timely action and a sense of urgency on behalf of the international community, but also cooperation among the various states and international organizations. Since the OSCE has no military means at its disposal, it has to combine its moral and political persuasive force with more material incentives or disincentives to be provided by others. While, by its very nature, preventive diplomacy cannot be proven to have been successful, the example of the Yugoslav conflict as opposed to the crisis in the Baltics underlines the critical importance of these conditions. In short, the successive Paris, Helsinki and Budapest Summits have turned the former CSCE into an organization which provides the conceptual basis, the mechanisms and the instruments needed to tackle the new challenges of the present time.

Notes

1 In the context of this contribution, the term 'Central Europe' will be used for those countries formerly known as 'People's Democracies' which constituted the Soviet Union's western sphere of influence, including former Yugoslavia which broke away from satellite status in the late 1940s. The term 'Eastern Europe', on the other hand, will refer to the former Soviet republics, including Russia proper, but excluding the Central Asian republics which do not belong to the historic or geographical area of Europe. Of course, that in no way diminishes their membership of the OSCE of which they are as much a part as the other non-European countries, namely Canada and the United States of America.
2 Christoph Bertram (1995–96) 'Multilateral Diplomacy and Conflict Resolution', *Survival*, **37**, (4), p. 66.
3 Ibid., p. 69.

14 The Role of Memory and Identity in the Process of Change, with Special Reference to the Former Soviet Union and Eastern Europe: Psychological Perspectives

Rita R. Rogers

Introduction

This chapter addresses four issues:

- **The impact of change since the collapse of the Soviet empire.** These changes are viewed as an identity crisis which promotes regression to old patterns of adjustment, a romantic view of the long-term past and a denial of the recent past.
- **The concept of individual identity.**
- **Collective identity (national consciousness).** This is discussed from the perspective of an 'imagined community', a cultural artifact invented by few but irrationally powerful to many.[1] National consciousness is easily manipulated. Two examples of the creation of a collective community are used for illustration: the strategically designed foundation of the Solidarity movement in Poland in 1981, which is contrasted with the creation of the politically conscious Turkish minority

in Bulgaria resulting from the imposition of Bulgarian name changes on the Turkish minority.
- **The role of memory in the foundation of personal and collective identity.** Differentiation is made between the impact of memory of emotionally loaded events (such as wars and concentration camps) versus everyday events. It will be argued that the skilful inflammation of hurtful memories can be a dangerous tool in the hands of political merchants of hatred.

Current tensions and changes in the former Soviet Union (FSU) and its former satellites represent different stages in identity formation and transformation. Stressing sovereignty as a symbol of independence is a transitory signal of insecurity, while acknowledgement of interdependence represents realistic adjustment to time and space.

In times of crisis (especially in an identity crisis) the individual falls back on earlier patterns of adjustment. In psychiatric terminology, he or she regresses to old behaviours with which he is familiar and which protect him from the difficulties of adjustment to new situations. In assessing the identity of an individual, one needs to evaluate the gap which exists between his or her perceptions of his or her identity and aspired identity (in psychiatric terminology, ego ideal).

The Impact of Change in the Post-Soviet Empire

The international and intranational changes which have occurred since 1989 have been difficult to absorb. They have challenged established patterns of adjustment in East and Central Europe, as well as in the Western European and American international equilibrium. For Eastern European soldiers who patrolled the Brandenburger Tor guarded the identity of the West as much as they guarded the rule of the communist regime. From a psychopolitical perspective, one has to consider the current tensions as a collective identity crisis which forces the countries of the FSU and its satellites to redefine themselves, their institutions, their beliefs and their relationships with each other. Until the collapse of the Soviet empire, the satellites of the FSU identified themselves with the paradigm of the 'prisoner' which permitted West Europeans and Americans to identify themselves with the paradigm of the 'missionary'.[2] Both sides have now lost their identity paradigms but sometimes act as if the past were the present, because of the insecurity created by the current chaos. Since chaos increases uncertainty, it is natural to try to combat such insecurity by regression and by falling back on old patterns of adjustments – patterns which do not fit current realities. While the satellites of the FSU saw themselves as prisoners, their focus was on the jailer. Now the jailer has gone they need to look for other scapegoats – other ethnic groups, Jews, gypsies, villains – which divert attention from themselves, their own abilities and strengths and their own shortcomings. Insecurity of identity increases the craving for exhibitionistic sovereignty. The West Europeans and Americans can no longer see themselves as 'missionaries'. The West, but especially the United States, has become the world policeman and instructor.[3]

Reform in Russia will never fit the American model.[4] Attempts to bring Central and East European countries into line with the perceptual models of the Western countries increase the craving for exaggerated sovereignty and demonstrable independence. Yet this craving is in profound discord with current trends towards interdependence arising from globalization and instant connectedness through electronic mail, faxes, mergers and the worldwide web.

The countries which previously belonged to the Soviet empire are undergoing a profound change in their collective identities. For nearly 50 years previously that identity was determined by the nature of their relationship with the Soviet Union.[5] It is now tempting for them to erase from the public record any reference to the communist era, as though it had been but an unhappy and transient interlude in their existence. In its place is substituted a more distant past which is used as a source of identity and reference.[6]

The romanticized view of the long-term past, together with the discontinuity with the immediate past, prevents newly established, independent countries from adjusting to current realities and precipitates the emergence of cults, feverish religions and unassimilated caricatures of the 'imagined' West. In chaos, there is a tendency to search for answers and avoid questions, particularly those pertaining to self-identity: who we are, what is in us from our recent past, and what part does that, as well as our long-term past, play in our current identity?

The West European and American paradigm of 'missionary turned instructor' demands the imposition of democracy in Central and East European countries without questioning whether democracy can be imposed on people who are not democrats. George Schopflin compares imposing democracy on non-democrats with the failed attempt by communists to impose a proletarian revolution without a working class.[7] The West has to learn to see the Central and East European countries through those countries' lenses rather than through its own. It can achieve this only through a thorough knowledge of history and geography and by discarding the rose-coloured, romantic spectacles through which it views itself and others. But the perception of the 'otherness' of another group is only possible when one's own identity is embedded as a continuing, stable point of reference. For the West, that continuous, stable point of reference for almost 50 years was the Cold War.

Currently, a re-emergence of old fault lines is also evident: societies which have had the Western experience of the Reformation, Renaissance, Enlightenment, and Revolution – the Europe of Protestantism and Catholicism – are confronting the societies of Orthodox Christianity and Islam. The profound change in identity in East and Central Europe has indeed provoked insecurity in identity in the West (being analogous to how the colonizer also absorbs and is influenced by those whom he colonized). Western plans to turn the western fringe of Europe (Poland, the Czech Republic and Hungary) into Euro-suburbs will leave former Byzantine Europe to stew in its provincial juices.[8] It will reawaken in Orthodox Christians in the former satellite countries the painful memories of feeling excluded from Europe by the West, will precipitate a regression to old intra-ethnic and interethnic rivalries and prevent adjustment to current realities and tasks. Ethnic legends increase the need to justify one's own group's misdeeds by ascribing them to the misdeeds of others (scapegoating).

Identity

Identity is a conscious sense of self. The self here is viewed as a conscious mind and body agency not entity.[9] The concept of identity has persisted over eight decades. Its origins can be traced to the earliest interplay of the infant's temperament with the mother's attitude.[10] Throughout its growth, the infant absorbs the attributes of others and identifies with others; its identity acquires its final shape by integrating contradictory identifications.

Psychiatrically, an individual is considered to have a cohesive identity when he or she possesses a realistic body image, constant attitude, gender authenticity, ethnicity and a feeling of subjective sameness. Identity arises both from intrapsychic and environmental factors. The term 'identity', was introduced by V. Tausk;[11] it is a continuous process, through which people experience themselves anew while possessing a persistent feeling of sameness. The ability to achieve flexibility in adjustment while feeling a continuum in one's basic personality is an essential feature of identity.

In the 1950s E. Ericson reselected the term and used the term 'ego identity' to denote both a persistent sameness within oneself (self-sameness) and a persistent sharing of some kind of essential character with others.[12] In assessing the identity of the individual, the gap between an individual's ego identity and his or her ego ideal (namely, the way the person sees him or herself versus the way he or she would like to see his or herself) has to be assessed. Identity issues and conflicts arise in adolescence, creating a turmoil involving both progressive and regressive trends. Regressive trends overwhelm the individual during times of crisis. In late middle age, individuals tend to re-evaluate whether or not they have been true to their innermost desires.[13] The paradox that individuals with a consolidated identity change so much and yet, in many ways, remain the same is attributed to R.M. Emde[14] (there being an ever-present affective continuity in the psychic life). Individuals with a crystallized identity are true to themselves and have a sense of generational continuity.

Collective Identity and its Roots

National consciousness is a cultural artifact of a particular kind.[15] Such cultural artifacts change over time and under particular situations and circumstances. They command particularly profound emotional legitimacy. Philosophical poverty, indeed incoherence, of national consciousness increases the irrational power of nationalism.

Nationalism is not the awakening of nations to self-consciousness. Nationalism invents nations where they do not exist. A nation is born when a few people decide that it should exist.[16] While religion is a matter of pure feeling, one can think a nation or a radical separation between past and present.[17] Benedict Anderson traces the cultural roots of imagined communities to the development of print.[18] G.W.F. Hegel, quoted in Anderson, observed that newspapers serve modern man as a substitute for morning prayers,[19] creating the extraordinary mass ceremony, the almost precisely simultaneous consumption (imagining) of the newspaper as a fiction. What would Hegel have thought and written about Cable News Network (CNN) which spreads instantaneously, repeatedly and transglobally the news from around the world – news which affects and is perceived through different cultural lenses, often increasing the gap between existing realities and aspirations?

Print capitalism gave a new fixity to language which in the long run helped build the image of antiquity so central to the subjective idea of the nation.[20] Another vernacular of the printed page to which Anderson assigns the birth of a nation is the musical score.[21] He mentions Friedrich Smetana, Anton Dvorak, Leos Janacek, Edvard Grieg and Bela Bartok. The accumulated memory of print is, then, one of the sources of nation-building.

The Polish Solidarity Movement: an Example of a Strategically-designed Collective Identity

Collective identity can be fabricated through the utilization of collective memory. An example of an anticipatory strategy for creating a collective community is the formation of the organization of Solidarity (*Solidarność*) which was formed in 1980 and implanted into the hearts of Poles as a *unified mass movement* in possession of the truth about Poland.²² It attempted and succeeded in creating an imagined community of Poland. Solidarity used images in unofficial postage stamps which were actually stickers used in their communications with each other to oppose government discourse in several ways. First, it created satirical images to expose the absurdities of government language, and thus attempted to undermine governmental authority. Second, it tried to establish its own authoritative discourse of images – one that constructed a counter-hegemonic representation of national history and identity. Third, it transformed certain words into images in an effort to control meaning in the public domain and to resist linguistic co-option and semantic impoverishment. The 'argument of images' in which Solidarity was engaged was based upon a linguistic ideology that based authority upon truth. In these images, Solidarity claimed to be the holder of the truth about Poland, Polish history and the nature of the communist government – a truth expressed in the movement's use of language and imagery. Using stamps to present a view of Poland's history based on a sacrificial and religious tradition placed Solidarity alongside other uprisings in that tradition. This historical representation not only countered the official history propounded by the communist government, but also portrayed Solidarity as a unified mass movement in possession of the truth about Poland. In the 1980s, truth, especially truth in language, became an important basis for political discourse and opposition in Poland. The claim to truth was significant in Solidarity's claim to authority.

Through stamps, Solidarity accorded itself authority by using the visual emblems of Polish nationalism. Underground *Solidarność* identified itself as an independent society of people who, like their forebears, were culturally Western.²³ Adam Mitchnik insisted that a transformation of Polish society could be achieved only if the population acted as if they did, in fact, live in a free society.²⁴ He recommended, and *Solidarność* instituted, the use of stamps featuring saints, Polish literary figures, Solidarity leaders, and events in Polish history. The stamps, depicting historical events worked on memory, focusing on the history of oppression and Polish resistance, representing the German–Soviet Pact of 1939 (drawn up by Joachim von Ribbentrop and Vyacheslav Molotov) and the Katyn Forest massacre of 1940 by the Soviets. They compared the Polish uprising of the nineteenth century with the post-1945 workers' protests. There were also stamps portraying individuals, such as Marshal Josef Pilsudski, defeating the Soviet Union in 1920, thus linking present martyrs to past heroes. Other stamps depicted religious images, such as Pope John Paul II and the Madonna. Images of Chernobyl emphasized the catastrophes emanating from the Soviet Union.

Solidarność also created the collective community through the use of language – that is, it debunked governmental language, such as official statements that a prisoner died at the hands of medical professionals when, in fact, he had been executed by security forces. And it debunked statements by the government about normalization in international relations, identifying it as 'denormalization'. In short, Solidarity considered that the Communist Party's language colonized the Polish language.

Transforming an Invisible Minority into a Political Action Group: The Turks in Bulgaria

In his paper, 'What's in a Name?', Daniel Bates describes how a persecuted minority can become a power broker.[25] He warns against equating ethnic politics with ancient intractable animosities. Ethnicity can be initiated through selective utilization of hurtful shared memories. According to Daniel Bell, collective identity and organizations raising the idea of ethnicity require a perceived interest in common, as well as an affectual bond.[26] The most frequently used tool is the memory of collective suffering at the hands of an outsider.[27] Bates gives us an example of the minority population in Bulgaria who, prior to 1990, had no public voice and no organizational structure. Between 1990 and 1994 the rise of politicized Turkish ethnicity constructed a sense of a national Muslim political community and transformed the Turks in Bulgaria from persecuted minority to political power broker.

Although contemporary ethnic population figures were not reliably accurate, according to a 1989 Ministry of the Interior source, ethnic Turks, including Tartars, numbered 847 584 or 9.5 per cent of Bulgaria's 8.9 million population; gypsies numbered 576 927, or 6.5 per cent; Christians and Muslims were approximately equal in number; and Pomaks, a term that refers to Bulgarian-speaking Muslims, numbered 268 971, or 3 per cent.[28] In 1960 legislation, in the form of a population registration law, permitted Albanians, Armenians, gypsies, Pomaks, and Turks to take Bulgarian surnames.[29] Few complied at that time. However, in 1962, Pomak names were forcibly changed in one region, the order only being revised after a mass demonstration in 1964. From 1962 Turkish language schools were in effect eliminated by virtue of being merged with Bulgarian schools, and all instruction was shifted to Bulgarian. Educational cadres were also integrated. Shortly thereafter, all Turkish language training programmes, apart from the Turkology programme at the University of Sofia, were closed. Turkish theatre groups were merged with Bulgarian groups, and programmes were no longer offered in Turkish. Between 1968 and 1978, the government followed an intermittent policy of encouraging emigration, and 120 000 people moved to Turkey. Around 1971, forced assimilation, referred to as the 'process of rebirth' became the official Communist Party policy, although there is scant documentation of a formal policy decision and no legislation to this effect.[30] The years 1984 and 1985 saw a forced assimilation of the Turks in the form of a name-change programme. Beginning with rural areas of the Rodopis in 1984, Turkish speakers (including smaller numbers of Tartars, Allevians and gypsies) who had not already done so were compelled to take Bulgarian names. At the same time, Islamic religious practice and education were curtailed and the public use of the Turkish language was prohibited. The authorities in Bulgaria conducted a media campaign, including the publication of purportedly archaeological and physical anthropological investigations, to show 'evidence' that all Bulgarians were of one common racial stock and that minorities were forced to convert by the Ottomans. The communist Bulgarian media insisted that these minorities were 'grateful' for being allowed to assume Slavic names. In reality, the name-change programme was administered extremely harshly and, even though individuals were permitted to 'choose' Slavic names, if these names bore any similarity to Islamic names, new names were arbitrarily assigned.[31] People were forced at gunpoint to sign a 'petition' for name change so that it looked like a personal 'request'; this was perceived as an insult to the identity of Muslims of the Turkish minority.

The enforced name change mobilized the ethnic Muslim community from its previous state of invisibility in the 1960s to a heightened Turkish Muslim self-awareness. Their shared experience of injustice strengthened their communal ties. They viewed the attacks on their religion and language as an assault on their identity; this precipitated an intensity in the quest for their own social identity and a stronger attachment to their own language and religion. From being an almost invisible minority, they became a political action group.

I have conducted no personal interviews to examine the motivations of the Turkish minorities or, for that matter, the Bulgarian authorities when they decreed the name changes. However, it can be presumed that the authorities expected that their action would appease and gratify the Bulgarian people. One can only speculate that lingering subconscious memories of the great Bulgarian empire of the fifth and sixth century and its struggle with the Byzantine Empire might have been in the background. But our unconscious memories cannot differentiate between Constantinople and Istanbul when emotionally loaded with cravings for power, hatred and jealousy.

Conclusion

Nations can exist in the collective memory of a people when the country does not exist. For example, Poland existed for 123 years in the memory of its people, and this painful memory increased their sense of collective identity. '*Yeste Polska ne Zginiela*' ('Poland hasn't gone under yet'), has been the glue which held together the Polish people.

Collective identity in Central and Eastern Europe and the Balkans is linked to ethnicity and religion. Citizenships are exclusive and cannot be compromised. To the nations of Eastern Europe independence is a powerful motor, because most of them have had less than a century of independent existence. Their intelligentsia elaborated their past glories with messages that these had been stolen from them by the imperial overlords. The enemy is an organizing principle, and in times of uncertainty and chaos, there is an increased need to hold on to the enemy image. The certainty of East–West confrontation and animosity was a given around which both East and West could organize their worlds. At present, the West is certain of its democracy, and East and Central Europe are disappointed with the concept. Post-communist countries tried to model their countries according to their visionary model of democracy at a time when this democracy was tarnished in the West. Democracy in East and Central Europe was seen (erroneously) as total freedom and immediate access to Western levels of prosperity. The dream of rejoining Europe was particularly fervent in the 'new countries' – those countries which had felt themselves expelled from Europe because they had never felt quite accepted. The feverish ambition to rejoin Europe was thus tinged with disappointment. Ethnicity resounded in the cultural and affective sphere. Identity, because it is a product of imagination, is not open to compromise. The style in which citizens coped with communism thus influenced how they adapted to capitalism.

The Role of Memory

Humiliating experiences to the collective self can become enshrined as cherished glories. For example, the Serbs have incorporated into their identity their defeat of Kosovo in 1389 which has made Kosovo their Jerusalem. This intergenerationally transmitted memory has eclipsed current realities, such as that 90 per cent of modern-day Kosovo is inhabited by Albanians. The Muslims of Bosnia have been transformed in the Serbs' emotional memories into the Turks of 1389 who defeated them. The Serbs' immersion and obsession with history is brilliantly manipulated by their political leaders, such as Slobodan Milosevic and Radovan Karadzic, who, like all decision-makers, are intimately attuned to their constituencies' hurts and vulnerabilities.

To fight for national aggrandizement, one needs the binding mortar of hatred for the perceived enemy, and the fuel supplied by political arsonists, intellectuals, politicians and clergy who stoke the real and imagined grievances to fan the flames of fear and intolerance. When a group has been exposed to humiliating experiences which have been perceived as injuries to its identity, it tends to embrace hatred as its moulding link. Hatred, as defined by Otto Kernberg, is a complex emotion derived from rage.[32] Lack of access, as in Poland, or suppression of one's language, as in Bulgaria, is experienced as a threat to the group's survival.

Wars, victories, defeats, catastrophies, pogroms and hunger are stored differently in our memories than other quiescent events. Such 'peak events' create 'peak affective states' and these become seminal in moulding a group's perception of its role, self-perception, and position in the world. Memory structures acquired during 'peak affective states' are different from those acquired during quiescent periods. Memories during 'peak affective states' skew reality and promote assessment into primitive dichotomies – all good or all bad. With the help of hatred, the bad object is both needed and desired, and the destruction of this object is both needed and desired.[33] This becomes a sure stepping-stone towards dehumanization, defined by Viola Bernard as follows:

> A defense against painful or overwhelming emotions which decreases a person's sense of his own individuality and his perception of the humanness of other people. The collective self under the impact of hatred propaganda is capable also of misperceiving others as subhuman or bad, viewing them as nonhumans, very inanimate items, or dispensable supplies. As such, their maltreatment or even their destruction can be carried out or acquiesced in in the relative freedom from the restraints of conscience of feeling of brotherhood.[34]

How else could we understand the denial of common humanity by the German nation during the Holocaust?

Historical enmity is transmitted intergenerationally much more easily in cultures dedicated to the oral, rather than the written, tradition.[35] Hatred, unlike rage, is chronic and lends itself to intergenerational transmission. When children pick up the hatred from their parents towards a parental enemy, they do not embrace the parental cause out of love for their parents. They do so in order to outshine their parents by proving themselves more powerful than them.[36] It is a means of shaking off their own humiliation of having had a humiliated parent. Collective group hatred leads to violence in its craving for affirmation of one's identity.

Conclusions

In the FSU and Eastern European countries, there is increased tension. The unexpected, profound changes, without previous development of institutions to absorb these changes, and the introduction of democracy to non-democrats, has provoked chaotic changes in international relations, especially in the collective identities of East and Central Europe. Such a crisis creates the temptation to erase the recent past and substitute the distant past as a means of lying to oneself in order to rationalize one's behaviour. It re-exacerbates the old fault lines between Rome and Byzantine Europe. The changes which these countries have to undergo are profound and demand the incorporation, and indeed the assimilation, of the past with the present. The Russians have had to make the most profound changes: from dictatorship to democracy; from a central to a market economy; and from an empire to a nation-state. Most novel is the idea that individual rights override state rights. It can very well be assumed that the adjustment to the new realities of citizens within Russia is more difficult than that undergone by Russians or East Europeans who have emigrated to other countries. In their native countries they must feel 'lost in familiar places' (the title of a book by Edward R. Shapiro and A. Wesley Carr).[37] Such chaos intensifies the search for boundaries to counterbalance fragmentation. Only people with secure identities are able to develop an internalized interpretative stance which protects them from globally dichotomizing everything into good and bad. Insecurity can lead to people falling back on religion, which caters simultaneously for the needs of dependency and irrationality. For both rationality and irrationality are necessary for people to explain themselves to themselves.

It is amazing that the profound change in East and Central Europe has occurred without massive bloodshed. The waves of past patterns of adjustments conflicting with present realities has to be taken as a given. East and Central European countries have had to undergo profound identity transformations since 1989. It could be expected that they would attempt imitational caricatures of their perception of Western democracies. It is understandable that they would introject, like foreign bodies, their images of the West, and that they would ride the waves of glorification of the long-term past, accept alien religious movements and cults, and vacillate between their own identities and those alien assumptions of the identities of the 'Western democracies'. For countries which had excused themselves to themselves by considering themselves to be 'colonized' by the Soviet empire, it will take some time before they stop looking for 'who did it', but will instead look at themselves and at their own strengths and shortcomings. Feeling enamoured with independence is an exhibitionistic stance of bravado; it will hopefully make room for acceptance of interdependence. True independence means accepting one's need for connectedness, not only with those such as one's own ethnic group, but also with others – different groups who enrich our existence by their otherness.

Security of identity in individuals and collective groups is achieved by accepting one's own personality, shortcomings and strengths, and by assimilating those aspects of personal and collective models which fit one's identity while avoiding those which are alien to one's sense of self-worth, national consciousness, and cultural heritage. Adjusting to current realities while maintaining one's core identity and culture demands a successful exercise in remembering and forgetting and a successful blend of past and present.

Notes

1. Benedict Anderson (1991), *Imagined Communities: Reflections on the Origin and Spread of Nationalism*, London, p. 4.
2. Elmer Hankins (1994), 'European Paradigms, East and West, 1945', *Daedalus*, **123**, (3), p. 116.
3. Mark Medish (1994), 'Russia Lost and Found', *Daedalus*, **123**, (3), p. 87.
4. Vladimir Lukin (1994), 'No More Delusions', *Washington Post*, 3 April, p. 3.
5. Tony Judt (1994), '1989: The End of Which European Era?', *Daedalus*, **123**, (3), p. 8.
6. Ibid.
7. George Schopflin (1994), 'Post Communism: The Problem of Democracy Construction', *Daedalus*, **123**, (3), p. 129.
8. Judt, '1989', note 5 *supra*, p. 16.
9. Mardi Horowitz (1996), 'Self-Regard: A New Measure', *The American Journal of Psychiatry*, **153**, (3), p. 382.
10. Salman Akhtar and Steven Samuel (1996), 'The Concept of Identity, Developmental Origins, Phenomenology, Clinical Relevance, and Measurement', *Harvard Review of Psychiatry*, **8**, pp. 254–67.
11. V. Tausk (1919), 'Über die Entstehung des Beeinflussungsapparatus in der Schizophrenie', *Internationale Zeitschrift Psychoanalysis*, **5**, (1), pp. 1–33.
12. E. Ericson (1962), *Identity and the Life Cycle*, New York, pp. 50–100 and 104–64; idem. (1958), *Young Man Luther: A Study in Psychoanalysis and History*, New York; and idem. (1962), *Identity, Use and Crisis*, New York.
13. Otto Kernberg (1995), *Love Relations: Normality and Pathology*, New Haven, Conn.
14. R. N. Emde (1983), 'The Representational Self and Its Affective Core', *Psychoanalytic Study of the Child*, (38), pp. 165–92.
15. Anderson, *Imagined Communities*, note 1 *supra*.
16. Paul Ignotus (1974), *Hungary*, London, p. 44.
17. Anderson, *Imagined Communities*, note 1 *supra*, pp. 22–23.
18. Ibid., p. 35.
19. Ibid.
20. Ibid., p. 44.
21. Ibid., p. 75.

22 Kristi S. Evans (1992), 'Argument of Images: Historical Representation in Solidarity Underground Postage, 1981–1987', *American Ethnologist*, **19**, (4), pp. 749–67.
23 Ibid., p. 750.
24 Adam Mitchnik (1985), *Letters from Prison and Other Essays*, Berkeley, Cal., p. 48.
25 Daniel Bates (1986), 'What's in a Name? Minorities, Identity, and Politics in Bulgaria', *Identity*, **23**, pp. 201–25.
26 Daniel Bell (1975), 'Ethnicity and Social Change', in N. Glaser and P. Moynihan (eds), *Ethnicity*, Cambridge, Mass., p. 169.
27 Bates, 'What's in a Name?', note 25 *supra*, p. 204.
28 Julian Konstantinov *et al.*, 'Nation, State, and Minority Types of Discourse: Problems of Communication Between the Majority and the Islamic Minorities in Contemporary Bulgaria', *Innovation and Social Science Research*, **5**, pp. 103–4.
29 Shimshir Vilal (1989), *The Turks of Bulgaria, 1878–1985*, London, 1989.
30 Krustyu Petkov and Georgei Fotev (1990), 'Ethnic Conflict in Bulgaria, 1989', *Sociological Archive in Bulgarian with English Summary*, Sofia, 1990.
31 Konstantinov *et al.*, 'Nation, State and Minority Types of Discourse', note 28 *supra*, p. 78.
32 Otto F. Kernberg (1989), 'The Psychopathology of Hatred', presented at the Symposium on Rage, Power and Aggression, sponsored by the Columbia University Center for Psychoanalytic Training and Research and the Association for Psychoanalytic Medicine. New York, p. 3.
33 Ibid.
34 Viola Bernard, Perry Ottenberg and Fritz Redel (1965), *Dehumanization: A Composite Psychosocial, Psychological Defense in Relation to Modern War: Behavioural Science and Human Survival*, Palo Alto, Cal., p. 64.
35 Cvijeto Job (1993), 'Yugoslavia's Ethnic Furies', *Foreign Policy*, (92), Fall, pp. 64–65.
36 Rita R. Rogers (1990), 'The Intergenerational Transmission of Historical Enmity' in Vamik D. Volkan, Demetrios A. Julius and Joseph B. Montville (eds), *The Psychodynamics of International Relationships*, vol. 1, New York, pp. 91–96.
37 Edward R. Shapiro and A. Wesley Carr (1991), *Lost in Familiar Places: Creating New Connections Between the Individual and Society*, New Haven, Conn.

Index

Aarelaid-Tart, Aili and Siisiäinen, Martti 132
Abdulatipov, Ramazan 112
Abkhazia 155, 173–4
Academia Europaea 87
Academy for Natural Sciences 78
Academy of Sciences of the FSU 78
Academy of the Russian Federation 78
Akaev, A President 88
Albania 146, 150, 171, 184
Almond, Gabriel and Verba, Sidney 25
Anderson, Benedict 195
applied sciences 79–80, 81
Aquinas, Thomas 101
Arashti 99
Arbatov, Alexei 16–17
argument of images and collective identity 196
Armenia 49, 123, 150, 153, 160, 173
   access to FSU oilfields, interest in 67–8, 179
   conflict in 49, 173
   nuclear industry 73
arms control
   conventional 158, 159–61
   nuclear 161–4
Arsamikov, Isa 111
Association of Scientific and Engineering Societies 88
Avars and Chechens 99
Avturkhanov, Umar 113
Azerbaijan 49, 66, 67, 123, 150, 172
   conflicts 49, 173
   energy export routes 62, 65, 67, 68, 73–4, 178–9

   treaties 153, 160
   oil-equipment production 63, 64
   oil industry 61, 64, 66, 67, 73, 179

Baltic states 49, 150, 130–1, 175
   Russia, relations 145–6
   Russian minority in 18, 134, 146, 172, 184, 186–8
Bamut, fighting at 99
Barsukov, Mikhail, Marshal 99
Baseyev, Shamil 91, 111
Belarus 49, 50, 51, 150, 153, 160
   gas access and imports 69, 70
   non-nuclear status aim 161–2
   Russia, relations with 15–16, 69, 146, 151, 153, 160
Beria, Lavrenty 128
Bernard, Viola 200
Bertram, Christopher 186, 187
Bosnia-Herzegovina 123, 170, 171
   peacebuilding in 158, 161, 188–9
Bowers, Stephen 122, 127, 133, 135
Brazauskas, Algirdas 135
Bretton Woods 10
Brezhnev doctrine 171
Brezhnev, Leonid 144
Brzezinski, Zbigniew 124–5
Budyannovsk
   crisis 91, 92, 94, 95, 102, 103
   hospital seizure 91, 97
Bulgaria 2–3, 4, 116, 127, 145, 150
   minorities, actions against 191, 197–9
Bunce, Valerie 39, 40
Barbulis, Gennadi 19

Burg, Stephen 122

Caspian oil fields *see under* oil fields of FSU; Azerbaijan; Kazakhstan
Caspian Sea, definitions of 66–7
CFE (Conventional Forces in Europe) Treaty 158–9, 160, 163
  achievements 159
  arms control 159, 160–1
  cooperation among armed forces 159, 164–6
  failures to comply 159–60
  information exchange/verification 159, 163–4
Chechen policy of Russia 47, 91–103, 108–9, 111, 112
  actions against Chechens 106, 107, 128, 172
  Agreement on Cessation of Hostilities 91, 92–3, 95, 97, 101
  agreement on relations with Chechen Republic 94
  Chernomyrdin-Zavgayev Accord 94–6
  effect on Russia's world position 116
  military solution 99, 100, 105, 114, 115, 116
Checheno-Ingushetia Autonomous Republic 94, 105–6, 109–10
Chechnya
  corruption and criminal activities 110–11, 112
  elections 94, 95, 96, 102, 109
  energy access routes 68, 73, 96, 179
  genocide 9, 102, 105
  historical background 94, 105–6, 106–7, 110, 128, 172
  hostages, taking of 91, 97–9, 102, 114
  independence, *de facto* 105, 109, 169
  oil industry in 73, 105, 110, 111
  Russian population 110, 115
  self-defence groups 92–3
  Sufi orders in 107
  Vainakh messianism 107

Chechnya conflict 5, 23, 105, 114, 185
  casualties 96, 97, 99–100, 106
  Dagestan 97–9, 115
  Gudermes and villages, attacks on 94, 96–7, 99–100
Chechnya crisis
  Chechen perspective 105–6, 107–8
  consequences 19, 20, 21, 105–17
  Constitutional Court 112, 114
  Cossacks 114
  Dagestani leaders' role 97, 98, 99
  effect on Caucasia and Islamic world 107, 115, 116–17
  international guarantees 100–2
  negotiations and future issues 92–6, 100–2, 106, 112–13, 114–15
  observers 92, 93, 101
  religious conflict avoidance 115, 116–17
  Russian perspective 105
  Vek (Century) publication of draft treaty 95
Chernobyl nuclear station 71, 72, 73, 82, 196
Chernomyrdin, Viktor 15, 69, 91, 94–6
Chernomyrdin-Zavgayev Accord 94–6
CIS 8–9, 154, 156
  Eurasian security split, danger 155–6
  NATO relations 153–6
  organs of 153
  peacekeeping in FSU 150, 154–5, 174
  security and military integration 152–3, 153–5, 156
civil society levels, differences 132–3
Clemens, Walter 129
CMEA 34, 50
coalfields in FSU 70–1
Cold War, end of 1, 11–13, 52, 80, 117, 157–8
collective memory 195–7, 198–9
Comecon 6, 169, 177
Communism, Soviet
  economic legacy 141, 146–8

ideological legacy 141–2
imperial legacy 141, 145–6
imposition of 127
living standards under 145
military legacy 141, 143
one-party police state legacy 141, 143–4
Communist ideology 141–2, 168–9
Communists, former 4–5, 116, 135, 144, 178
Confederation of Peoples of Caucasia 111
Conflict Prevention Centre (CSCE) 182, 185
Congress of the Chechen People (OCCP) 109, 111
Copenhagen Meeting on the Human Dimension, Declaration 181, 183, 185
Council of Europe 188
Council of Heads of State (CIS) 153
Crimean Tartars 128, 172
Croatia 170, 185, 186, 188
CSCE (Conference for Security and Cooperation in Europe) see OSCE
cultural experiences, Western and Eastern 194, 201
Czech Republic 4, 69, 146, 150, 151, 184
Czechs, undue perceptions 131
Czechoslovakia 2, 145, 171, 175

Dayton Agreement on Bosnia-Herzegovina 158, 160
democracy
  explanatory models in transition to 23–44
  factors for 24, 25, 26–7, 37, 41–2
democracy, transition to
  comparative approach 39–40
  economic basis of theories 24, 25, 26–7, 37–8
  imperatives of liberalization theory 24
  institutional problems 175–6

internal restructuring of society 180, 181, 190
international factors 37–9, 179–80
legacies of the past 24, 28–9
literature 32, 40–2
mixed school 25, 35–6
process orientated school 24–5, 25, 31–5
security environment, contribution to 180
structuralist school 25, 26–31
theories generally 24–5, 26, 27–8, 39–42
Deutsche Forschungsgemeinschaft 85
Di Palma, Giuseppe 32
Dnestr Republic 174–5
Dobbs, Michael 135
Dudayev, Dzhokhar
  Chechen military actions 91, 94, 96, 102, 114
  Chechen opposition to 105, 108, 112, 113–14
  corruption allegations 105, 111–12
  political power, acquisition 108, 109, 112, 113
  Russia and 108, 109, 112, 113
  support for 105, 108, 109, 110, 111
Dulles, John Foster 142
Dzerzhinsky, Felix 128

East German Academy of Sciences 88
East Germany 1, 4, 127, 145, 146
Eastern Europe
  change, impact of 178, 191, 192–4
  common problems and factors 1–5, 127, 171
  Communism, imposition of 127
  cooperative security and NATO 5, 157–66
  cross-regional comparisons 39–40
  democratic experience, previous 2, 175–6
  ethnic problems 171
  ethnicity and religion, links to collective identity 198, 199, 201

gas exports to 69
identity and change 191–203
instability in, OSCE role 167–90
living standards fall 178
psychological perspectives 191–203
science, reforms and changes 77, 87–8
see also Communism, Soviet; instabilities in the FSU and Eastern Europe
ego identity 194–5
Emde, R.M. 195
empires, disappearance and vacuum 169–70
Ericson, E. 194
energy, international security and 73–4
Estonia
   Communism in 126–7
   deportations and Russification 128
   economic aspects 49, 50, 123, 131, 134
   Finland, comparisons with 123, 130, 132
   social group interests 132, 133
   undue burden perception 131
Estonian Popular Front 133
ethnic conflict, meaning 122
ethnicity and religion, and collective identity 198, 199, 201
ethnos, meaning 120
EU 38, 143, 177, 185, 188
   membership, future 145, 146, 189
Euro-Asian Physical Society 88
European Physical Society 88
European security, East-West divide 155–6, 185, 189

free market, transition to 177–9, 179–80, 190
French Revolution, *Grandes Ecoles* 81
FSU (Former Soviet Union)
   border and energy access problems 61–2, 67, 172–5, 178–9
   changes, impact of 178, 191, 192–4
   collapse of 5, 107, 130, 177

Communist legacies 141–8
conflict resolution 150, 154, 155
defence expenditure 52–5
democracy transition problems 2, 175–6
disintegrationist trends 130–1
economic peaks, table of 49
economy, collapse of 45, 48–9, 49–50
economy, transition 3, 45–52, 55–8, 147
electricity production 71–2
energy in 61–75
energy resources 61, 62, 63–4, 67, 68, 178–9
identity and change 107, 191–203
instability in, OSCE role 167–90
international scientific institutions, obligations 86
living standards, fall 178
minorities 128–9, 170, 171, 172–5
oil production, Western investment 65, 67
psychological perspectives 191–203
reform programmes 45–6, 46–9, 49–50
Russia as dominant nation 129
science, reforms and changes 77, 78, 80, 87, 88–9
scientific associations, reorganization 88
structure of 105–6, 129–30
struggle for survival 45–59
trade and investment, reorientation 177–8
see also coal fields in FSU; Communism, Soviet; gas fields of FSU; instabilities in the FSU and Eastern Europe; oil fields of FSU; Russia
FSU and Eastern Europe
   collective identity, profound change 193, 201
   prisoner paradigm 192, 193
fundamental science in Russia 79–81, 83

Gaider, Yegor 7, 15, 18, 19, 50, 112
Gamsakhurdia, Zuiad 135
gasfields of FSU
  Russia 61, 64, 69, 70
  Turkmenistan 61, 69, 70, 178–9
GATT and 'shock therapy' 34
Gazprom 69, 70
Gellner, Ernest 132
Geneva Convention 100, 102
Geneva Expert Meeting on National Minorities 181, 182
Genschel, General 149
Georgia 49, 153, 160
  access to FSU oil fields 68, 73–4, 179
  conflict in 5, 150, 154, 171, 173–4, 185
German Democratic Republic *see* East Germany
glasnost, reform catchword 106, 144, 177
globalization 55, 56–7, 124, 147, 148
Glukhikh, Victor 53
Goble, Peter 125, 129
Gorbachev, Mikhail
  Estonia's subsidized economy 131
  Marxism-Leninism, decline 142
  military conversion strategy 53, 54
  power struggles 109, 144, 169
  reforms 7, 17, 23, 78, 130, 177
  science students 83
Gowan, Peter 34
Greater Caucasia 108
Greenfield, Liah 124
Grozny 100, 110, 111, 112

Hague Convention, The 100, 102
hatred for perceived enemy, and memory 199–200
Havel, Vaclav, President 168–9
Hegel, G.W.F. 195
Helsinki Final Act 181, 183, 190
High Commissioner on National Minorities (CSCE) 182, 183, 184, 187, 188
historical emnity, intergenerational transmission 200
Hitler, Adolf 63, 121, 144
Hungary 3, 145, 175, 177
Huntington, Samuel 29, 35–6
Huttenbach, Henry 127

identity, collective (national consciousness) 191, 195–99, 202
identity, individual 191, 194–5, 202
IFOR 158, 161, 165
IMF 3–4, 7, 10, 34, 46–7, 177
INF (Intermediate Nuclear Forces) Treaty 161
Ingushetia 94, 105–6, 107, 109–10, 115, 128
instabilities in FSU and Eastern Europe
  anti-Russian sentiment in Eastern Europe 171
  anti-Western sentiment 170–1
  causes 167–8
  economic problems 168, 177–9, 189
  ethnic problems 168, 171–5, 189
  institutional problems 168, 175–6, 189
  political and psychological problems 168–71, 189
invisible minority, transformation (collective identity) 197–8
Iran 18, 47, 73, 145, 173
  FSU energy resources, access 67, 68, 70, 74, 179
Islam and FSU 107, 116–17, 145
Izyumov, A., Kosals, L. and Ryukin, R. 53, 54

JCG (Joint Consultative Group) of CFE Treaty 159, 160–1
John-Paul II, Pope 196
Joint Air Defence System of the CIS 153
Jowitt, Kenneth 39

Kabardino-Balkaria 115
Kaganovich, Lazar 128

Kalmyks 128
Karachai-Circassia 115, 128
Karadzic, Radovan 199
Karaganov, Sergei 16–17
Karl, T.L. 31, 33, 35
Katyn massacre 128, 196
Kazakhstan 15–16, 105–6, 153
  economy 51, 55, 66
  energy access routes 62, 65, 67, 68, 72, 178–9
  energy production 61, 64, 66, 71, 74, 178
  non-nuclear status aim 161–2
Kennan, George 142
Kennaway, A. 51
Kennedy, John, President 147–8
Kennedy, Paul 124
Kernberg, Otto 200
Khasbulatov, Ruslan. I., 93, 95, 108, 113
Khruschev, Nikita 144, 147
Kirgizstan 88, 153, 172
Kitschelt, Herbert 26, 30
Kizlyar, Dagestan, attack on 91, 94, 97–9, 102, 103
Klaus, Vaclav 4
Koedjajev, Sjelov 187
Kohn, Hans 125
Kosovo 185, 186, 199
Kozyrev, Andrei 15, 19, 20
Kravchuk, Leonid 135

Labazanov, Ruslan 111
Latvia 49, 50, 128, 134
Lebed, Alexander 16, 175
Lenin, V. I. 24, 128, 144
Lipset, Seymour 25, 27, 28
Lithuania 49, 50, 73, 128
Lobanov, Mikhail 128
Lukin, Vladimir 16–17
Lysenko, Nikolai 17

Macedonia 171, 185
Macmillan, Harold 147–8
Manstein, von, F.E., Field Marshal 63

Marxism-Leninism
  effects on FSU and Eastern Europe 144, 146, 148, 168–9
  principle tenets 141–2
Maskhadov, Aslan 93, 99
Maynes, Charles 122
memory and identity in change in FSU and Eastern Europe 191–202
memory and personal and collective identity 192, 199–200, 202
Meri, Lennart 128
Meszaros, Sandor 93
Michels, Robert 24
migration pressures, future 124–5, 136
military expenditure, decline and response 46, 52–6, 79
Milosevic, Slobodan 134–5, 185, 186, 199
Minatom 73
Minogue, Kenneth and Williams, Beryl 126
minorities in Eastern Europe 171, 184, 185, 191, 197–9
minorities in FSU 8, 128, 170, 171, 172–5
  Baltic states 18, 134, 172, 184, 186–8
  states, other 110, 115, 128, 146, 172, 185
Mitchnik, Adam 196
mixed school of transitional theory 25, 35–6
Moldova 49, 51, 153, 160
  conflict in 5, 150, 154, 171, 174–5, 185
Montenegro 186
Montreux Convention 1936 68
Moore, Barrington 27–8
Moscow Institute for Physics and Technology 81
Munck, G.L. 29–30
musical score and collective identity 195

NACC (North Atlantic Cooperation Council) 150, 155, 156, 162, 163

peacekeeping 149–50, 164, 165
Nagorno-Karabakh
   conflict in 5, 150, 154, 155, 172, 173
   ethnic violence 171, 172, 173, 175, 185
Nakichevan 172, 173
Naqshbandiya orders 106
nation and nation-state, meaning 120, 121
national consciousness 191, 195–9, 202
National Science Foundation (US) 85
nationalism
   aims of 120–1
   concept of 120–2, 195
   constructive 122, 123
   destructive 122–3
   future pressures 124–5, 136
   globalization and 124
   post-Communist theories 119–39
   Russia 7–9, 122, 125
   see also post-Communist nationalism
nations, construction and destruction, Communist 119, 128–30
NATO
   arms control 158–60, 160–1, 162, 163
   Combined Joint Task Force 158
   continuation, likely 143, 157
   enlargement 21, 47, 145, 150–5, 183–4, 189
   European security 155–6, 157
   groups on specific issues 163, 164–5
   instabilities in Eastern Europe, role 157–66, 188
   instability, areas of, and cooperation 150, 158
   Operation Joint Endeavour 166
   peacekeeping 150, 154, 158, 164–5
   purpose and role 149–50, 154, 157, 158, 165–6
   relations with NACC and OSCE 149–50, 152, 164–5
   relations with Russia and CIS 149–55, 155–6, 158

science and technology centres in FSU 162
   see also Russia and NATO enlargement
neo-imperialism in Russia 7–8, 9
new industrial revolution 55–7
'new world order' 12
non-interference in internal affairs, reconsidered 100–1
North Ossetia 115, 174
Novecon 53
Novogroznenskoe 100
nuclear disarmament and proliferation 161–4
Nunn-Lugar fund 162

O'Donnell, Guillermo, Schmitter, Philippe C. and Whitehead, Laurence 32
oil price increase, OPEC 1973 46
oil, world consumption 62
oilfields of FSU
   access, Russian control over 66, 67, 178–9
   access schemes, regional interest 67–8, 73–4, 178–9
   Azerbaijan 62–3, 64, 65–6, 67, 68
   Kazakhstan 62, 64, 65–6, 67, 68, 74
   Russia 61, 63, 64, 65
Oman 67, 68
Ormerod, Paul 46
Orwell, George 142
OSCE (Organization for Security and Cooperation in Europe) 181, 182, 189–90
   accomplishments 184, 185–9, 190
   Baltic states, Russian minorities and 184, 186–8, 190
   Bosnia-Herzegovina, peacebuilding 188–9, 190
   conflict forestalling 182–3, 183–5, 190
   Chechnya talks, observers at 92, 93, 101, 102
   CIS and 153, 154, 156

Code of Behaviour 183
Cold War functions of CSCE 180, 183
Declarations, meetings and summits (CSCE) 167, 181–2, 188, 190
free market transition 181, 190
FSU and Eastern Europe, role in 150, 154–5, 167–90
international organizations, relations 152, 156, 164, 165, 183–4
minorities 181–2, 183, 184, 187, 188
missions 183, 184, 185, 187, 188
Moscow Meeting on the Human Dimension 183
NATO and 164, 165, 183–4
norms for interstate and intrastate behaviour 182, 183, 190
objectives, main 182–5, 190
organs of 182–3, 184, 185, 187, 188
Permanent Council (CSCE) 182, 184
political dialogue, aim for 182, 183–4, 190
security, Euro-Atlantic area 167, 179–85, 189–90
Yugoslavia, conlict and 154, 184–5, 188, 190
Ossetian-Ingush conflict 112

Pakistan 173
Paris, Charter of 181, 182, 190
Park, Andrus 120–1
Päts, Konstantin 127
peak events in memory 200
perestroika reform catchword 2, 11, 54, 78, 144, 177
Pervomayskoye, attack on 98–9, 103
Peter the Great 169
Petrossian, Lev, President 173
PFP (Partnership for Peace) 158, 160–1, 163
   NATO 149–50, 157, 164, 165, 166
Phare programme 38
Physical Society of the Soviet Union 88
Pilon, Juliana 125, 129
Pilsudski, Josef, Marshal 196

Poland 3–4, 70, 147
   collective identity 195–7
Poltoranin, Mikhail 19
Posen, Barry 126
post-communist leaders 123, 123–5, 135
post-Communist nationalism 121–2
   adoption by former Communists 135
   causes of 119–20, 123–36
   Communist construction of nations 119, 128, 129–30
   Communist destruction of nations 119, 128–9
   conspiracies by political elites 119, 134–6
   economic factors 119, 130–2, 133–4
   ethnic cleansing backlash 128–9
   lost opportunities, perception 130–1, 133
   pre-Communist causes 123, 125
   responsibility for imposing Communism 119, 126–8
   social and political vacuum 119, 132–3
   specific Communism-related causes 123, 125–33, 134–6
   swing theory 126
   undue burden perception 131
   'unfreezing' following collapse of Communism 119, 125–6
Pridham, Geoffrey 29, 37
print capitalism and collective identity 195
process orientated school
   conflict resolution 33
   democratization 31–3
   impure model 33–5
   literature 32, 40
   shock therapy 33–4, 35
   time dimension and choice 41
   transition, modes of 33
Przeworski, Adam 29, 30–1, 32–3
Putnam, Robert 28–9

Qadiriya orders 106

Radnyer, Salman 91, 96, 97, 98–9
Reagan, Ronald, President 46, 64, 148
Remmer, Karen L. 32, 37, 38–9, 40–1
Romania 2, 4, 129, 145
Romanov, A., General 93
Rosvooruzheniye (Russian arms export agency) 54
Rueschemeyer, Dietrich, Stephens, E.H. and Stephens, J.D. 28
Russia
  anti-Russian nationalist feelings 127–8
  anti-Western sentiment 170–1, 189
  Black Sea Fleet 160
  CFE Treaty, failure to meet 159–60
  Chechen policy 91–103
  China, joint ventures with 57–8
  CIS and 153, 170
  Communist group, active 16, 21
  Communism, links with 127–8
  defence costs and production 18, 46, 52, 53–5
  democracy in 11, 18, 39–40, 143–4
  domestic politics 15–21
  economy 6–7, 10, 46–8, 50–2, 57–8, 147
  energy consumption 62
  energy export routes 62, 65, 66–7, 68, 69, 178–9
  energy, natural resources 61, 62–5, 69, 71, 179
  energy production (oil) 61, 62–5, 179
  energy production (other than oil) 47, 61, 69, 70–1, 71–2, 73
  far abroad and 16, 19, 20
  fascists 17
  free market economy, and 7, 37–8, 147
  FSU, boundaries and republics 6, 8–10, 47, 129
  German wartime oil objectives 63
  instability, sources of 7–8, 16, 21
  Iran, nuclear exports to 47, 73
  languages, ethnic 172
  legacies of the past 29, 30
  liberal pragmatic group 16–17, 21
  nationalists and nationalism 7–9, 17, 122, 125
  near abroad and 6, 15, 21, 145
  neo-imperialism in 7–8, 9, 16, 21
  nuclear arsenal 143, 162
  pro-Western group 15–16, 21
  reactionary pragmatic group 17, 21
  reform programmes 46–9, 49–50
  social group interests 132
  undue burden perception 131
  Tatarstan treaty 113
  see also CIS; Communism, Soviet; FSU; Russia and NATO enlargement; Russian foreign policy; science in Russia
Russia and NATO enlargement 149–51, 155–8
  application to join 18, 149
  'CIS military integration as alternative' approach 152–5
  'Enlargement is inevitable but let's negotiate conditions' approach 152
  'Humiliated Great Power' approach 151
  relations 5, 149–55
  'Worst-case planning' approach 151–2
Russian Academy of Sciences 78, 82, 83–4
Russian Communist Party 16, 21, 116, 143–4
Russian foreign policy
  Balkans, peacekeeping 21
  domestic opinion groups 15–17
  FSU republics and 15–16, 18, 150
  geopolitical considerations 15–21
  'Monroe doctrine' 20, 146
  phases in 17–19, 19–20, 21
  Strategic Defense Initiative 18
  see also Chechen policy of Russia; Russia and NATO enlargement
Russian Parliament 113, 116, 178

Russian Revolution 81, 126–7
Russian national identity, sense of 170
Russification 128, 172
Rustow, D.A. 27, 30
Rutzkoi, Alexander, General 149
Rüütel, Arnold 135
Ruutsoo, Rein 133

Sachs, Jeffrey 33–5, 147
Sakwa, Richard 30
Salambekov, Yusup 111
Samashki 97
Samuel, Maurice 68
Sartori, Giovanni 24
Scmitter, Philippe, and Karl, Terry L. 38, 39
Schopflin, George 193
science in Russia
   anti-scientific and anti-intellectual trends 79, 82, 84–5, 87
   decline of 77–8
   exchange trends and developments 83–5
   finance and investment 78, 79–81, 88
   fundamental science 79–81, 83
   help from ouside 83–4, 85–6, 87
   military dominance 77, 80, 87
   morale 86–7
   need for education/training 81–2, 84–5, 86, 87
   new conditions and departures 81–3, 87–8
   present state and future 77–89
   reforms and changes, effect of 77, 78, 80, 88–9
   students in USA 83
   world science, integration with 83–5
security of identity 202
Serbia 132, 170, 199
Sernovodsk 99, 100
Shakhrai, Sergei 112
Shapiro, Edward R. and Carr, A. Wesley 201
Shevardnadze, Eduard 18, 135
shock therapy 3–4, 33–5, 146, 147

Shushkevich, S. President 88
Skidelsky, Robert 147–8
Slovakia 69, 171
Slovenia 123, 134, 170
Smith, Anthony 120, 124, 125
social Darwinism 56
Solidarity movement in Poland 191, 195–7
Soros Foundation 85
Soros, George 122–3, 133
South Ossetia 174
Soviet Communism, legacies of 141–8
Stability Pact 188
stability, post-Cold War challenges 1–13
stabilization, quest for 10–13
Stalin, Josef 105, 128, 129, 142, 144, 169
Stalingrad, Battle of 63
START (Strategic Arms Reduction Talks) Treaties 143, 161
Stavropol 113–14
Strategic Defense Initiative 18
structuralist school 25
   criticisms 30–1
   economic institutionalists 28
   legacies of the past 28–30
   total societal level 26
   transitional 26–7, 41
   variables and choices 26, 27–8
Suleimanov, Ibrahim 111
Suny, Ronald 135–6
Suslov, Mikhail 142

Taagepera, Rein 134
Tacis programme 38
Tadjikistan 5, 20, 150, 153, 154, 185
Tatarstan 107, 113
Tausk, V. 194
Thatcher, Margaret 46, 148
transitologists 24
Treaty on the Collective Security 153
Trotsky, Leon 127, 142
Turkey 67–8, 70, 74, 173, 179
Turkmenistan 61, 67, 69, 70, 178–9

Index   215

Ukraine
  deportations under FSU 128
  economy 49, 50, 51, 57, 61, 164
  energy needs and resources 61, 62, 69, 70, 71
  military 'closed' towns and regions 54, 55
  nuclear considerations 72, 161–2
  relationships 15–16, 146, 153
Umalatova, Sazhi 108
UN 153, 164, 165
  peacekeeping, former Yugoslavia 150, 154, 185
Union of Scientific and Engineering Societies 88
US Office of Technology Assessment 56
USA, FSU energy, interest in 63, 67, 68
USSR *see* FSU
Uzbekistan 61, 70, 153

Vainakh Democratic Party 107–8
Verdery, Katherine 120
Vojvodina 185, 186
Volga Germans 172
Volsky, Arkady 92

'waves of democratization' 30, 35–6
Welsh, Helga 33
West, the
  anti-West sentiment 170–1, 189
  'missionary' paradigm 192, 193

  'otherness', perception of 193
  'world policeman and instructor' paradigm 193
WEU 156, 165
WMD (Weapons of Mass Destruction) 161, 163
World Bank 10, 34, 177
world energy projections 62
WTO (Warsaw Treaty Organization) 6, 141, 145, 149, 169, 177

Yavlinsky, Grigori 16–17
Yeltsin, Boris
  Chechnya crisis 94, 99, 109, 112–13, 114, 115–16
  foreign policy 17, 19, 20, 114
  power struggles of 47, 108, 109, 135, 144
  reforms 23, 47, 78, 147
  Russian Federation republics and sovereignty 108
  successors, possible 143
Yugoslavia 18, 127, 170, 184–5
Yugoslavia, former 1, 3, 150, 154
  conflict in 175, 184, 185, 188, 190

Zaslavsky, Victor 41
Zatulin, Konstantin 16
Zavgayev, Doku 91, 94–6, 97, 100
Zhirinovsky, Vladimir 17, 171
Ziuganov, Gennadi 16